Contents

Terminologies

2nd Degree: A Super-S with powers created by design or accident.

Academy of Higher Development: An educational establishment specialising in the training and development of children displaying superpowers.

AFV: Military slang for when a mission goes wrong. A 'fuck-up' (acronym for 'America's Funniest Videos').

A.W.O.L.: An acronym for "absent without leave".

B.P.P.: An African-American revolutionary organisation established to promote Black Power, and by extension self-defense for blacks. Active in the United States from the mid-1960s into the 1970s.

Council Flat: A form of public or social housing, primarily referred to in the United Kingdom.

C-Section: A surgical procedure in which incisions are made through a mother's abdomen and uterus to deliver one or more babies.

Exo-S: A Norman or Super-S that utilises a type of armoured battle suit.

Flambo: A derogatory term for a Super-S that can control fire.

HALE-CRITERION: The test designed by Dr. Montgomery Hale in 1969 which can predict the presence of superpowers in an unborn baby; more commonly known as 'the Super-S test'.

Hazmat: Hazardous materials 'clean-up' team.

Inter-Meta: A union (usually by marriage) of a Norman and a Super-S or 2nd Degree.

Invo: Slang term for a Super-S with invisibility powers.

Lob-Job: Slang term for a mentally unstable individual.

M8: The busiest motorway in Scotland. It connects the country's two largest cities, Glasgow and Edinburgh.

M.I.: Military Intelligence.

NHS: Name commonly used to refer to the publicly-funded healthcare system of the United Kingdom.

Norman: Super-S slang for an ordinary, everyday human being.

Perv: Slang term for 'Pervert'.

S-Book: Popular online community site similar to Facebook, commonly used by those with superpowers.

S.o.B.: The shortened term for 'Son-of-a-bitch'.

Solo: A Super-S that operates on his own.

Spook: Slang term for a Super-S with the ability to 'detect' invisible or cloaked objects and/or people.

S.T.A.R.T. Program: Super-S Toxic Addiction Rehab Trust.

Super-M: An extreme mutation of a Super-S, usually resulting in physical alterations.

Super-S: The generic term for those born with abnormally high human development markers; a superhero.

S-Zone: A tightly controlled government-monitored area, normally a town, where Super-S possessing powers considered too dangerous to the general public are relocated. Sometimes called a "Freak-Tank". Most common in the United States of America.

Take the Mickey: To tease or make fun of someone.

Tracksuit: An article of clothing consisting of two parts: pants and a jacket. Originally intended for use in sports, nowadays it has become commonly worn in other contexts.

Vader: The term used to describe a superhero that is, or has become, 'evil'.

Yurei: Spirits in Japanese folklore, analogous to Western legends of ghosts.

Dedicated to:

My wife, Natasha.

My son, Zack.
Born 7th June 2008 at 5.34am

So I once worked as a copywriter for Marvel Comics. Before Justice. Before Earth X. Even before Footsoldiers. I wrote ads. If Captain America were going to take on the Red Skull again, it was my job to write an ad telling potential buyers and fans why this time it was going to be different. Why this time, Cap himself could actually lose. While there, I was privy to an amazing number of candid words given by editors, artists and executives alike. Things you would never expect to hear.

One such testimonial came from one of the editor-in-chiefs I worked with. He was asked what he would do if he were given the power of flight. I will never forget his answer. He said that he would never fly more than five feet above the ground because he was afraid of heights. I think that was the moment I both lost respect for editors, and also discovered the humanity behind having powers. It wasn't Alan Moore. It wasn't Grant Morrison. Wasn't even Alan Grant who turned my heard towards thinking about what mankind might be like if we had super powers. It was this statement by this editor.

The book you hold in your hands is jammed with such interesting little thoughts. Really, it's not like anything I've ever read. Please understand that I love British comics. I always have. I wouldn't be here in this industry if it weren't for Moore Swamp Thing and Captain Britain. Or Morrison's Zenith and Animal Man. I still hold up Volume 1 of Knights of Pendragon as the best comic book series of the 90s. I'm the only American I know who buys every issue of 2000 AD (I do know that many out here buy it. I'm just the only one I know of). The artists in this book are the best British artists working today. That would have been enough for me to buy it.

If you've only leafed through it, you may not realize what you've stumbled onto. It's a one-page view into 45 different stories. 45 different hints of what it would be like to have super powers in the world AND have all your only hidden faults. For me, this is a book of ideas. For some of the characters within, I'm perfectly happy just finding out that they walked the Earth (or walked above it) and finally settled down and had a family and retired. But for others, there's a whole story just waiting to be told.

I especially enjoyed the guy with super powers who couldn't come up with a "code-name" because all the good ones were being used by made up heroes from American publishers. Yeah. Little insights like this are what makes this book loads of fun.

I imagine I'll be picking this book up often. Sometimes only to page through it. Sometimes only to read one page and let the creators' imagination effect my own. This is great work. And you should count yourself privileged to have picked this up. But of course, this is ComX. So if you're smart enough to know who they are, you're smart enough to pick something up on their logo alone.

If I had the power of flight, there are a lot of things I'd do. One would be to get back to England to shake of the hands of this crew and congratulate them on such a fun read. And then, since I'm there, I'd probably try to figure out how I can get my hands on one of those Zenith Hardcovers I heard were printed and never released.

Grateful to be a part of this.

Jim Krueger *Earth X, Justice and Footsoldiers*

I read a lot of comic books. Even before I started my current stint as the world's most foul mouthed reviewer on Ain't It Cool News, my longbox collection was already causing marital strife due to the amount of closet space it was consuming.

Being a veritable encyclopedia of the comic medium, you begin to recognize patterns; cyclical similarities that at times make me wonder how I can continue to love a medium that essentially revels in sameness from month-to-month-to-month. Well the answer is quite simple, for all of the hundreds of books that seem to roll off of a creative assembly line, hidden between them are sparks of sheer brilliance that force you to say "Yeah, I never saw this coming."

Well, I never saw 45 coming. Even after I had done a fairly extensive interview with Andi, I still just didn't get what 45 was truly about. And that's the thing with books that spit in the face of convention. You simply don't get them until you experience them. Think about the industry game changers and if in concept they would have bowled you over. Dark Knight Returns — batman is middle aged and the imagery will be almost indecipherable. Astro City — you know a city about superheroes. Marvels — we're going to look at super heroes from the perspective of the reader. Nothing about these concepts should have led to being landmark books. Yet, they were.

After my interview with Andi, this is how I was feeling about 45. Everything about the book's concept was so different from the norm how could it possibly be good? 45 interviews with more words in each interview than you get in a handful of regular weekly comics and only one picture per interview. No word balloons, no panel breaks, no thought blocks that gave the much needed exposition the artist was too lazy to render. 45 disparate interviews that stand-alone, but also meld into a greater whole, sort of like Voltron.

Where some would shun these very concepts I dove in feet first, partly because of my job as a reviewer and sometimes train wrecks are just fun to watch (as long as you aren't on the train).

At every turn of the page where I expected disaster to befall Ewington's brain child, I found myself becoming more engrossed in the story. Not just the solitary interview I was reading, but also in the life of the interviewer. This was not only connective tissue tying together this world of super beings, this man was a super being in his own right with enough heart and virtue to expend all of his resources simply to understand his unborn child.

My reservations about one picture per story were quickly abated during the first few interviews. These are more than mere pictures; they are standalone works of art. A barrage of collages and imagery that convey the life, turmoil, joy and in some cases death in each super powered individual's life. Granted it takes a different eye to read a "comic" in this fashion, but after the hundreds of thousands of panels I've read in my life, it was a most welcome diversion from the norm.

If I had to surmise 45 into one concise pull quote I would say something along the lines of, "45 explores the world around us and the very nature of existence inside a world far more interesting than our own." But you know what? I've hated pull quotes since I believed that one bastard in 1982 that promised the play I was going to see "was better than cats." So I leave with the following, "stop reading my verbal diarrhea, turn the page and be thankful you had the courage to break from the norm."

Optimous Douche (a.k.a Rob Patey) *Ain't It Cool News*

In some instances in this book, names and locations have been changed in order to protect interviewee identities from those that may wish to do them harm.

"For rarely are sons similar to their fathers:
most are worse, and a few are better than their fathers."

Homer (800 BC - 700 BC), The Odyssey

Prologue

The reason for these interviews is a simple one: in a little over four months I'm going to be a father.

My wife and I agreed to forego the Super-S test (technically known as the HALE-CRITERION test); a test that would determine whether our unborn son or daughter carries the extra chromosome that could potentially alter our lives forever. Yet even though we decided against it, I couldn't help but wonder, "What if our child is born with superpowers?". Could I cope with the pressures of a child bestowed with a gift to do extraordinary things? Here in Britain, our Government monitors rather than regulates Super-S activity and only steps in to isolate the more dangerous ones, primarily for their own benefit, employing patriotic Super-S to resolve or diffuse situations, whereas other countries have taken more drastic measures to ensure public safety. So what future can my son or daughter look forward to? If he or she is diagnosed as a Super-S, will they be free to live a normal life? What physical and psychological hurdles would they face growing up? With these and numerous other questions preying on my mind, I felt it necessary to find out more from those who are blessed with enhanced abilities, in preparation for understanding my own child better.

As a parent, you aspire to be a role-model for your children, someone they can look up to, learn from, and admire. But how can you possibly be a hero to a child that is potentially destined to become one?

I needed to discover more about the world that could be waiting for us as a family. During my time as a freelance journalist I have taken thousands of photographs of superheroes and written of their amazing feats and courageous deeds. Now, I wanted to read between the lines and delve deeper than the usual media I am forced to report on. We all think we know a Super-S, but do we *understand* them? Have we ever wanted to? Like most Normans, I have taken the guardians of our cities for granted, without consideration for their thoughts and feelings.

It had been my intention to interview as many superheroes as I could; from a Norman parents' discovery that their child is Super-S, to the growing pains of adolescence and the reckless years of adulthood, to the critical years of mid-life and beyond. Once I had made my preliminary calls, word spread quickly. More and more Super-S came forward. I still don't fully understand why. Maybe it was a need to share their experiences, a desire to be truly heard above the standard media speculation and press reports? I know for some it was an opportunity to unload psychological burdens that had been carried for months, if not years; for others, it was a chance to simply set records straight. My voyage of Super-S discovery has enabled me to lay several myths to rest and in turn uncover truths I never could have dreamed of.

We, the privileged many, have much to learn from the gifted few that fly above our cities while we sleep safely in our beds.

James Stanley
August 18th 2009

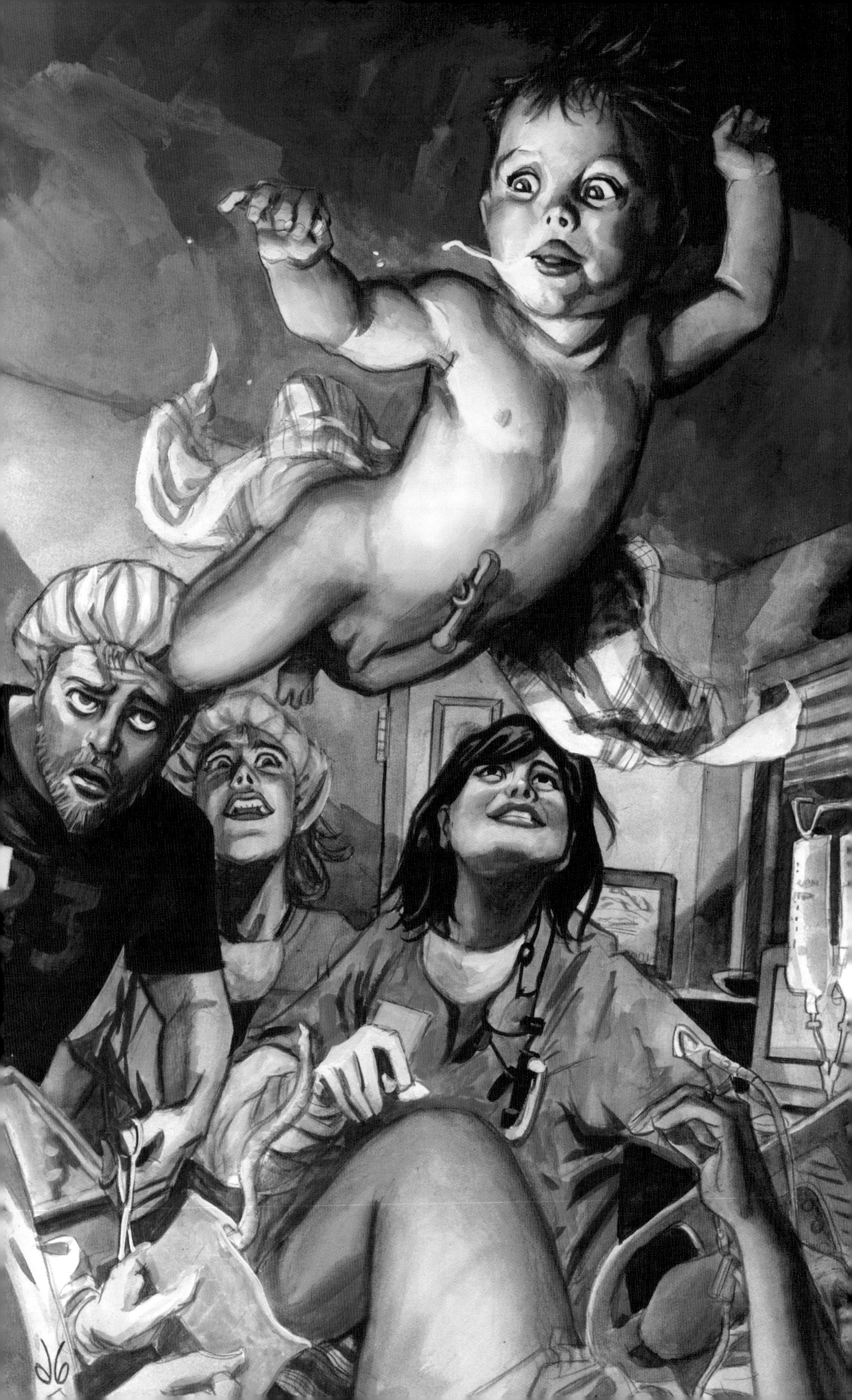

I am somewhere in the southeast of England, sitting in a private hospital ward with Michael and Felicity Brown* and their five hours-old son.

Felicity is happy but exhausted. She's holding her newborn child in her arms; one end of a cord is attached to her wrist, the other is attached to her child buried somewhere deep in his blanket. Michael sits next to them, holding a digital camcorder. His face is a picture of delight.

JS: Firstly, congratulations to you both, you must be very proud. Michael, how are you feeling right now?
MB: Thanks! It's incredible! You got kids?

JS: My wife's expecting our first. It's a rollercoaster of emotions at the moment; I'm both apprehensive and delighted at the same time.
MB: Congratulations to you, too! The ride just becomes wilder and wilder. Take that constant feeling of nervous excitement you have right now, multiply that by a thousand, and you're still nowhere near the euphoria you'll be feeling when your child's born. Are you hoping for a Super-S?

JS: We'll just settle for healthy to be honest. Thank you for seeing me so soon after the birth. Felicity, how are you feeling?
FB: As elated as Michael, except with a lot more soreness! It still hasn't sunk in yet that he's really here. He gave me a bit of trouble early on, but I was determined for a natural birth and not a C-section. In the end, all the effort was worth it. My beautiful boy.

Felicity glows proudly, doting over the bundle in her arms.

JS: Did you take the Super-S test?
MB: No, we chose not to.

JS: Did you suspect anything during the birth?
MB: Everything happened too fast. Felicity was incoherent; the pethidine meant she was flying – metaphorically speaking! When he appeared we were expecting him to be drowsy from the drugs, but no sooner had I cut the cord then he was off, whizzing around the room! We couldn't believe our eyes! Felicity thought she was hallucinating and I almost fainted from shock, but there he was, actually flying, buzzing overhead like a heat-drunk fly, screaming the delivery room down! There was meconium falling out of the air, and he was peeing and pooing everywhere-

FB: Michael!

MB: Sorry, but it WAS utter chaos; a right stinking mess. Everything was covered; from the baby, to the delivery team, to us. Looking back now it was pretty funny, but at the time it was sheer pandemonium.

JS: How did you manage to catch him?
MB: Luckily for us, he tired really quickly. The midwife caught him just as his ability waned. Good hands, that one! I joked that she should try out as goalkeeper for West Ham – God knows they need one although, personally, I blame the defence. Unfortunately, being a Chelsea supporter, she didn't see the funny side.

JS: How do you both feel, now that his ability has been confirmed?
MB: We're both walking on air! For the record, neither of us are Super-S, we're both Normans. Nothing can truly prepare you for the experience; there's no mention of super-powers or how to deal with them from the midwives or antenatal classes, I guess with such a variety of talents out there it's impossible to offer practical advice. Like yourself, we felt that if we were going to waive the test, then we would be acceptive, no matter the outcome.

JS: With your "special" arrival, you're going to have your hands full 24-7. Have the NHS given you any indication of the postnatal support that's out there for you?
MB: You're kidding, right? They're stretched as it is with Norman babies. No way do they have the infrastructure to cope with something like this.

JS: So what are you going to do? You clearly need extensive help and guidance for the foreseeable future.

Michael and Felicity glance at each other. Michael produces a business card from his pocket and hands it to me.

Ms. T. Lorien
Executive Administrator & Liaison Director
XoDOS

JS: She gave this to you? There's no telephone number, no logo, no contact details. Don't you think that's a bit strange?
FB: I said the same thing. She told us she'd be in contact to see how we were coping. Michael thinks she's something to do with National Security.

Felicity stifles a laugh.

MB: I'm just repeating what she told me!

JS: When did Ms Lorien arrive?
MB: About an hour before you. It was a very brief visit.

JS: Did she explain why she was here?
MB: She said she represented a U.S. presidency initiative that offered support and financial stability to families in our position.

JS: But you're English, why is the American Administration offering assistance here in England?
MB: That's what I wondered.

Felicity nods in agreement.

FB: Do you know much about XoDOS, Mr. Stanley?

JS: Only as much as the next Norman.
FB: They must be a reputable organisation. They wouldn't have the backing of the UK Government to be over here talking to us in hospital if they weren't, would they?

JS: I'm sure it's fine.
MB: Ms. Lorien said she'd be in touch in a few weeks. She also said there would be the possibility of a grant to help us financially. We'll certainly need the extra money to help support the little 'un.

The bundle in Felicity's arms yawns.

JS: What do you plan to call him?

Michael looks sheepishly at Felicity.

MB: We're not sure yet. I really like The Hammer, The Mighty Iron, or maybe The Claret & Blue Avenger, but Felicity isn't having any of it; she wants something like WonderKid or SuperBoy. I've already explained that those names are fine when he's younger, but he'll hate them when he's older. But you know women, always got to have their own way- ouch!

Felicity slaps Michael ruefully on the arm.

JS: Sorry, I meant his real name?
MB: Oh... we haven't really thought about that yet. We were pretty convinced that *he* was going to be a *she*.

FB: Well, I like Ross.

MB: We can't have Ross. I work with a Ross. Everyone will think the baby's his! I'll never hear the end of it. How about Bobby?

FB: I'm not naming my son after a football player.

MB: Bobby Moore wasn't just a player, he was a legend! Hang on, I like that! The Legend! Kinda catchy – I like it. The Legend!

*Interviewee names have been changed

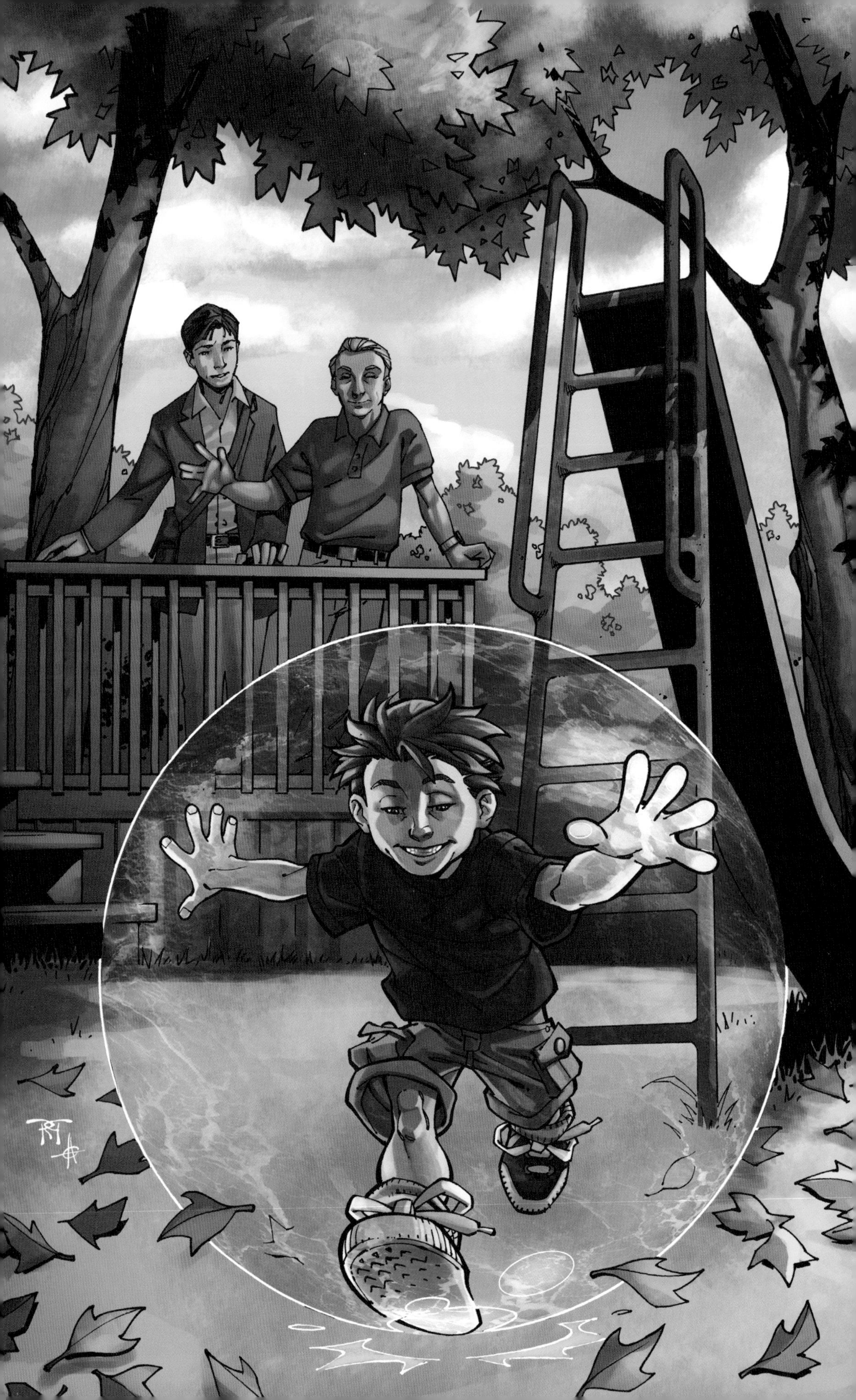

Ben Wallace* is an excitable five year-old. Tomorrow will be his first day at school. His father, Eddie, has decided to send him to a special Super-S Academy of Higher Development in Santa Monica, California.

I'm standing next to Eddie, in a park, watching his son playing on the playground equipment. Our meeting has purposely been scheduled early to avoid any unwanted attention from members of the public or press.

JS: Are you looking forward to Ben attending an Academy of Higher Development?
EW: Of course! Sending Ben to a Super-S school is the right decision. It'll be good for him to mix with kids that have comparable needs. He has Norman friends and he's pretty good at suppressing his powers when he's around them, but a Norman school could potentially propagate too many problems. I don't want to run the risk of Ben being the center of attention.

BW: Dad! Dad! Look at me! I'm King of the Hill!

Ben has climbed to the top of a slide.

EW: Very good, King Ben!

JS: You're fortunate to be in a position to send him to such a school.
EW: It's been a struggle. We're certainly not a rich family. We sold the house and had to rent a place. It was the only way we could lay our hands on the amount of money needed to support that kind of education. Banks do offer specialized loans but the interest repayments are exorbitant, so we opted to sell the house. We've enough funds for the first few years. After that, I'm not sure what we'll do. I guess I'll have to keep buying lottery tickets. Ultimately, the sacrifice is worth it to see Ben do well. We both want what's best for him. I speak from experience when I say I know what it's like to be different from the other kids.

JS: So you're not a Norman?
EW: I'm a Norman to my friends, but I'm actually a lot like my Ben. I've just always felt I should keep my power secret.

Eddie laughs.

I don't know, thanks to Ben, maybe I'm having second thoughts about keeping it under wraps. We have similar abilities, Ben and I, but having a superpower when I was a kid was very different to how it is now. Back then the system didn't have the support in place to deal with people like us; no special schools or funding. As a youngster I heard so many horror stories of kids being taken away from their parents. I didn't want that. I was scared. So I suppressed my ability and denied its existence. I'm ashamed to say, I chose to ignore my true potential.

JS: So you could inhibit your power completely?
EW: No, not completely. There would be instances at school when my power would naturally manifest itself in some way, usually if I felt threatened. People knew that there was something not quite right about me, but not what exactly. The public didn't understand people with powers in those days; not sure they do now, either. It was perceived as some kind of disability. I changed Norman schools more times than I care to recall. They kept inventing reasons to expel me.

JS: How did your parents' react to your expulsions?
EW: They had no idea what was *really* wrong with me. Remember, the *HALE-CRITERION* wasn't introduced until 1969; there was no way to diagnose kids with the Super-S gene when I was young. They just assumed I was a difficult child. Once I'd realized I was different, I kept it from them. I preferred it that way, rather than they think of me as some kind of freak. Oh, I had lots of counselling, all of it fruitless. I had never discussed my gift with anyone, so I was hardly about to start talking about it with a complete stranger. I made up excuses for my problems at school just to keep them from finding out. I don't ever want Ben to go through what I did.

JS: And yet here you are now, divulging your secret. Do you ever regret the decision to suppress your power?
EW: I regret not disclosing the truth to my parents. They've both passed away now. They never knew Ben. And, well, ...um, well, they never really knew their own child.

Eddie becomes emotional. We take a break from the interview.

Ben's birth has enabled me to see my life from a new perspective. I've been able to exorcise my demons. He has the chance that I denied myself; to be the incredible man he ought to be. I know you shouldn't attempt to fulfill your dreams through your children's life, but he has the chance to use his gift for the good of society, if he so chooses.

JS: And what if Ben decides not to rise to the challenge?
EW: The important thing is, that's his choice to make, not mine. I'll stand by him regardless. All I can do is show him the road to potential, it's his decision whether he walks it or not. He can have a Norman job like me and live a quiet, respectable life if he wants to, but I also want to give him the chance to be something greater than that, if he so chooses.

Ben runs over to us and jumps into his father's arms.

BW: Did you see me, daddy? Did you?

EW: Yes, we did! What a brave young man you are!

JS: Hello, Ben. My name's James. Your father tells me you're about to go to a special school. Are you looking forward to it?

Ben looks to his father for guidance.

EW: It's okay. I've told him about our secret.

BW: I'm going to a place that will teach me how to use my power! Daddy says I'll make lots of new friends – friends just like me.

EW: Like you in certain ways, Ben, but not exactly the same.

JS: So what's your secret, Ben?
EW: Why don't you show him?

BW: Mommy said I wasn't to do it outside.

EW: Don't worry, Daddy says you can, just this once. Nobody's watching, except us.

Ben runs to the slide and climbs the steps. He reaches the top and waves at us, enthusiastically. Just as I wave back, Ben jumps. My natural instinct is to run over to catch him but Eddie holds me back. I see a small, white flash emanate from Ben, then a force-field envelop his body, cushioning his fall. The field dissipates as Ben's feet make contact with the ground. He runs back to us, smiling.

EW: Good boy! That was a good one!

JS: He already appears to have good control over his ability.
EW: Sticks and stones aren't going to break his bones, that's for sure. It's just the other stuff that I have to shield him from. No protective barrier he creates is going to stop the verbal and mental abuse. That's why he's going to an Academy.

JS: Are you tempted to hone your own power, now that you're comfortable with it?
EW: I think it's time for me to enjoy my current life, without thinking about manufacturing a new one as some kind of superhero.

Ben is back on the slide. He jumps off again, replicating his force-field with ease. He waves at us.

JS: Don't forget, Eddie, there are all kinds of heroes.

Artwork: Randy Green - Ben Wallace

**Interviewee name has been changed*

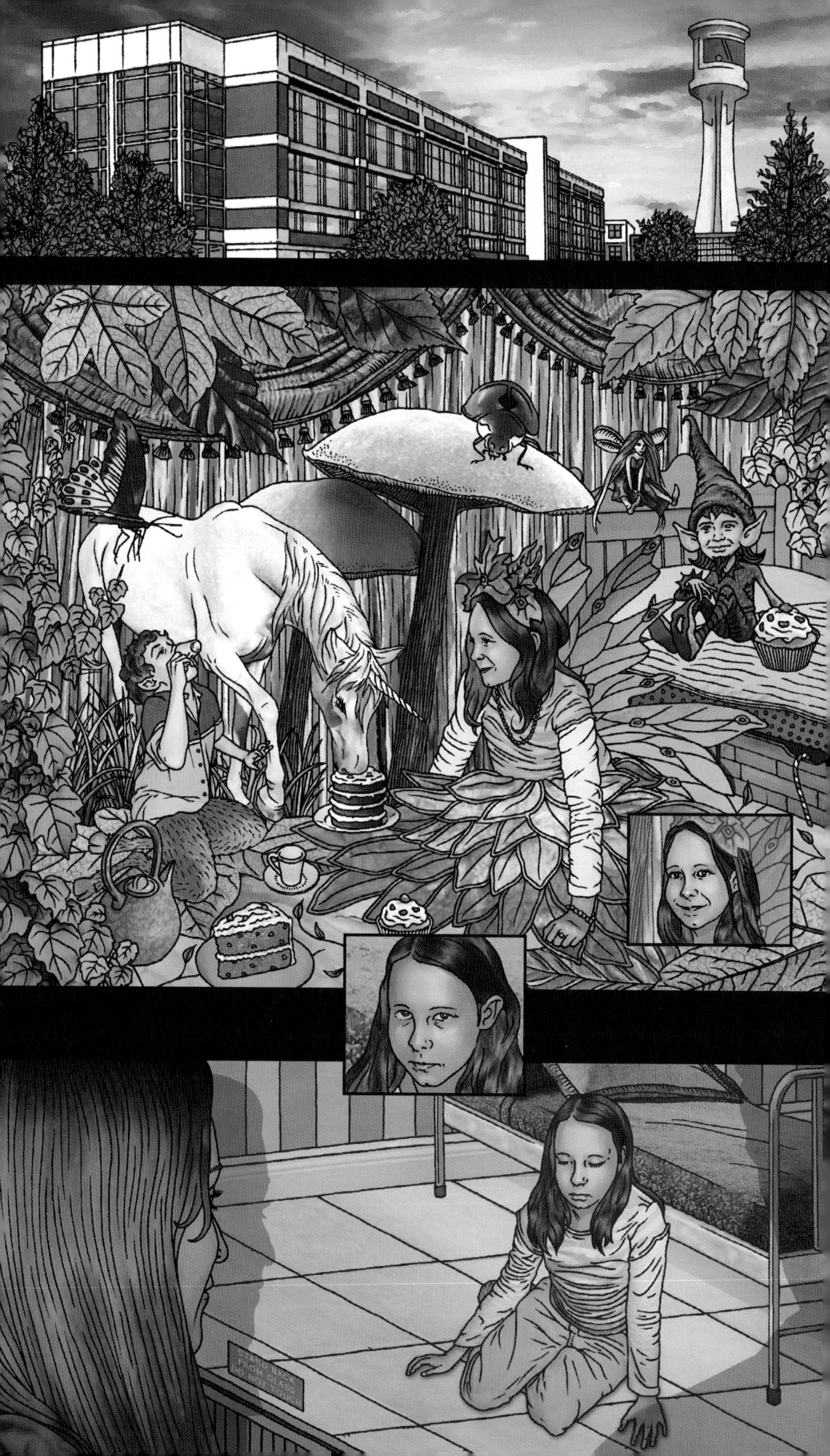
STAND BACK FROM GLASS DO NOT TOUCH

Sarah Berkley* is seven years-old. She sits playing in an observation room at the charity, HomeLight. She was born a Super-S. She knows neither of her biological parents.

I watch Sarah's powers in full-flow. She has created a fantastical woodland tea party with unicorns, leprechauns and other fabulous creatures in attendance. The director of HomeLight, Claire McCarthy, stands beside me as we observe the young girl through a two-way mirror.

JS: What's Sarah's story?
CM: It's one we see all too often. Her mother turned up at HomeLight one day, heavily pregnant with Sarah. She literally went into second-stage labour there and then on our doorstep. She pleaded with us not to take her to a Norman hospital; she knew something was different about her unborn baby. Don't ask me how as she'd never taken the Super-S test. It must have been her maternal instinct, I suppose. Sarah arrived about thirty minutes later, which is extremely quick for second-stage labour. Actually, it's rare for Normans, but not for a Super-S baby, so we knew straight away that Sarah was going to need special care.

JS: What happened to Sarah's natural mother?
CM: Unfortunately, it's the usual, common story amongst Norman mothers who give birth to Super-S; she couldn't cope with the added pressure of bringing up a daughter with extraordinary gifts. It's our policy to encourage young mothers to care for their special babies and help guide them through post-natal but sadly, some simply don't want to know. Sarah's mother left the facility a month after she had arrived.

JS: Was there any sign of the father?
CM: None. Sarah's mother never spoke of him. I had the impression it was an accident, a one night stand.

JS: Has any attempt been made to try to find him?
CM: We wouldn't even know where to begin. Powers or attributes aren't hereditary and Berkley isn't her real name so, unless he's a convicted criminal, he isn't going to turn up on any DNA database.

JS: What happens to Sarah now?
CM: She'll live with us for the time being. We'll take care of her here at HomeLight. She'll be taught how to use her powers within a controlled environment, such as this observation room. Young people need to be treated very carefully when it comes to their abilities. Mastering them can be quite a traumatic experience, so we support them in the utilization of their gifts, as well as providing the love and support necessary for proper maturation. Sarah is extremely bright but emotionally deprived. I think it will be some time before she accepts who she really is. She'll make a positive addition to the world one day, I'm sure of it, although she requires a great deal of encouragement. Many of the children left with us usually do. Being abandoned is an enormous burden to overcome for a little girl.

JS: How long will she stay with you?
CM: Until she's 23. We're not an adoption agency and besides, Norman foster parents don't generally cope well with Super-S kids. So we persuade those in our care to stay with us until they're 23. I think 18 is too young for them to make their own way in society, especially after coming from a specialist institutionalized environment.

We watch as Sarah interacts with the illusions she's creating. She cuts some cake and feeds it to a faun, then pours tea for what can only be described as a Hobbit.

JS: How successful is HomeLight? Have any of your past-minors "turned Vader"?
CM: I am pleased to tell you that almost all of our children successfully integrate back into society.

JS: Almost?
CM:There was one particular child we were unable to assist. It's extremely rare you encounter someone past saving, especially at such an early age, but she was completely uncontrollable. I blame myself. I completely misread her. We all learnt a harsh lesson that day.

We pause as the fantasy tea-party continues to unfold before our eyes. Several satyrs have now materialised. Sarah sits before them, dressed as a fairy princess.

JS: How did HomeLight begin?
CM: It was my father's vision. He was a Super-S fortunate to be blessed with both great power and wealth. Cruelly, his prosperity became insignificant once he found out he was unable to have children of his own.

JS: But you just said...
CM: I was adopted. My father was a true pioneer. He recognized that many Super-S children were not fulfilling their potential. Many were either neglected or exploited. He wanted to do something to help, so he created HomeLight, a charitable organization that now protects over three hundred children within its walls. We have one hundred staff and security personnel on site, not to mention hundreds of colleagues working off-site on the charity's behalf. We offer hope where there was once darkness and despair. It's a mantle I was honored to take up when he died.

JS: I hope you'll forgive the question, but wasn't it ironic that he should take his own life whilst he gave life to so many others? Did the pressure of caring for so many drive him to it?
CM: No, I don't think his commitment to this organization was the chief murder suspect.

JS: Murder suspect?
CM: My father was in a perfect state-of-mind. There was no way he was considering taking his own life the day he died.

JS: So you believe he was killed?
CM: Undoubtedly. There are many people out there who wish to see HomeLight fail.

JS: Any you would be prepared to name?
CM: Not specifically. Vaders, foreign governments, multinationals, billionaires – many people have tried to infiltrate our organization and invalidate the work we do here. Fortunately, I have my own method of screening prospective employees. My father certainly knew what he was doing when he chose me as the sole heir to his legacy.

Claire affords me a knowing smile.

JS: You have the ability to read people's minds?
CM: Something like that. I can decipher thoughts, evaluate emotions, even predict intentions if the individual I'm monitoring is committed enough. So when I tell you that there wasn't a suicidal thought in my father's mind the day he died, then you'd better believe it. I knew his mental state that day; I knew it better than he did. There was nothing there but love and commitment to the future of HomeLight. He was even planning to set up a new facility in New Jersey to add to the one we established here in Wisconsin.

JS: Well, I wish you all the best in continuing your father's vision. You're doing valuable work for the young and vulnerable.
CM: Thank you. There are still so many out there that need us, need our support. It's a constant struggle, both maintaining the facility and defending it against forces that are just waiting for us to fail. No matter what happens, I'm committed to the end; if it wasn't for the love of my father, I couldn't begin to imagine where I would be right now. You see, I know what it's like to be that little girl on the other side of this mirror.

Before I leave, we watch Sarah's picnic scene slowly unfold and disappear before our eyes. Gone are the unicorns, satyrs, hobbits and leprechauns; gone is the tea party with it's cakes, candy and culinary delights. Sarah, a princess no more, sits on the floor of the white observation room, alone.

Artwork: Sally Hurst - Sarah Berkley

*Interviewee name has been changed

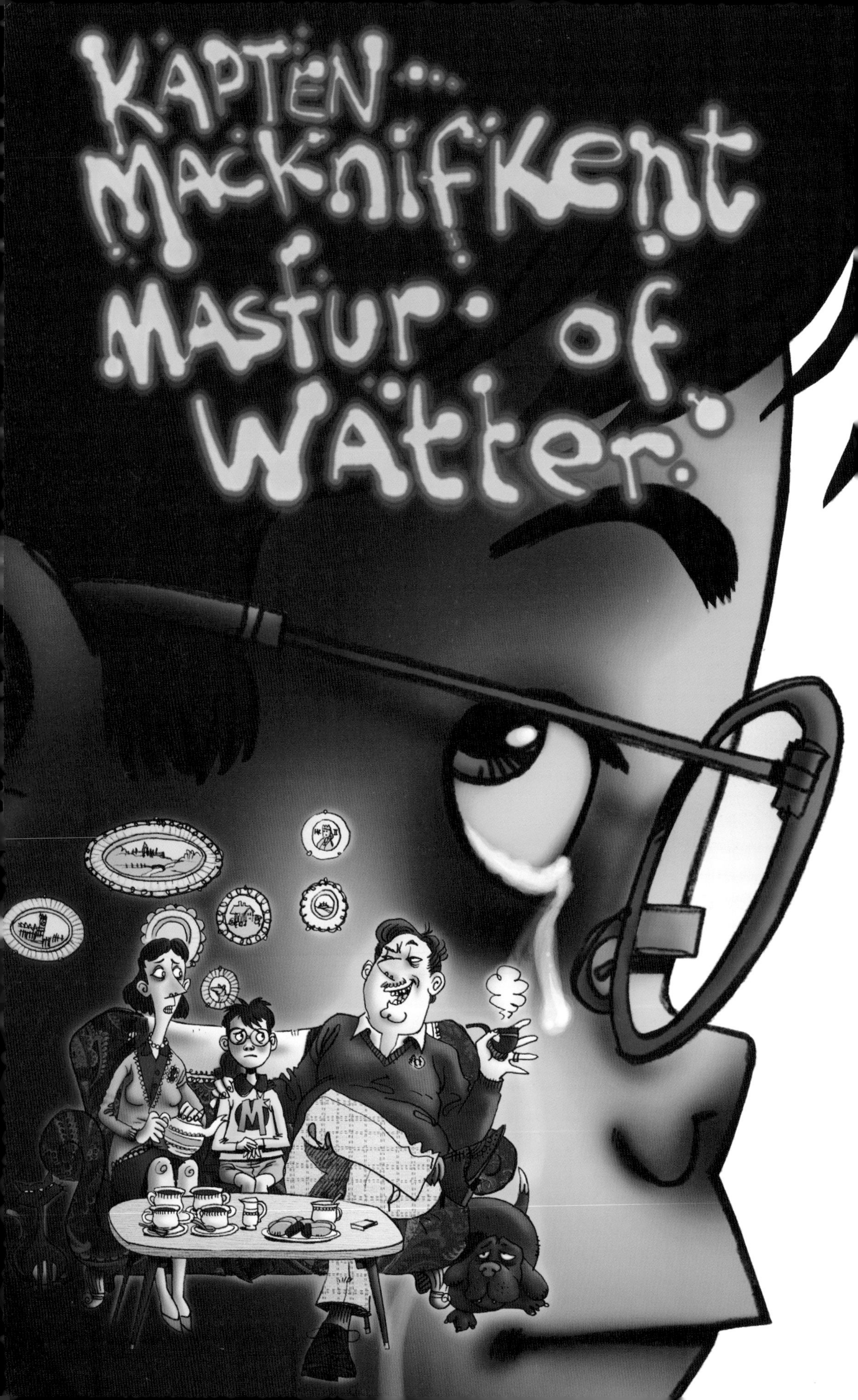
KAPTEN...
MACKNIFKENT
MASTUR OF
WÄTTER.

I am in the West Midlands, United Kingdom. I am here to interview Arthur Miles-Miller, his wife, Valerie, and their nine year-old Super-S son, Nathan.

The house is typical 'Middle England' in style. A traditional, bone-china tea set sits on the table; alongside it a neat regiment of biscuits on a small, white plate. Porcelain and brass ornaments adorn the walls. Arthur Miles-Miller is a portly man with an air of money and arrogance about him. His wife, Valerie, is quite the opposite; she appears quiet and withdrawn. Sandwiched between them sits Nathan, wearing a rather incongruous looking superhero costume; it looks like a cross between Eaton schoolboy and Sherlock Holmes. He appears very self-conscious and uncomfortable. Arthur is anxious to begin the interview.

JS: Thank you for allowing me to interview you. I actually used to live about ten miles from here. Have you been here long?
AMM: Over twenty years now. Moved here in the summer of '87, a few months before the great storm. You remember that?

JS: Yes. Our home only suffered minor damage.
AMM: Lucky you. We lost more than a few roof tiles that day, I can tell you! Mind you, things would have been different had Captain Magnificent been around.

Arthur ruffles his son's hair. Nathan appears unsettled by his father's attention.

JS: Is that your Super-S name, Nathan?

Nathan begins to form an answer, but his father interjects.

AMM: Of course it is! Captain Magnificent, Defender of Justice. Flying the flag for the British Empire. None of that Yank stuff, you know; just good, honest, English heart!

Valerie lets out a gasp, just as she is raising her cup to her lips, spilling tea onto the carpet.

AMM: You stupid woman.

VMM: Sorry, how clumsy. Excuse me while I clean this up.

Valerie hurries to the kitchen and returns with a cloth.

VMM: I'm really sorry Arthur, it was an accident.

Arthur mumbles something under his breath that I can't quite hear. Nathan watches as his mother scrubs feverishly at the stain on the floor. I'm a little embarrassed and can't help feeling that this isn't exactly a happy family. I move the interview on as quickly as possible.

JS: Nathan, can I ask you how it feels knowing you're going to be a superhero when you grow up?
AMM: He's obviously thrilled by it all, isn't he? Normally, he would have followed me into the family business, but now he can make much more money from his abilities and enable me and his old mum to retire early, can't you, son? You mark my words, the Miles-Millers stand on the cusp of greatness. I've done some genealogy research to see if there's evidence of any Super-S blood in my ancestry but surprisingly, nothing's come up yet. I am proud to tell you however that my great-great-grandfather, Albert Miles-Miller, was awarded the Distinguished Conduct Medal for his service during the Crimean War; a surefire sign of the greatness that was to follow. With my expert guidance, I expect Nathan's profile to be appearing on future bank notes!

VMM: I... I have a distinguished ancestor too, one who travelled with the first Pilgrim Fathers that left Plymouth in 1620. He was quite important in his day, mentioned several times in history books for his heroic deeds and-

AMM: Do stop troubling the man with unnecessary drivel, dear. Your ancestor had no claim to greatness whatsoever. In fact, I'm pretty sure it was quite the reverse. He was a Nonconformist who was practically kicked out of his country for his wild beliefs and attitude. Not before his time, if you want my opinion. Now if you don't mind, Mr Stanley is here to discuss Captain Magnificent's superpowers, aren't you, sir?

VMM: Sorry, dear. Of course.

I notice the milk jug rattling on the tea tray Mrs Miles-Miller is holding. Pre-empting another spillage, I reach forward to steady the tray. She gives me an appreciative look. Arthur is oblivious to the situation.

JS: Your family history does sound very interesting Mrs Miles-Miller. How do you feel it contributed to Nathan's Super-S abilities?
VMM: Well, I've always thought-

AMM: Pshht!

I ignore Mr Miles-Miller's interruption but decide to change the subject.

JS: So, tell me Nathan, what makes you special?
AMM: He can do anything he puts his mind to, can't you, my boy? He can fly, move objects with his mind, crush steel with his bare hands-

VMM: Erm... no, he can't, Arthur. He can control water, that's what he's able to do. No flying. No-

AMM: What are you talking about? It's obvious his powers are going to develop further. All Super-S can crush steel and fly! You don't think he'll get to the top just by making pretty shapes out of water, do you? He's got to push himself if he wants to achieve greatness.

JS: I think the ability to control water is a power that needs careful nurturing. After all, 70% of our planet is covered in the stuff and 80% of our brain is made up of it.
AMM: Sorry, Mr Stanley, but that's rubbish.

NMM: Father...

AMM: No son, you have to stand up to these people. How else are you going to learn to defend yourself? Don't let them put you down. Give them an inch now and they'll take everything from you later. You mark my words.

My attention turns to the tea pot, which has started vibrating. Froth is bubbling at the spout and lid.

VMM: Arthur, please...

AMM: Please WHAT? What are you interrupting me for?

I ignore the parents and focus on Nathan.

JS: Nathan, do you want to be a superhero when you're older?
NMM: Actually, I want to be a fireman.

AMM: Don't be stupid, you can't be a fireman!

VMM: Arthur!

A crash is heard from the kitchen. I can hear the sound of water gushing from somewhere. Drips fall from the living-room ceiling, from what I assume is the bathroom above. Valerie rushes out.

AMM: Right, I think that's enough interviewing for now. Nathan and I don't need to answer any more of your banal questions. Putting stupid ideas into my boy's head; what kind of journalist are you? Turn off the recorder, take your stuff and leave, please!

I glance at Nathan as I leave the room. Despite his water-controlling abilities and the chaos he's inadvertently instigated, it's apparent the poor boy has no control over his own tears.

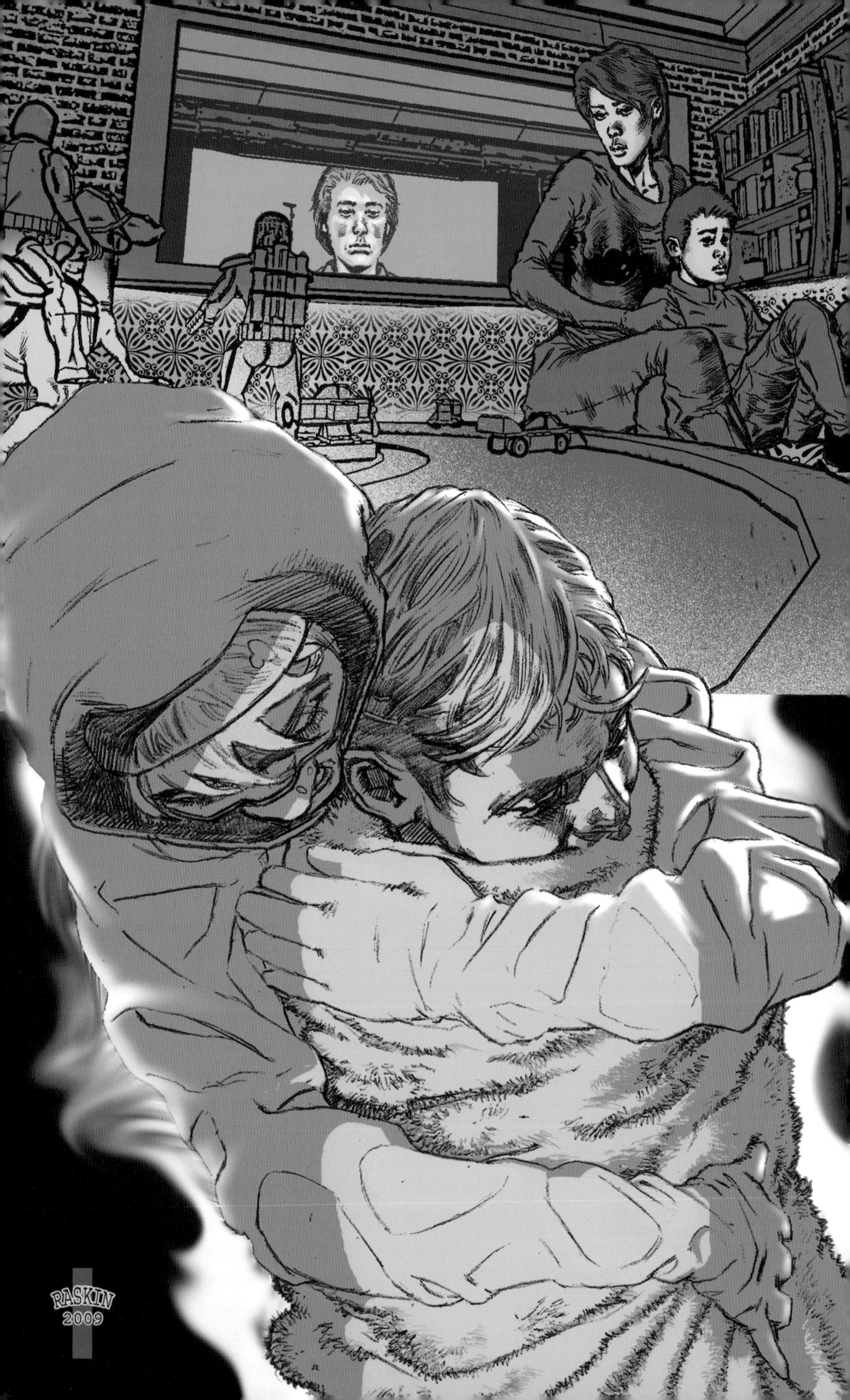
RASKIN
2009

Like any regular eleven year-old boy, Richard Lewis* enjoys watching TV. But Richard is far from normal. For his own and other's safety, Richard's mother has chosen to shield him from the outside world. They reside in a secluded suburb, not far from Detroit, in one of the new Government-monitored S-Zones.

I am sitting with Richard and his mother, Laura, in his bedroom. He is rocking back and forth on a chair, watching a wall-mounted television and juggling the remote in his hands. Laura is wearing a custom-made, latex suit.

JS: Hello, Richard. Do you know why I'm here?

Richard doesn't break his stare from the television.

RL: You're here about my power.

JS: That's right, your mother contacted me and said it would be okay to talk with you. Is it okay if we talk?
RL: 'Suppose...

JS: So, tell me what you can do.

Richard doesn't answer.

LL: Honey, Mr Stanley asked you a question. Please answer.

RL: I hurt things.

JS: What do you mean?

Richard shrugs his shoulders.

RL: I dunno. I touch them and they just... go bad. I hurt Mom, too.

JS: Can you elaborate?
LL: I was pregnant with Richard when my husband Jeff, died. I was devastated. After losing him, my baby became even more precious to me; my only living connection to Jeff. When Richard finally arrived the labor was an incredibly painful experience; I knew the process would hurt, and you prepare yourself for it mentally, but this pain was like no other. I felt like I was on fire. Thankfully, the labor didn't last long. The midwives handed him to me as soon as he was born. They encouraged me to breastfeed straight away, so naturally I embraced the idea. But as he suckled, a searing, intense heat shot through my chest. I looked down to see my breast rotting away before my very eyes. I screamed for help. They pulled us apart and I was rushed to surgery to have the tissue around the wound neutralized before the decay could spread any further.

Laura pauses. She touches her chest, remembering.

LL: They removed the whole thing.

JS: I'm so sorry to hear that.
LL: He wasn't to blame. No-one could have known.

JS: Why weren't the midwives injured when they handled him?
LL: Surgical gloves. It quickly became apparent that his ability to decay only triggers when his body is in contact with organic matter.

JS: Did you know he was a Super-S before he was born?
LL: No, Jeff and I didn't feel it necessary to take the test; no family member on either side has ever been diagnosed as having the Super-S gene.

JS: How do you cope, not being able to touch Richard?
LL: It's unbearable. I can't cuddle him without protection, I can't comfort him if he scrapes his knee; I've been denied that all-important, physical bond with my son. I think we've both suffered because of that.

She runs her latex-gloved hand through Richard's hair. His initial reaction is to flinch, but slowly, he warms to his mother's actions.

LL: I haven't touched him properly since the day he was born. We endure life through plastic, rubber, anything dense and non-organic that his touch can't react to.

JS: Richard, do you ever play outside with other children?

Richard ignores the question.

LL: Richard?

RL: I don't like playing outside.

LL: It was never his intention to harm anyone. I want to make that clear; he's a good boy. The accident just... happened.

Laura's voice drops to a whisper.

It wasn't his fault. They were playing together. I blame myself. I should have been watching them more carefully. Richard's glove tore, but he hadn't realized; neither of them did. And he accidentally touched Michael on the head.

JS: Michael?
LL: He was Richard's friend that lived next door.

JS: Was?
LL: After the funeral, Michael's parents moved away. The police asked a lot of questions and I thought they were going to take Richard away. There was bad talk coming from the town's folk. I feared for our safety.

JS: Were there any repercussions?
LL: Probably, had we stayed. But some government men visited us, said they understood what we were going through and could help with Richard's situation. I was so grateful to them. They gave us so much support; money, a new home here. It's not so bad being monitored and at least the other parents in the 'Zone talk to me. There are many other families here in a similar position, and Richard has the opportunity to make new friends, when he's ready.

JS: Which government department were these men from?
LL: They called themselves the XoDOS Initiative.

JS: Did they ask for anything in return?
LL: No, nothing. All they do is visit us once a month to talk to Richard and run a few tests on him. Other than that, they leave us alone. Sometimes they'll call to see if we need anything. Last month they bought Richard this brand-new, widescreen TV for his bedroom. He hasn't stopped watching it.

JS: So, Richard, what's your favourite program?
RL: The news. Some cartoons, but mainly the news.

JS: Why's that?
RL: I can see what's happening in the outside world. It helps me protect my Mom and keep her safe.

LL: Don't be silly, honey. Who do I need protecting from?

RL: The bad people.

JS: What bad people?
RL: The ones on TV.

Richard points at the screen. Whilst I've been interviewing his mother, he's been watching a newsflash. A reporter and camera crew are reporting from Toronto, where a new super-villain called Memento is laying waste to the city.

LL: Can I ask you something, Mr Stanley?

JS: Of course.
LL: When your child is born, be sure to give it a big hug from me.

05

Artwork: Jordan Raskin - Richard Lewis

*Interviewee name has been changed

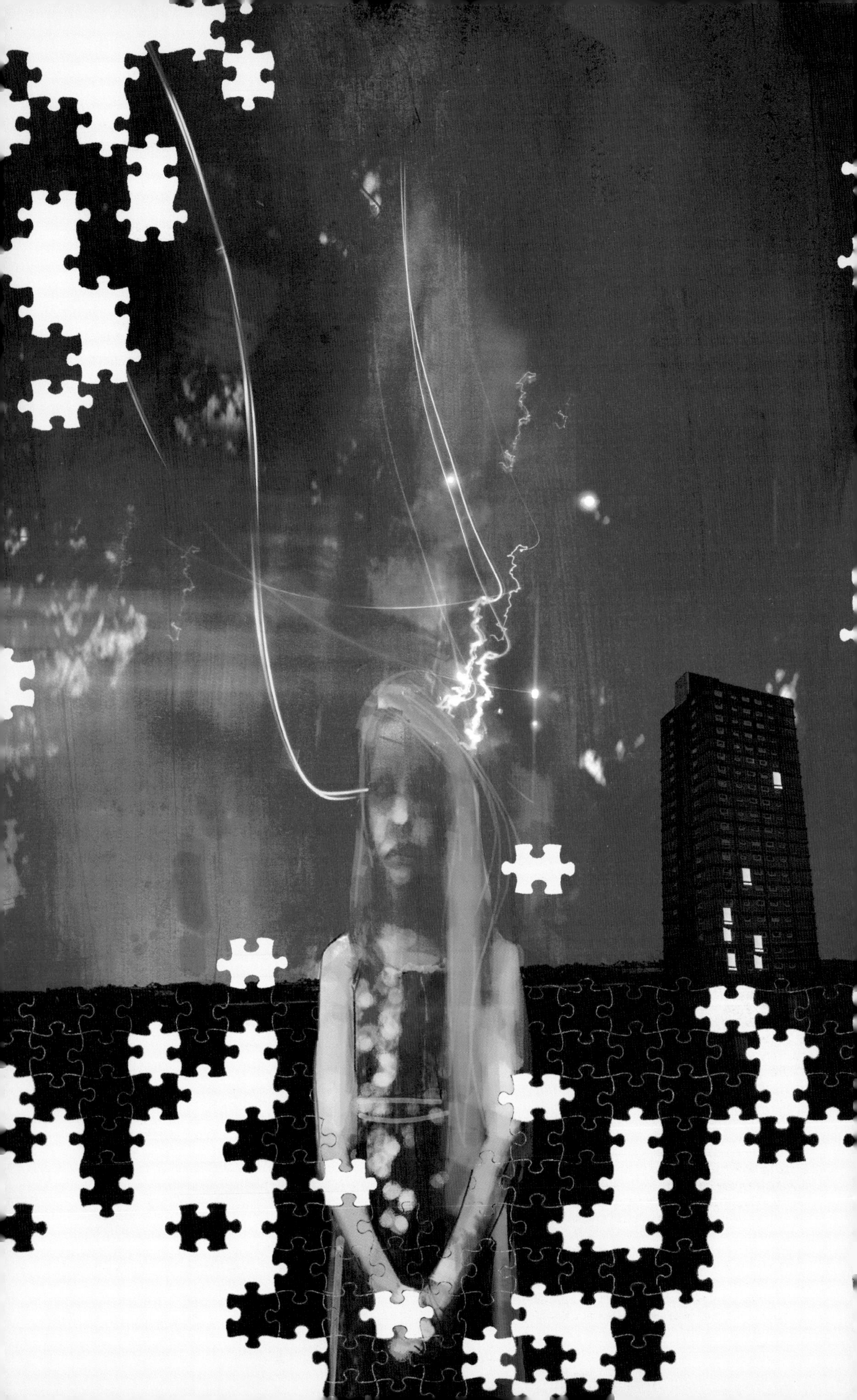

Jennifer Turner* is a single mother living in a council flat in Dagenham, Essex. She has three children by three different men; Josh (5), Ryan (8) and Amy (12). Amy is Super-S.

Jennifer's flat is located at the top of an apartment block on the notorious Brown Estate. Childrens' drawings adorn the living-room walls, wedged between tourist souvenirs from holidays long past. Amy is sitting on the floor, piecing a jigsaw together. Josh, her youngest brother, is trying to help her whilst Ryan is preoccupied, watching television. Jennifer lights a cigarette and slowly exhales.

JS: How are you coping? You look like you have your hands full!
JT: You tell me. I'm stuck in this shitty flat with barely enough space to swing a cat, I'm struggling to put food on the table an' pay the bloody rent. Benefits don't cover it. Josh is gonna be startin' school soon, so maybe I'll be able to go out an' get a job and bring in more money. But then, my tax credits will stop, so I'll be back to square one again. Typical.

JS: Is there any additional support you can apply for, for Amy's circumstances? Anyone that can help?
JT: You're joking, aren't ya? I get no additional benefit recognition for Amy whatsoever. Nuffin'! This soddin' government don't recognise her rights as a Super-S. I get normal child benefits, that's all. If she was disabled I'd get more, but she's put in the same bracket as Norman kids. But she ain't the same.

JS: How do you cope with her abilities?
JT: It's bloody hard, I won't lie. There are times I wish she weren't Super-S. It's bad enough bringing up three kids on your own, let alone when one of them can do the sort of things she can. It gets too much, know what I mean? I don't sleep well at night, I wake up at the slightest sound. I mean, *every* sound. As you might have gathered, this ain't exactly a quiet neighbourhood.

Jennifer shakes her head and looks over at Amy, who's spinning several pieces of jigsaw in the air in front of her. She picks one of the pieces out of the air and tries it in one of the empty spaces on the puzzle. It doesn't fit. She lets go of it and it floats back to rejoin the other floating pieces. Josh sits, fascinated by the whole scene.

JT: Nah, she ain't the same.

JS: Where's her father? Does he pay maintenance?
JT: Does he 'eck, he's long gone. Left as soon as he found out I was pregnant. Said I was a fuckin' whore and a stupid slut that should've taken precautions. Wanker. Good riddance. We only saw each other the once an' look what he left me with; a freak kid. He can stuff himself, I don't want anything to do with him.

JS: Can't the courts track him down and force him to pay for her upkeep?
JT: What's the point? I hardly knew him. Guys like him probably got a dozen women like me all over the world. I think he used to work on the ships, an' you know what that sort are like. I don't even know where he is. The bastard can rot in Hell, for all I care. We don't need him. We'll survive somehow. We always manage to. Men! All bastards, every last one of them. Present company excepted, of course.

JS: Do you remember anything else about him?

Jennifer shrugs her shoulders.

JT: To be honest, it's all a bit of a blur, it was about twelve years ago. I can't remember being drunk when we got together, but I guess we must have had a few. Either that, or I've tried to shut the bastard out of my mind and move on.

JS: What about your parents? Are they supportive?
JT: They don't want to know. They're scared of Amy, of what she can do. Sometimes, I know how they feel; she can scare the crap out of me too. But she's my kid, y'know? You have no idea what we put up with; the other families on the estate whispering about us behind our backs, kids slaggin' us off as we walk past. I've had graffiti sprayed on me front door, bricks through the windows, the lot. They treat us like we're some kinda freak show.

JS: There are Academies of Higher Development that can help her, to teach her how to use her powers properly.
JT: I'll use some of me Lottery winnings for that then, shall I? Do I look like I was born with a silver spoon in me mouth? Schools like that cost money. Lots of money. Amy has to go to a Norman school, like all the other kids. It's free.

JS: There should be some sort of funding available for her.
JT: We've already had some people 'round here talkin' money an' training an' stuff. Amy doesn't want to go, though. Can't say I blame her, they gave me the creeps; could be bloody pervs for all I know.

JS: Who were they?
JT: I can't remember their name, but they were American. At least, they spoke with American accents. I don't trust yanks. Not from what I've seen of 'em on the telly.

JS: Was it an organisation?
JT: I told ya, I can't remember. They weren't here long enough for me to know the ins-and-outs of what they did or what they 'ad for lunch.

JS: So how will you allow her to nurture her ability? How will she understand not to misuse her powers?
JT: Misuse? Look we might be struggling, but that doesn't make us criminals.

JS: Sorry, I didn't mean it that way.
JT: Then what fuckin' way did you mean?

JS: Well, she might feel the need to protect you, from the abuse you're suffering. But in doing so, she may not realise her own strength and she might hurt someone. Possibly kill them.
JT: Well, more fool them then. Teach them not to mess with us. They'll think twice about doing it again.

Jennifer stubs out her cigarette and lights another, just as Josh stumbles into Amy's part-finished jigsaw puzzle. Puzzle pieces spill across the floor. Amy screams in frustration. Suddenly, Josh's feet leave the floor and he's pressed, spread-eagled, against the ceiling. He starts crying.

JT: Amy, put your brother down!

AT: He ruined my jigsaw!

JT: AMY! PUT YOUR BROTHER DOWN NOW OR GOD HELP YA. I WON'T TELL YA AGAIN!

Josh becomes hysterical. Jennifer pulls Amy to her feet and shakes her, violently.

JT: What have I told you about using your powers on us? LET HIM DOWN, NOW!

Josh floats back down from the ceiling. As his feet touch the floor he runs to his mother, burying his tear-soaked face in her tracksuit bottoms. Amy pulls free and runs to the corner of the room, where she sits with her back to us, sobbing. The jigsaw pieces strewn across the floor vibrate angrily and float towards Amy. They reposition themselves around her protectively, like a shroud.

JS: I'm sure she didn't mean to hurt him, her emotions obviously triggered her power. She's too young to really understand what she's capable of doing.
JT: She'll do as she's told, or she'll feel the back of my hand.

The puzzle pieces freeze mid-air for a second before dropping to the floor.

JS: Is that really necessary?
JT: Never done me no harm.

06

Artwork: Jock – Amy Turner

*Interviewee name has been changed

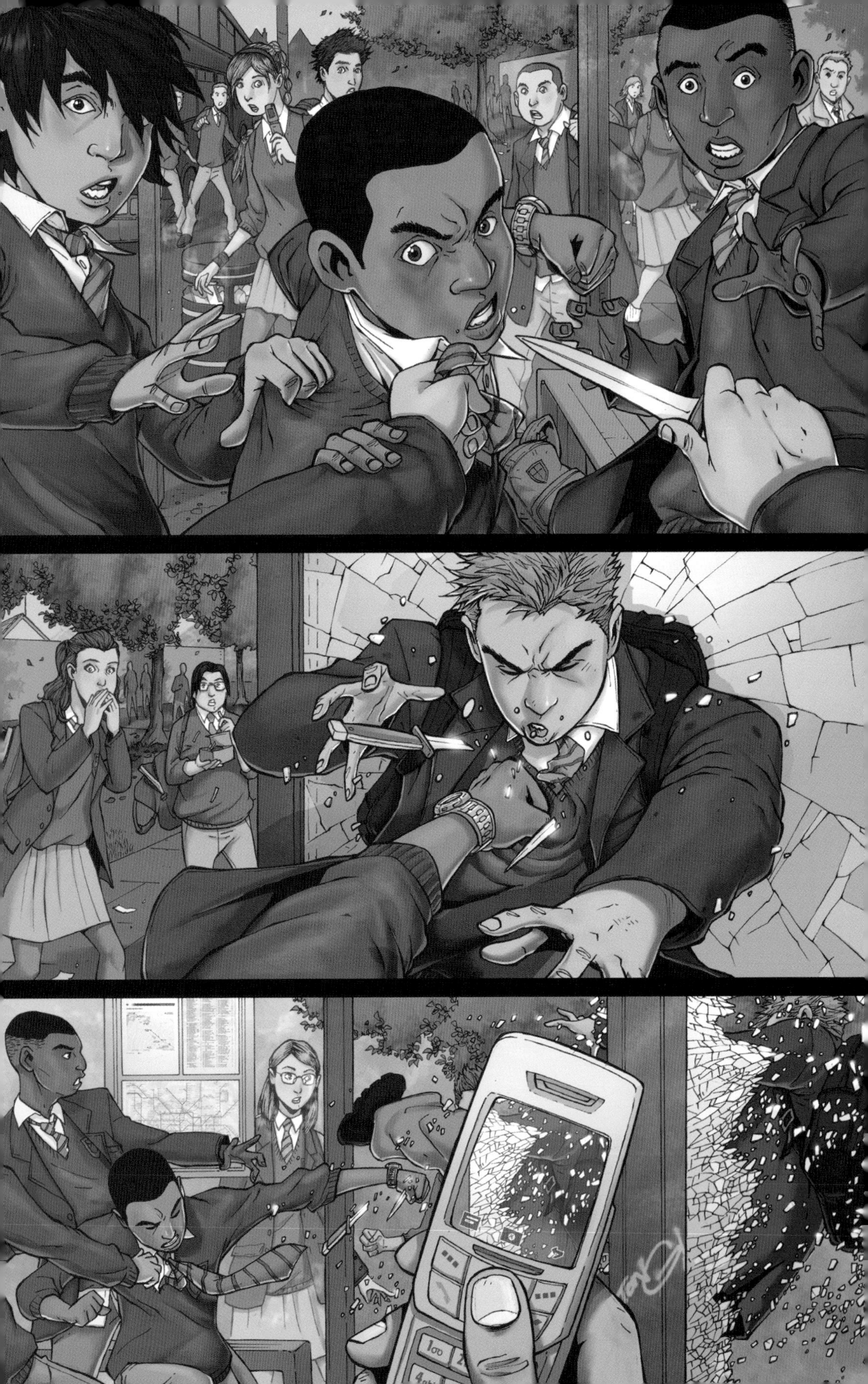

Simon Bakersfield* is fourteen years-old; a self-assured boy for his age. He attends a Norman school in Leicester, United Kingdom.

We're in the school canteen; not the quietest of locations to conduct an interview, but Simon insisted I meet him here. Both his parents and the school have given me consent to interview him.

JS: You had the option of attending a Super-S school but chose a Norman comprehensive instead – why is that?
SB: I want to be treated like a real person, not a sideshow freak.

JS: Do your parents support your decision?
SB: They're both Normans, so they're happy I'm getting a similar education to the one they had.

JS: Super-S schools offer a system that helps develop the special gifts young people like you have. Isn't that something you'd prefer?
SB: I don't think I'm *special,* and I don't want to be surrounded by people that think they are. At first, my Headmaster tried to keep my gift a secret, leaving me to blend in with the rest of the pupils, but it's a small school and rumours get around quick. Deep down, I think he was delighted to have me come here; it opens the door for more to follow.

JS: Has the school coped well with you being acknowledged as a Super-S?
SB: They've been great. I'm their first one. Off the record, I'm looked upon as a bit of a celebrity by the staff. But I try not to encourage them or take the mickey. You know, by handing homework in late and stuff like that.

JS: What about the pupils?
SB: Most of them are great; I'm pretty much treated like one of the gang. I don't try and show off to get noticed in any way, but of course, not everyone is cool about it.

JS: What do you mean?
SB: Well, I don't like to name names, but Billy Horn and his crew were a little rough on me when I joined. I stress *were.*

JS: What happened?
SB: Typical 'new kid' stuff. Billy and his gang thought they would teach me a lesson. I was waiting at the bus-stop; I'd stayed behind for football practice – I play right-back for the school team.

Anyway, Billy and his mates turned up at the same bus-stop. They must have had detention or something, as there's no way they would be hanging around that late after school for any other reason. Two of them started pushing me about and grabbed my bag and threw it on top of the bus-shelter. The usual intimidation tactics. It was all pretty mindless stuff, but I was in control of myself, I wasn't reacting to them. Maybe it was my calmness that got to them, because they suddenly turned real nasty; spitting at me, slapping my face. Then one of them pushed me to the ground and stopped me from getting up. That's when Billy started kicking me, hard!

JS: What did you do then?

Simon looks around to see if anyone nearby is listening before he continues.

SB: It got worse. One of the crew said the word 'shiv' and some of them backed away. Billy was standing over me with a blade in his hand. To think he would be cowardly enough to do that, that's what made me mad. I got up and hit him. I know I shouldn't have but I had no choice in the matter, he was going to cut me.

JS: It sounds like you showed admirable restraint. It was clearly self-defence.
SB: Yeah, but I slammed him right through the glass bus-shelter. His mates just looked at me. They were scared. I mean, *really* scared. Billy was the toughest boy in our school and I had just bust him through the shelter like a rag doll. He ended up in hospital; a hundred and sixty-seven stitches! They didn't dare touch me after that. No one did. Billy moved away after his recovery. I paid him a visit before he left the school, though.

JS: Not to apologise, surely!
SB: No way! To give him a 'little' lecture on knife-crime. And to let him know he would always be in my thoughts, if you know what I mean.

A bell rings in the canteen. Everyone returns to class, leaving myself and Simon alone.

JS: How did the school treat the incident?
SB: I was suspended for two weeks. My parents grounded me for a further two months. The police asked lots of questions but nothing 'came of it. They spoke to Billy too. Turns out, he'd been in trouble with them before. There was no more hiding what I was after that.

JS: How did you feel going back to school after your suspension?
SB: I shat myself! First day back I didn't know how everyone was going to react. I worried that my new friends would be scared of me. You hear horror stories of Super-S in other Norman schools, where they're treated like lepers and such, but everyone was great; I was suddenly the coolest kid in school.

Besides, I had sorted out a common enemy. They even called me "Bionic Billy-Basher" for a while. I don't think I'll be keeping that name for when I'm older! I did find there was an up-side and a down-side to the incident, though...

JS: What was the up-side? Let me hazard a guess. Was it female attention?
SB: Yeah. I really could do without it right at this moment, I've got too much on my plate with my studies to get involved with girls. I know they're not really interested in the real me, more the power I wield. They were friendly to me before the incident with Billy, but not *that* friendly. And it's worked out better for my mates, too. They now get attention from those girls who want to get closer to me and at the same time, the bad kids steer clear of them.

JS: And the down-side?
SB: I was kicked off the school football team.

JS: How did that feel?
SB: I was upset at first, but I understand why.

JS: Because they knew your superpower was physical?
SB: Yeah. I'd tried so hard to suppress it and not make it obvious. I would be lying if I said I hadn't been tempted in the past to take on the entire opposition and score the winning goal, busting the net and the goalkeeper's hands in the process, but I kept my head down and made myself useful as a right-back.

When I was rumbled as a Super-S, it didn't take long before the other teams found out about me. And I don't like the idea that my school team would have been labelled as cheats just because of me. I'm not a great footballer; my superpower doesn't give me the natural skill to play like say, Beckham, but I'm very fast and very strong. The team weren't happy when I had to leave but they still let me go to practice after school. We have a great time; I go in goal, and the challenge is to score a penalty past me.

JS: Has anyone succeeded?
SB: Not yet! That's one game I'm playing to win!

JS: So what plans do you have for your future?

Simon looks at the clock hanging in the canteen.

SB: Well, right now there's a math's lesson and I'm late! Sorry, I know we have permission to chat longer, but I have exams in a week. Laters!

Artwork: Andie Tong - Simon Bakersfield

**Interviewee name has been changed*

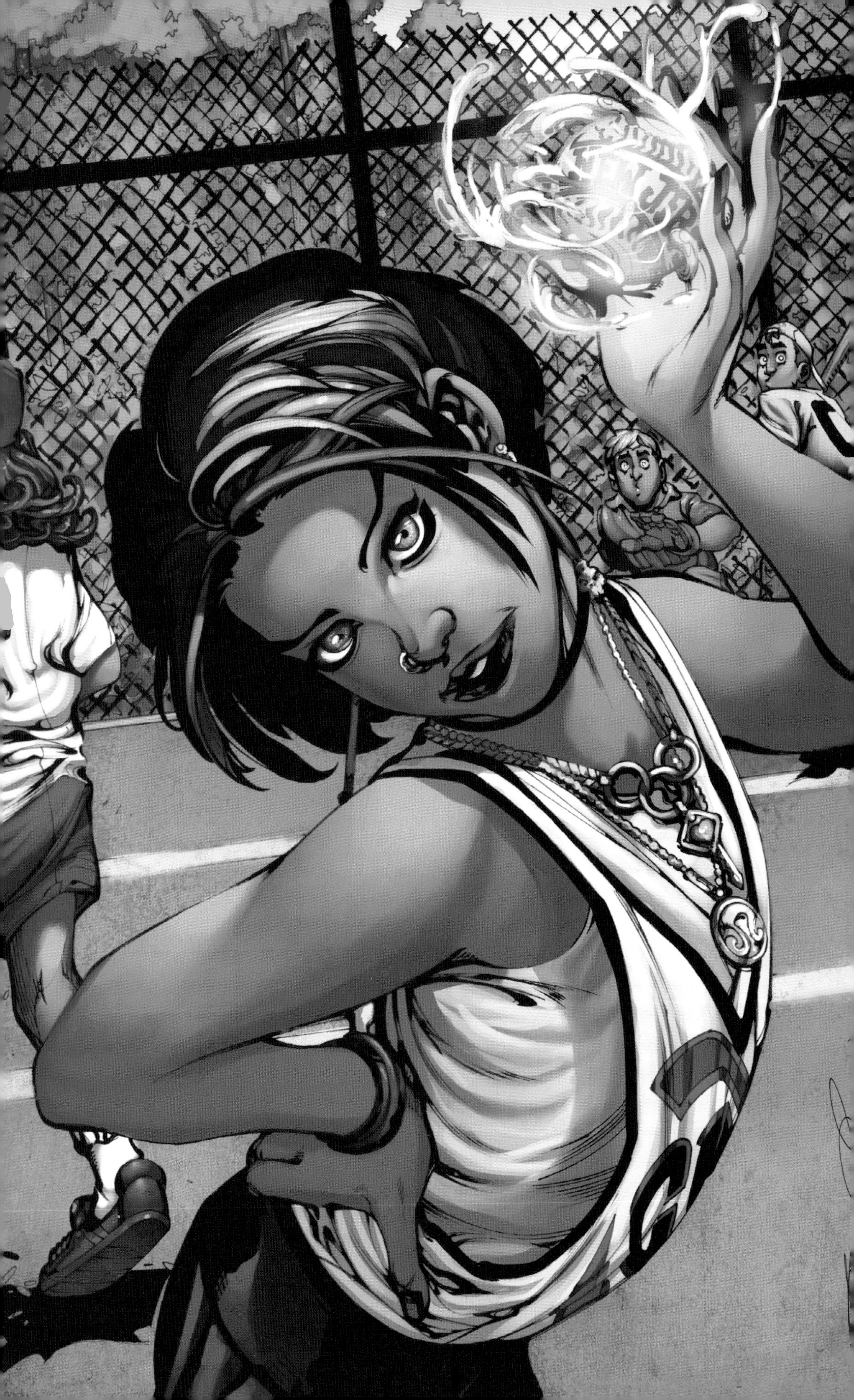

Monica Bentley is a sixteen year-old student at the EvenSeed Academy of Higher Development, New Jersey. It's a school dedicated to training those gifted few who are Super-S.

We're standing in the middle of a playing field. A mixed game of softball is in progress. Monica should be fielding deep, but she's taking five minutes out from the game to talk to me.

JS: Are you enjoying your time at EvenSeed?
MB: Oh, yeah! It's so awesome. It's great being surrounded by kids like me. Well, not exactly like me, but you know what I mean. We're all special.

JS: Have you found being "special" has it's drawbacks?
MB: Well, kind of. EvenSeed has a policy of no mixing with Normans during school term, or any communication with Norman high schools – a BIG drawback in my book.

JS: You mean Norman boys?

Monica blushes.

MB: Maybe. Some of us do manage to sneak out after hours to hang out with a few Norman boys from the next school. Suzanne Garcia is an Invo. You know what an Invo is?

JS: She has the power of invisibility?
MB: Yeah, but she's not like any old regular Invo; she can project. You getting this? Like, the size of a pickup truck! It means a whole group of us can sneak out without being spotted.

JS: Where do you go?
MB: Nowhere special. Mainly, we just hang out at Quakerbridge Mall. But we only go if old Mrs Warner isn't on patrol. She's a Spook; got some weird, funky kind of special-vision thing going on. None of us are entirely sure how it works. All I know is, every time Suzanne tries to sneak us out when Warner is on duty, we end up getting caught. And that usually means detention or cleaning out the locker rooms; both the girls AND the boys! That sucks so bad. We don't chance it anymore when she's on duty.

Crack! Someone shouts as the ball is hit deep in the outfield. Monica runs for the ball but another fielder phases into the ball's path in mid-air, plucking it out the sky. He reappears back on the ground, triumphantly holding the ball aloft.

MB: No fair, Tom! You know the rules. No powers!

The shrill of a whistle is heard over a chorus of protests from the side that are batting. An umpire walks over to Tom and reprimands him. His team are penalised.

MB: Jerk. He's always doing that.

JS: Why was he penalised?
MB: For using his powers, of course.

JS: But I thought you were encouraged to develop and embrace your powers?

Monica laughs at my puzzled expression.

MB: It's not about using powers to do everything. Here at the school, we're taught not to rely upon them, but to understand when and how we should use them. Just because Tom can use his power to catch the ball, doesn't mean he should. You get me?

JS: Of course.
MB: You can't always rely on your power for every given situation, so you have to be able to trust all your abilities, super-powered or not. The school teaches us that confidence in yourself and optimism are the most powerful weapons anyone can have. Some of the kids here say I'm too positive sometimes, too out there. I think they feel a little intimidated. I can't help it.

JS: Who, the Boys?
MB: Yeah, mostly.

JS: Do you date the guys here?
MB: Date the boys? Ewww! No, thank you! I've tried a few times; some of them are good-looking, but most of them are jerks. They're all on their mini-ego trips; "Yo, I can bench-press a Jeep", or, "My eyes can burn thru steel". Yadda yadda. Always the same, totally into themselves and trying to outdo their buddies. It's sooo boring.

I much prefer Norman boys. Most of us girls do. Once they know you're a Super-S, they try harder to impress you, to show you that it's just as cool to be Norman as it is to have powers. There's something cute about that.

Monica giggles.

You think I'm silly?

JS: Not at all. I think it's admirable that you don't judge someone purely on the extent, or lack, of special abilities.
MB: Who knows? Maybe I'll marry a Norman one day, instead of some high-profile, Super-S dude.

JS: Speaking of the future, what are your plans after you graduate?
MB: I haven't thought much about it yet. Some of my girls here want to start a girls-only superhero group. I kind of like the idea of that, but you have to be careful – girls can get real bitchy. I don't like the idea of joining a group with so much back-biting and mind games. Imagine the mess they would make out of one another if it all went wrong? Still, it would be fun to watch from the sidelines.

Monica laughs.

JS: What about going alone?
MB: No way. You hear too many horror stories about those going "Solo". You have to be extremely talented to even think about doing something as brave as that. We were told a shocking statistic the other day: only 6% make it Solo. That leaves a huge proportion that end up in teams, duos or as military support; and that doesn't even include those that retire early, have mental break-downs or "go Vader".

JS: What are your other options?
MB: We had a presentation from an organization called XoDOS recently. They're recruiting for the government; that sounds pretty cool. I could be tempted by something like that. You know, doing good for your country. They wore these totally rad outfits and handed out glossy brochures and gave us a slide-show presentation on the opportunities within their organization, like working abroad and stuff. That appeals to me, but...

JS: But what?
MB: I dunno. I've heard different things from people. You know, rumours on web forums, S-Book, places like that.

Another crack! The ball is hit in our direction. Monica studies it as it flies over our heads.

MB: Hey, did they tell you what my superpower is?

JS: No, they didn't.
MB: Better stand back then. Things are gonna get hot, real quick!

Monica's body transforms into molten mass before my eyes. She bursts into the air and catches the ball, incinerating it in an instant. She lands back on the field, her burning shape returning to normal. Her clothes smoking but still intact. Another whistle stops the game. Tom shouts from his fielding position.

T: Hey, Blastarella! Who's cheating now?

MB: Bite me!

Artwork: Eduardo Francisco / Colours: Teodoro Gonzalez – Monica Bentley

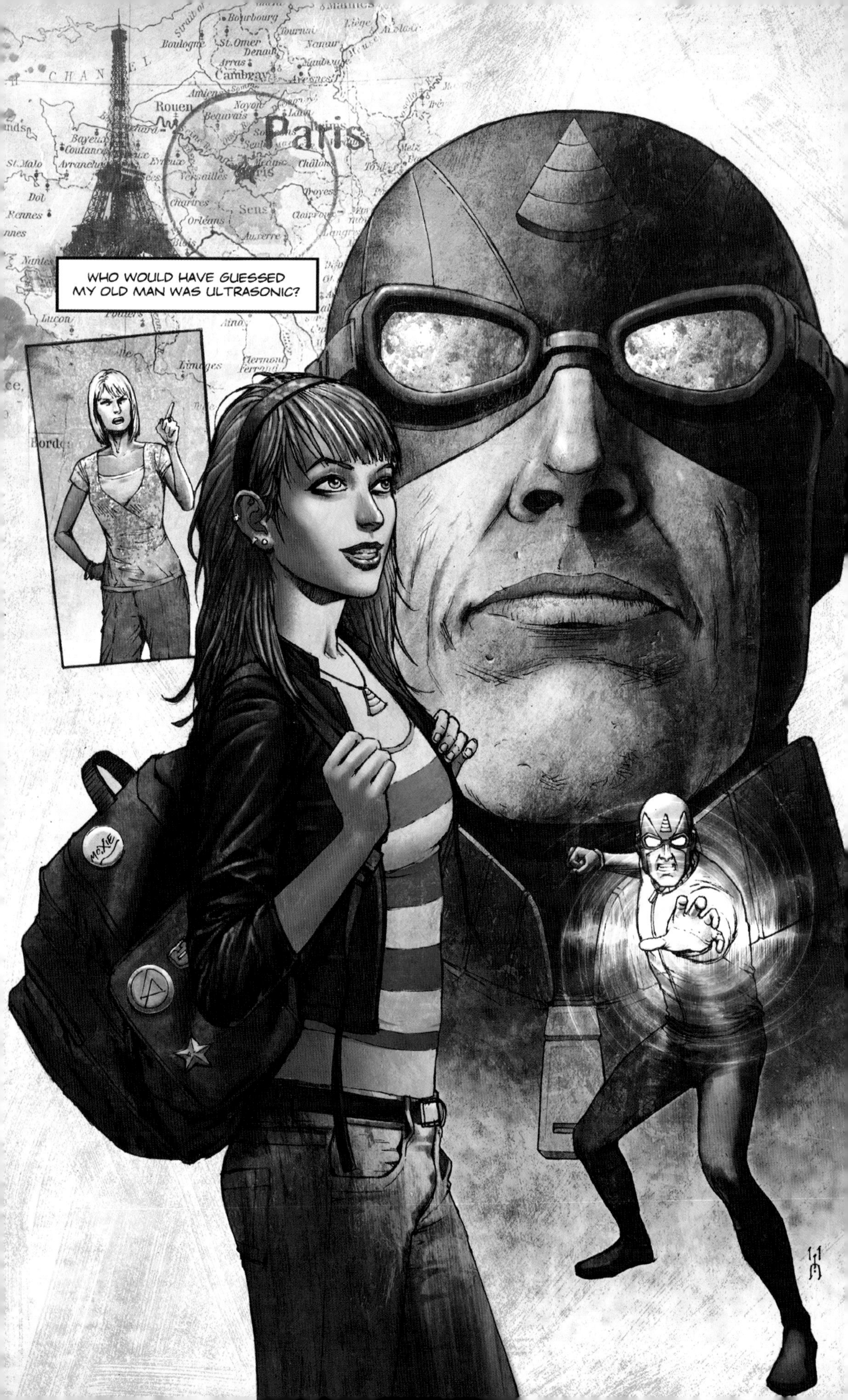
WHO WOULD HAVE GUESSED MY OLD MAN WAS ULTRASONIC?
Paris
MOXIE

St. Pancras Station, London. Seventeen year-old Hannah Hawkins should be enjoying her teenage years but instead, she's growing up a lot faster than most, with just her Norman mother for support.

It's extremely early in the morning. I'm sitting at a table, with a cup of coffee, waiting for Hannah to arrive. I'm not sure she's going to turn up; she's already an hour late for our interview (but it wouldn't be the first time I've been stood up by an interviewee). I'm about to leave the station, and its hoards of early-morning commuters, when a young woman carrying a backpack approaches me.

JS: Hannah?
HH: Hey! You must be James? Pleased to meet you! Sorry I'm late; bloody London Underground! So, you'd like to talk to me about dad?

JS: Yes please.
HH: Who would have guessed my old man was UltraSonic? A Super-S – and a famous one at that! I was eleven when I found the letters he'd written to my mum hidden in her bedroom wardrobe. She wasn't happy and refused to discuss the situation until my sixteenth birthday; she felt I wasn't old enough to understand. What she told me was very hard to accept, which is why I need to find him and hear his side of the story.

JS: Have you established contact with him?
HH: No, but I can't wait until I do!

JS: You seem to have a burning desire to uncover your past. How do you plan on finding him?
HH: I've been following his recent movements. I heard that he's living in Paris – at least, that's what the papers say. I booked myself on the Eurostar. I'll find him somehow, even if I have to throw myself off the Eiffel Tower to do it!

JS: You're being quite optimistic. Don't you feel somewhat bitter that he abandoned you?
HH: Not really. Mum told me that it was safer for everyone if he wasn't around us anymore. Even now, I think she's still worried about me, I reckon she thinks that someone will hurt me to get to him. But I don't mind the risk, he's my dad, I can look after myself.

JS: I can understand your eagerness to see him but what if the answers you're looking for fall short? What if he doesn't want to meet you?
HH: I have to know, I have to meet him. He's not gonna refuse to see me, right? I *will* find him. Besides, UltraSonic seems a solid kind of guy; he'll be cool with it, won't he?

JS: Does your mum know you're on your way to Paris?
HH: Not exactly. When I mentioned that I wanted to contact my dad, she totally flew off the handle! She accused me of not loving her and wanted to know why I was punishing her. She said that I would be putting myself in danger if I decided to try and find him.

Hannah sighs.

JS: But you're still going?
HH: She thinks I'm off to Sheffield, to visit friends. I know, I know. I'll call her later and tell her where I am. This is important to me.

JS: Have you inherited any of your dad's abilities?
HH: I wish! But I do think we look alike! I don't have his powers but mum says I'm irrational and I get that from him. Typical – all I get is a difficult attitude when I could've had something cool, like his SonicWave! But, y'know, the main thing is that I have a dad.

JS: Would you like to be a superhero?
HH: Seriously? Who wouldn't want to do the things he does? Those that say they wouldn't are totally lying. Not that my mum would approve; she'd have kittens if I followed in his footsteps! But I don't think there's much chance of me suddenly developing super-powers, just because I've met my dad. It would be pretty cool, though, wouldn't it?

JS: What was it like growing up without him, yet seeing his image adorned across the front page of the news or on a TV report?
HH: Well like I said, I didn't know who he was until I was eleven, but like any kid without a dad, it was tough. Constantly seeing his face splashed across the media all the time really hurt. Mum would tear his picture out of newspapers and magazines or change channels if he was on TV, as if he didn't exist. I kept a secret scrapbook on him. She never found out.

JS: Do you blame your mother for what she's tried to do?
HH: Yes... no... oh, I dunno, it... it's difficult isn't it? I'm sure she had her reasons but I'm an adult now and I can make my own decisions. And that includes looking for Dad. Mum's only trying to do what she thinks is best. It's not easy being a single parent.

JS: Do you think your mum was right to protect you from the dangers attached to being the daughter of a superhero?
HH: I guess so. But there's violence and pain everywhere, you can't hide from it. I don't see why my life is any more dangerous to that of, say, any other Norman, really. Plus, there are plenty of heroes out there that balance private lives with their public work, so why would my world be any more hazardous if my dad was a part of it?

JS: Do you think he's been successful *because* he had no family to worry about?
HH: I hope not, 'cos he's about to meet his daughter and I intend to stay in his life! Boy, this is a tough interview!

JS: I'm sorry. I'm just interested in your opinion.
HH: Well, I hope he can care about me as much as he does about others. He does incredible good, saves countless lives. It's comforting to know that he puts the general public before himself; he's got to be a caring man, right? How could he not feel something for his own flesh and blood? I guess I'll find out soon enough. Plus, I've been thinking about it, I want to do good like he does. I know I don't have powers but there's lots of jobs I can do where I can help people-

The station Tannoy barks into life as boarding for the Eurostar to Paris begins. Hannah picks up her bag.

-Oops. Sorry to cut the interview short, but gotta go. This is one train I can't afford to miss!

JS: Well, thank you so much for your time. The best of luck and I hope you find what you're looking for.
HH: Thanks! I just hope he likes what *he* finds.

09

Artwork: Wayne Nichols - Hannah Hawkins

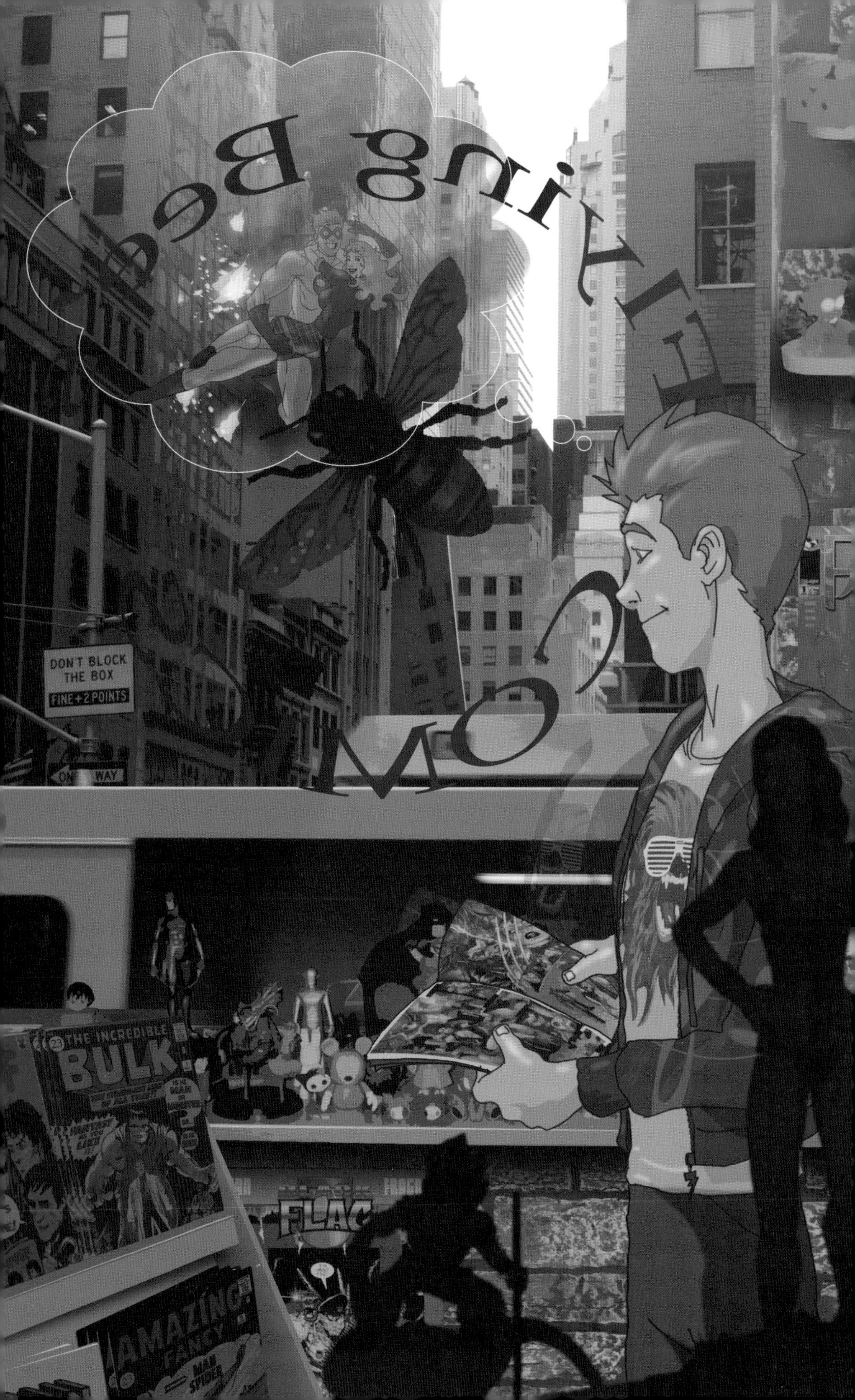
DON'T BLOCK
THE BOX
FINE + 2 POINTS
ONE WAY
23 THE INCREDIBLE
BULK
FLAG
AMAZING
FANCY
MAN
SPIDER

When not at Norman school, eighteen-year-old Peter spends his spare time working at his parents comic shop, just off Times Square, New York. Peter was born a Super-S but didn't discover he had a gift until he reached puberty.

Midday. The shop is quiet. Peter is behind the counter, doing an inventory check of the latest delivery.

JS: Just for the record, you aren't really...

Peter laughs.

PP: Nope. My parents have a wry sense of humor. This is my dad's store and, as you can probably tell, he's into his comics, big-time. With a surname like mine it was inevitable I was going to be called Peter.

JS: Where is he today?
PP: He's out at one of the 'Cons, I watch the store when things are slow. It's alright – gives me a chance to chill-out and recharge the batteries and shit.

JS: Do you mind being named after a fictitious alter-ego?
PP: Man, it sucked growing up. Try going to public school in this city with this name. I caught all kinds'a shit from the older kids, especially as I didn't go to an Academy of Higher Development. But it was a different matter when I discovered my power. I was in Ninth-Grade; a "late starter", as they say.

JS: I have to ask; your power doesn't have anything to do with spider-abilities, per chance?
PP: Fuck, man, I wish! Could you imagine it? A litigation lawyer would have a field day with that one! Having not only the name but also the abilities of one of the most famous comic characters? No, I'm thankful my super-power is only energy manipulation. I say "only", but energy manipulation is kinda cool!

JS: How does it work?
PP: Yo, It's like this; objects and people generate an energy field which is invisible to the naked eye, right? Well, I have the ability to both see and manipulate that energy. For example, I can stop a bullet fired from a gun, or contain an explosion; I can even fly.

JS: You have the ability to fly?
PP: Nah just hovering, but I'll figure it out in the next few months! Shit, I've only been a Solo for a year so I've had to work on other areas of my power.

JS: What aspects are you making most progress with?
PP: I'm enjoying the creative side. Moving tanks and planes is all macho and predictable and being a Solo means you have to be able to think outside the box, so I've turned my training towards complex stuff like, magnifying or suppressing an energy field and shit. I'm not a strong guy but if I can magnify the energy in a punch it'll feel like you've been hit by a fuckin' bulldozer! Shit like that can be just as devastating if applied correctly in the right situation.

JS: What's the hardest thing about being a superhero?
PP: Easy – Picking a name that isn't corny.

JS: Really? Is it that difficult?
PP: Oh, HELL yeah! The good ones are all gone, thanks to comics. Even though they don't actually exist, the names of fictional superheroes are all trademarked and copyrighted. Not even a real, living, breathing Super-S would be stupid enough to take on the corporate giants over an important issue such as a name. Shit, there's no foe that strikes fear into the heart of a Super-S like a fuckin' lawyer. You try picking yourself a name – go on! You're a limey, right; so pick a name for yourself that sums up where you come from.

JS: Let's see... Captain Britain?
PP: Taken. Have another go.

JS: Union Jack?
PP: Nope.

JS: Captain UK?
PP: Sorry Bud, gone too. See? I racked my brain for weeks trying to come up with something that fit. And everytime I thought I'd found a name, I'd Google™ it, only to find some other guy already had it. I'd be all, give me a fuckin' break, man.

JS: I can see your point! But, joking aside, is there anything else that you've found difficult coming to terms with?
PP: I guess I'm a bit young to have much of a list to pick from, but if I had to choose something, it would be trying to second-guess where an incident is gonna present itself and having the instinct to know what to do- Hold up a sec – EY'YO! Either buy something or bounce, library's over on 5th Avenue!

Peter is talking to a huge, thick-set man wearing an overcoat and beanie, who is hanging around on the other side of the store. He must be at least eight-feet tall. Peter does not seem intimidated by this – I guess you wouldn't if you had abilities like his.

Fuckin' crackhead's always in here, checking out the same old back-issues. He hangs out here for hours and never buys shit, dunno why the old man puts up with him. I swear I know that dude from somewhere. Anyway, you were saying...?

JS: Could you elaborate?

Peter picks up a comic.

PP: Yo, take this comic here, or any comic in this store for that matter; I bet you a hundred bucks that the hero of the story always turns up in times of trouble. Guaranteed. Not only will they defeat the villain, but they'll also save the world and get the fuckin' girl. Every time. You know why? Because the audience fuckin' *demands* it! We love a winner. Yeah sure, we might see them falter and stumble a little, but ultimately they have to come out the other side victorious and saving the day and shit. The audience loves drama but no-one wants to see a Super-S fail; that's the bottom line. You can spin the same story any way you like, but the end result will always be the same – Good triumphs over Evil.

Doesn't work that way in the real world though. There's no second-sense, no serendipity. Hell, I've turned up so late to a burning building before that all I could do was watch them bringing out the crispies. No-one prepares you for that kind of shit when you're a superhero. No-one. And I'm only eighteen, man. That shit's no joke, and I'm gonna do this for the rest of my life?

JS: So why do you surround yourself with comics then? Do they offer a false sense of reality? A way of escaping for 25 minutes?
PP: You fuckin' kidding me? I love these things. They've been a lifeline for me since I was kid. I wouldn't go as far as to say they're lifestyle guides or instruction manuals, but they've certainly given me lots of inspiration and comfort over the years. Without comics I wouldn't have been able to cope when I discovered my power at the age of fourteen. Puberty was a bitch, yo! Comics helped me identify with who I was and who I could potentially become. Even though I had no guidance when it came to coping with my powers at school, I had role models to look up to printed in the very pages of the books my Dad sold at his store.

Peter stares at the cover of the comic he's holding.

Yo, just think, all the writers, pencillers, inkers and colorists it took to create these characters, and I bet not one of them is a Super-S or a 2nd Degree. Crazy, huh? I wouldn't be half the superhero I am today without their help.

It just goes to prove, you don't have to have a super-ability, or experience in teaching Super-S and shit, to be able to educate one and introduce them to the ways of their world.

10

Artwork: Dan Fraga - Kinesis

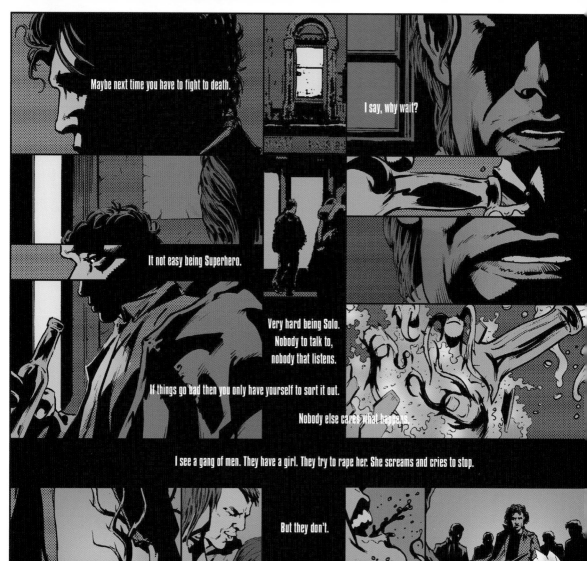

Maybe next time you have to fight to death.

I say, why wait?

It not easy being Superhero.

Very hard being Solo.
Nobody to talk to,
nobody that listens.

If things go bad then you only have yourself to sort it out.

Nobody else cares what happens.

I see a gang of men. They have a girl. They try to rape her. She screams and cries to stop.

But they don't.

Did I kill him?
I don't know,
maybe. He is on
floor, clawing
at his neck.
He may live... yet.

Hard sometimes
to do right thing.
You understand?

My hands, they are strength and a curse.

Marek Zawadzki* is a Polish-born Super-S; he's nineteen years-old and lives on his own in London, UK. His family live in Myszków, Poland. By day he's a labourer on a building site, by night he roams the streets of London under the guise of Kolec, the name by which he wishes me to address him.

The bedsit is located above a curry-house in Shepherd's Bush. The only illumination is from a fluorescent strip coming from the bathroom. Kolec sits hunched in an armchair opposite me, a beer in his hand.

JS: Do you have any regrets about leaving your family and coming to London to attend an Academy of Higher Development?
K: No, it was for the best. My parents agreed also. Not many Super-S types in Poland, so no chance of development. If I have no success in London, maybe I go to America. Maybe I try luck and become really big Super-S there so that I can bring family and look after them. London is good but too small; I think I don't stay here long. Not like DarkMatter, yes? He get most of your attention here, I think. No chance for son of Polish shoemaker from Myszków when he around.

JS: Do you think about visiting your family in Poland?
K: It is difficult. I cannot go home. I will bring family over as soon as I am success, when Kolec is front-page news.

JS: Why so much pressure on yourself to succeed?
K: I owe my people much. My family, friends, they all raise money for me to attend your Academy. I let them down.

JS: How did you let them down?
K: I was asked to leave Academy.

JS: Did you leave, or were you expelled?
K: So, they tell you? Yes, that is correct word for it.

JS: Can you elaborate for me?
K: I don't want to talk about it.

JS: Please, I'd very much like to hear your side of the story. To set the record straight.

Kolec shifts in his chair, uncomfortably.

K: They make comment, yes? About my sister. I thought school would teach them control. But some do not have this; they live too close to edge. The schools, they are idiots. They know who walk the bad line but they do nothing, nothing! Those few, it will be the last time they fight me. I make sure they don't forget Kolec name fast; make sure they respect my family. It is possible that you will come up against these people again, you know, in next life. Maybe next time you have to fight to death but I say, why wait? They already choose the line. You understand?

JS: Do you think your actions could have been misconstrued as a like-minded act of aggression?

Kolec swigs from his beer. I notice his fingers transforming into thorny, sharp vines. They wrap around the bottle, tightening. The bottle shatters.

K: You think I go Vader? That what you say? You think I follow their path and want to be like them?

JS: No, I wasn't inferring-
K: Forget it. It is the same, wherever I go. I am Super-S and foreigner to your country. You stare at me and judge me; I am two-times bad in your eyes. I am immigrant. People think I come here to steal your money, your women, your work? To burden your taxpayers, yes? All day, I work hard on building site; making new school and house and office for the English people. You use us because we work hard and we are cheap; we do not complain. Tell me, if we are hated so much, why is there always work for us to do?

Always is the same; people think about their own situation. If there is much unemployment problem, then people must question Government and their policies. It is their fault, not mine. People have no fight, no pride. I come to this country to be better; I want to learn, be success. Send money back to help my family and make them proud. My sister, she is eight and we think she is Super-S. My father is sick. My mother, I want to help her.

JS: I'm sorry if you felt I was judging you. I'm just trying to understand what it's like for you, both as a Super-S and a migrant.
K: Then understand quick, my friend. It is not easy being superhero. Even harder being Solo, like me; nobody to talk to, nobody that listen. If things go bad then you have only yourself to make good again. Nobody else care what happens.

JS: What problems have you encountered being Solo?
K: Every night, many problems. I go out in the city and walk the streets, looking for trouble. Not to start it, just make sure it not happen. I see many, many, bad things; men and women with drink and drugs. The city at night is not a good place.

JS: Can you give me an example?
K: One night, I see a gang of men. They have a girl. One man, he try to rape her while his friends watch. I know they will try next. She screams and cries to stop. But they don't. So I walk up to them. They do not see me, they are too busy with their entertainment, so I place my arm around his neck and-

Kolec demonstrates. His arms form a mangled mess of twisted vines and razor-sharp thorns.

JS: Did you kill him?
K: Maybe. But I am in dangerous situation, yes? There are many more of them than me and I am alone; no-one to help if I am injured. Did I kill him? He was on floor clutching at his neck and there was much blood. But it was not up to me. It was up to his comrades. They have the choice to save him or fight me; his life was in their hands, not mine. His fate was theirs to control.

JS: What did they choose to do?
K: I see the girl on the floor, almost naked. She crawls away from them so I know she safe. The man, he could not scream, but he make noise as he lie bleeding, like a wounded dog. His friends turn to see what I have done to him. Then one man, he has a knife. The others follow, too. More knives. And one break a bottle. So I know then they have made their choice.

They circle me. I wait. They curse me as their friend struggles to breathe through his ripped throat. Still, I wait. They come at me, all at once, and I destroy them before they even touch me. I leave one alive; let him crawl away on his broken stomach, like a bleeding snake.

JS: Why did you spare his life? Couldn't he identify you, report you to the police?
K: That is what I want; for these people to fear the name of Kolec. This man I let escape? He is scum. If he survives, he will tell other scum how he saw Kolec tear the friends apart with his bare hands. They will learn that it is not safe to commit crime, to disrespect people. This is why I do this.

JS: And the girl? Was she ok?

Kolec stares down at his re-formed hands.

K: I go to girl. I tell her it's okay, that she is safe. I make my hands normal again. I reach out to her, to help her. But the girl's face... I remember her stare... the horror and fear. I save her but this is how she see me; not as man, but monster. So I walk away. It left me empty. Things like that girl, they make me question, why? It is too hard sometimes to do right thing, understand? My hands, they are both strength and curse.

I look again at the young man before me, opening another bottle of beer. I wonder if he's closer to the line than he realises.

Artwork: John Higgins - Kolec

*Interviewee name has been changed

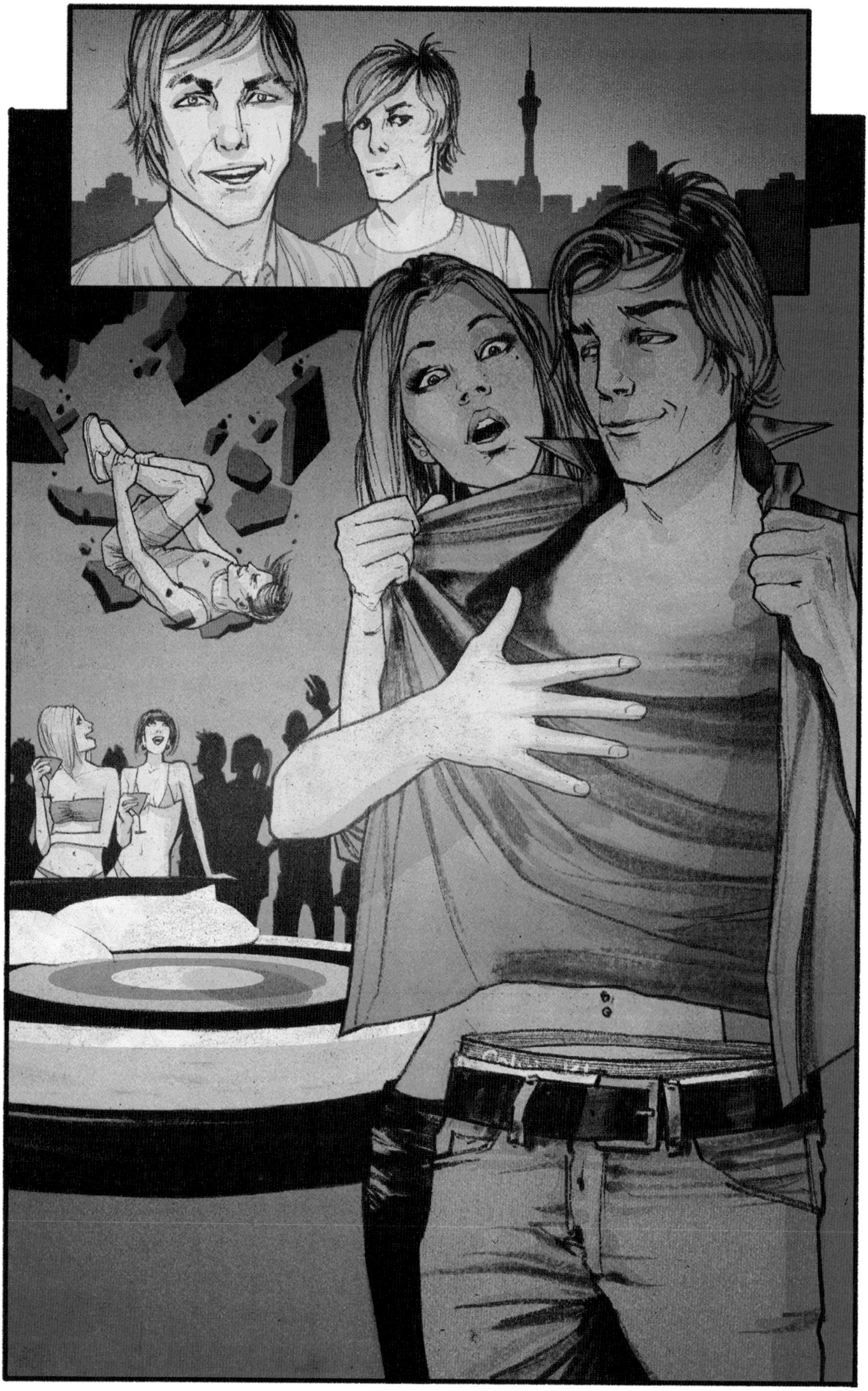

Adam and Brad Poole are twins – twenty years-old and living life to the full. They are studying at the Auckland Academy for Higher Development in New Zealand. They are a year away from graduating.

We're out by One Tree Hill, looking over Auckland. In the distance, the Sky Tower dominates the compact cityscape.

JS: Do you find that, being both twins and Super-S, this gives you certain advantages over your fellow students?
AP: Without doubt, like. We're always looking out for each other. Actually, mainly I look out for Brad here, seeing as I'm the older brother.

BP: By four minutes!

AP: Still makes me older, mate. Mom'll confirm it.

BP: If Mom knew what you got up to, she wouldn't say you acted like it; she'd be grounding your ass for a month.

JS: Sounds like you enjoy getting up to no good, Adam...?
AP: Nah, I wouldn't say that. We just goof around a bit. You know, as you do when you're in school.

BP: Adam's an *Invo*. Though he can't project or anything, he can camouflage himself; so guess who's always sneaking into the girls' changing room? He's known as *Invoperv* at the Academy.

AP: Hey, what red-blooded male wouldn't, right? Some of the sights I've seen, man! That Melanie Langford... awesome rack... ain't no problem in that shelving department, I can tell you. Mmm... Anyway, hypocrite warning! What about you? You're no saint!

BP: Me? I haven't done anything!

AP: So the demolition of fourteen walls inside school grounds had nothing to do with you, right?

BP: I told you before, I slipped.

AP: Right, right... slipped. Fourteen solid brick walls. Count 'em. Four. Teen. Sure you weren't showing off for a certain Emma Cox?

BP: Shut up, dude. You don't know what you're talking about!

JS: Fourteen walls? What happened?
AP: Ol' *Dense-Kid* here has the ability to affect his density. One minute he's a 150-pound weakling, next thing you know, he's a fully-charged 100-ton wrecking ball – and without any outward physical changes.

BP: Don't call me that. I haven't chosen a name for myself yet.

JS: That's pretty impressive. Brad, do you have any plans in terms of how you'll use this power when you graduate? It doesn't appear to be as practical as other peoples' skills.
BP: You'd be surprised, the Academy teaches you to think laterally. I've got a few tricks up my sleeves already.

JS: Care to explain?
BP: Sure. Imagine, punching a concrete wall; the punch starts off like a normal punch, but by the time it connects, it ploughs thru the wall as if it were marshmallow. Or a runaway train whose brakes have failed; just sit me at the crossing, man, and wait for that sucker to connect with me. It's not going anywhere. If you understand your ability and what you're capable of, then the possibilities are endless.

AP: Cool, huh? Brad here might sound like a dork, but nobody's going to mess with him 'cos of what he can do.

JS: Have you had much trouble from the other students?
BP: No, not... much.

AP: Let's just say that the school can be a cauldron of egos. Everybody thinks they're going to be the big enchilada when they graduate, so there's lots of students vying for top position. Yeah, we've had our run-ins, but Dense-Kid here makes sure people know their place in the pecking order.

BP: I told you to stop calling me that!

JS: So, beyond school, out there in the big, wide world, what are your plans? Are you aiming to become a super-duo?
BP: I think so. Mom wouldn't forgive me if I left Adam to his own devices. He'd only end up getting into trouble that I'd have to fix.

AP: The only trouble I'd be getting into is the female kind. Man, I can't wait to get out there as a team, meet some nice girls, show off our powers, you know? Rip up the town. It's gonna be a blast!

BP: We've come this far together, I can't see why we'd change it. To be honest, I don't think anybody else could put up with his smell.

AP: Look who's talking! You ever smelt your pits after a 'heavy' session at the gym? Man...

BP: Of course, we'll have to work out where we operate from – a secret base or something. No way we're staying at home with the folks; that's not gonna do much for our street cred.

AP: Not a chance! Just imagine Dad – he'd be all like, "I want you back home by midnight." Yeah, like, dude! I'm twenty, going on twenty-one, I can stay out as long as I like!

BP: Could you imagine some thirty-something Super-S, still living at home and getting balled out for turning up thirty minutes after curfew?

AP: The dad would be all, "Where the Hell have you been?" and the dude would be like, "Sorry I'm late, Pops, I was Downtown quelling the wrath of Monkeytron. It won't happen again." No way. Got to get our own place, fast.

BP: We'll get an awesome bachelor pad, somewhere we can entertain the babes. With wireless and HDTV.

JS: Shouldn't you be thinking a little more responsibly? You have all this power and the intelligence and training to use it respectfully. Super-S don't receive great PR at the best of times; do you think this flippant attitude you have towards your powers will exacerbate the problem? People will look up to you. What kind of example would that set?
AP: Look, we're still kids – in hero terms, anyway. I've just completed an exhaustive period of my life, working hard at school-

Brad makes a derisory snort.

AP: Yeah – *real* hard. And a bunch of Normans aren't gonna dictate to me how I enjoy my post-grad break. So we'll be living large for a few months; getting drunk, having a laugh... 'cos that's what people our age do, mate. We've got our whole lives to be Super-S, saving women from burning buildings, that sort of thing.

BP: Always about the women. You notice that? Adam here is gonna have so many restraining orders slapped on him, he won't be able to operate as a Super-S.

AP: Dude, they'll have to find me first. If you can't see me, you can't sue me. That's my motto.

BP: Seriously, we know we'll have to change. I mean, it would be great to mess around for the rest of our lives, but we both know that can't happen, no matter how much Adam here wants it to.

AP: What's the line from that film? Something about, "With great power comes great responsibility"? Something like that? We get it. Just let us grow up a year at a time, will ya? Sheesh!

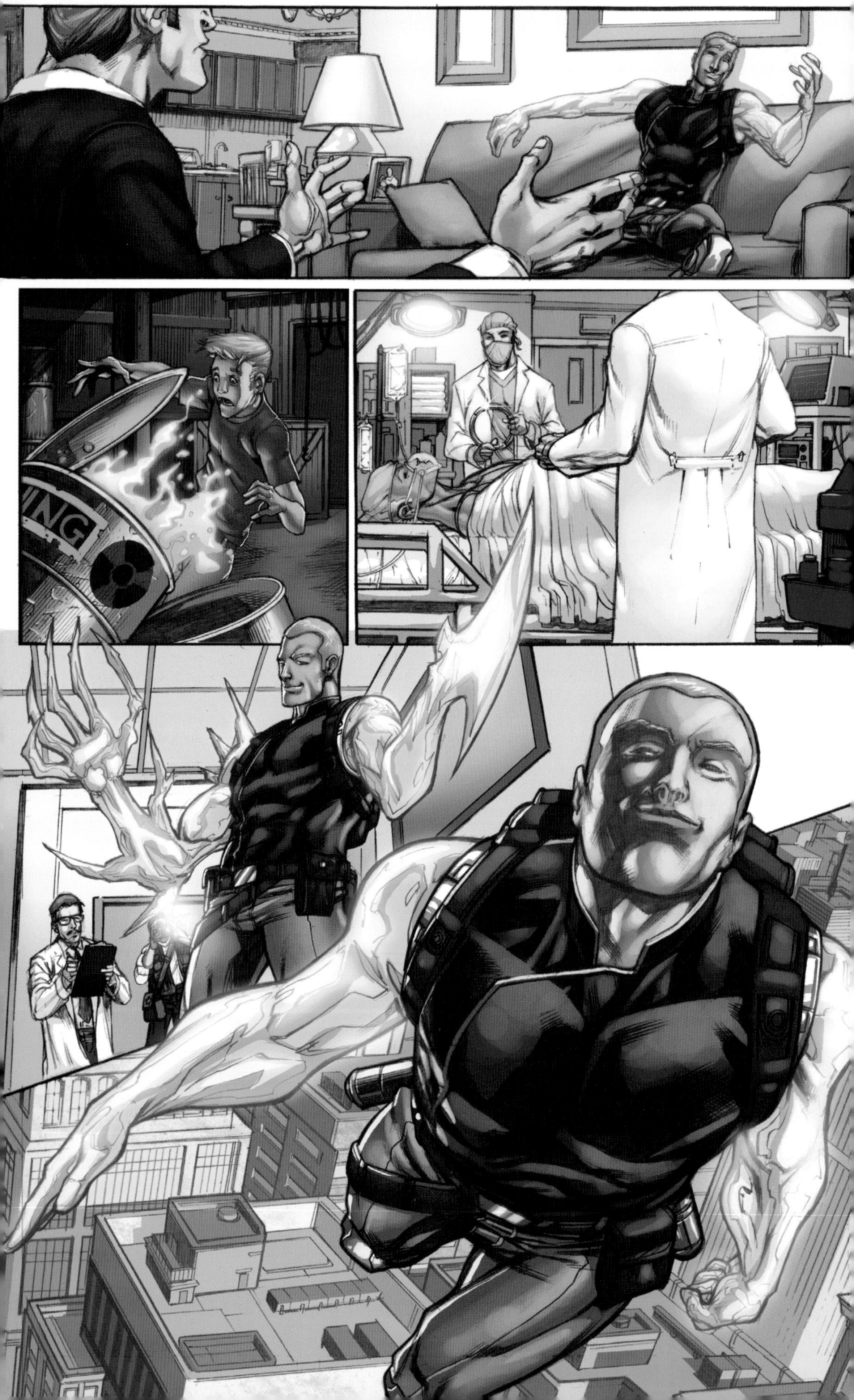

FullyArmed is twenty-one years-old. He lives with his parents in Chicago, Illinois. He is an amputee, having lost his arms in a freak accident when he was thirteen, but he has since been afforded a second chance at life as a *2nd Degree*.

I am sitting opposite FullyArmed in his parents' living room. The glowing energy that forms his new limbs is mesmerising to watch; the blue, pulsating current travels down from the energy rings attached to his shoulders, which act as a conduit, right through to his virtual fingers.

FA: They're quite something, aren't they?

JS: I'm sorry. I didn't mean to stare.
FA: Don't worry, I'm not offended. I quite enjoy it when people stare. To be honest, I often admire them if I'm walking past a mirror, or checking my own reflection in a store window. I still can't quite believe it; I love watching the energy forms adapt and change shape. They're totally state-of-the-art.

JS: Change shape?
FA: Sure. Watch this.

Almost instantaneously, FullyArmed 'morphs his appendages into a range of objects; from a shield, to a sword, to a pick and a shovel.

JS: That's amazing. Can you create any shape you think of?
FA: Almost anything. I can't create guns that fire bullets or anything overly complex, the Energy Rings don't work like that; whatever I generate has to be formed from a single, shaped unit. Apart from that, I can be as creative as I please. I just think about it and WHAM!, there it is.

JS: Amazing. Can I ask how you came to acquire your power?
FA: I'm what's called a 2nd Degree. Basically, I was born a Norman but got caught in a freak accident which manifested itself as a super-ability.

I was playing around a garbage dump when I was a kid, goofing around with some friends, you know the sort of thing. I spotted some discarded barrels, thought they looked interesting. So I decided to open one of them up. Before I knew it, I was covered in this nasty, green goop. Typically, I hadn't taken into consideration the radioactive warning signs pasted all over the sides of the barrel. The toxic shock almost killed me. A Hazmat Team that had arrived at the scene finally managed to pull me out, but I was covered in the stuff. It took ten months for it to pass through my system, by which time my arms had eroded so badly that they had to amputate. Right up to the shoulder sockets.

JS: That must have been devastating.
FA: Totally. As a Norman teenager, I was an excellent athlete; I'd been told I potentially had a huge career ahead of me in football if I continued developing the way I had been at school. Well, that dream disappeared, right away. I was mentally and emotionally destroyed; all I kept doing was breaking down in tears. Mom and Dad put on a brave face, organized counseling and stuff, but I just didn't want to talk. I didn't see the point. All I could think about was what I had lost; all those things I couldn't do anymore. Simple things, like waving, writing, clapping, holding someone... flipping someone off or wiping my ass.

FullyArmed laughs.

Sorry, I know I shouldn't joke, but being the one that it's happened to, you have to let it out somehow. Joking aside, I don't think I could have been any lower at that point in my life. I had most certainly contemplated suicide. Think about it; I was almost fourteen and all I wanted to do was end my life.

JS: What was the turning point that changed your mind?
FA: Turns out, that radioactive gunk I messed with was a bit of a double-edged sword; it triggered an ability in me which almost any kid would find hard not to think was extremely cool. It certainly took my mind off the depression and my lack of arms.

JS: What was that?

FullyArmed grins.

FA: Flight. The power of flight. Twisted, eh? I couldn't pick my own nose, but I could soar above the clouds, higher than a bird. I think someone up there must have a warped sense of humor.

JS: When did you discover you had the power of flight?
FA: While I was in the hospital, shortly after the docs had operated on me. One of the duty nurses came in to check on me that evening to see if I was ok, only to find me fast asleep, floating, five feet above the bed. Her screams woke me up and for some reason, gravity kicked back in and I fell back onto the mattress. I reckon she thought I was possessed or something, like out of *The Exorcist*. Looking back, it was pretty funny.

That was the point the docs considered the possibility that the waste material had somehow changed me. I was transferred to a Super-S ward for three weeks where I had specialist help in developing my new gift. Once they had confirmed my ability was permanent, they officially designated me a 2nd Degree. It wasn't long after that I had a visit.

JS: Who from?
FA: A suit turned up, said he was from XoDOS. Someone in the hospital had talked to them about me and explained my condition. He said they were developing something in one of their research departments that could help me; a prototype device that was almost custom-made for my condition. He said I was the perfect candidate.

JS: So you agreed?
FA: Not straight away. You have to understand, I was in a seriously bad place. As far as I saw it, I had no future, I was a freakin' mess. I told him to take a hike.

JS: What made you change your mind?
FA: I've got my Dad to thank for that. He came by after the suit had left and sat with me. He apologized, said he felt he had failed me as a father and that he wanted my forgiveness. He blamed himself for everything that had happened, for not looking out for me. There I was, lying in my bed, wallowing in my own despair, with my Dad in pieces next to me. I could see how my condition was affecting not just me, but my whole family. That was the point I knew I had to do something positive to get us all out of a rut. It was a sign.

JS: So you took XoDOS up on their offer?
FA: Yup, I signed up the very next day – if you'll pardon the pun – and was transported immediately to one of their private facilities. The operation to graft on the Energy Rings took four days. Once they had been attached, it was unbelievable; I fired these babies up and the power that coursed through me was like nothing I had ever felt before. It took some time to adjust to them; I'd generate all manner of shapes, my arms would be all out of proportion, but the XoDOS psychologists helped me adapt to them and become more precise with my creations. Soon, the shapes and forms became second nature to me. Now, I can pretty much create anything I set my mind to. I owe XoDOS my life. They offered me an alternative to being physically disabled for the rest of my days.

JS: So, do you feel whole again now?
FA: I feel so much more than that. Once, I was a multiple amputee, now I'm a multi-talented superhero. Instead of ten digits on my hands, I've got as many as I can think up!

JS: So what do you do at XoDOS?
FA: Mostly training. I've been honing my powers and testing my endurance, learning new skills, stuff like that. They tell me I'm becoming an extremely effective Super-S. They haven't given me a live mission yet, but I've heard a rumor that XoDOS want to integrate me into one of their new superhero Teams, which would be awesome. I can't wait! Oh, and it's great to be able to wipe my own ass again!

Artwork: Robert Atkins / Colours: Bob Pedroza - FullyArmed

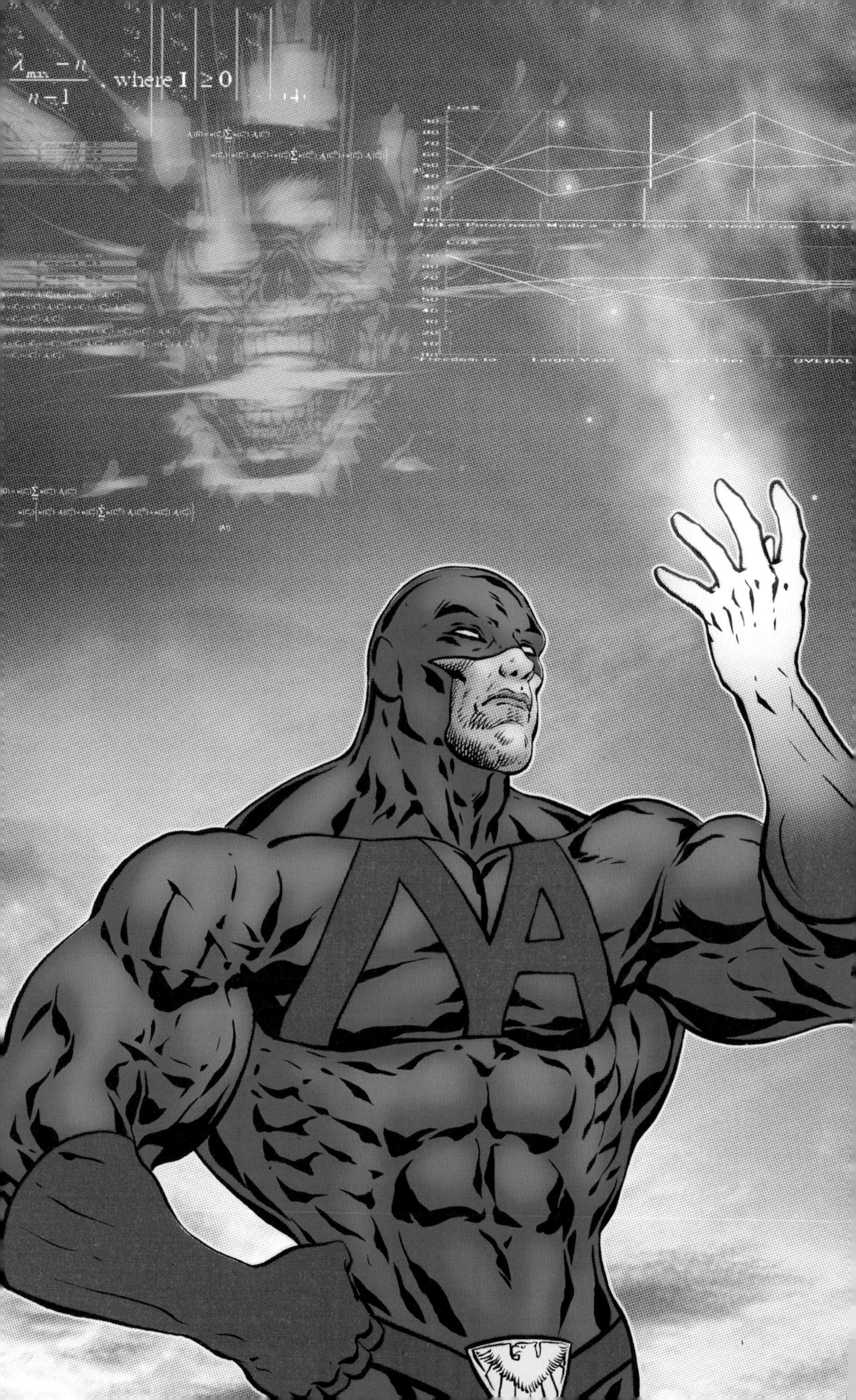
$\frac{\lambda_{max} - n}{n-1}$, where I ≥ 0

Major Action is twenty-three years-old. A former army boy, he's now a regular feature over the city of New York.

We're standing on the observation platform, on the 86th floor of the Empire State Building, overlooking 6th Avenue, towards Central Park. It's certainly one of the more unique locations I've held an interview.

JS: I don't think I've ever been this high up before.

Major Action takes a deep breath and puffs out his chest and assumes the classic superhero pose; arms on hips, stomach in, groin out.

MA: I wanted to show you my battlefield. I've made it my sworn duty to protect this city from anyone and everything that threatens it. I've made it my primary mission to acquire an in-depth knowledge of every sidewalk, alley, rooftop and underground tunnel. In my world, preparation and understanding of the terrain is half the battle.

JS: And the other half?
MA: Kicking the ass of the bad guys, of course!

He grins.

JS: You're a 2nd Degree. Could you tell me the story behind the procurement of your powers?
MA: I was in the Army for four years – 101st Airborne Division, America's finest. I was stationed in Fort Campbell, Kentucky, did two tours of Iraq and was awarded the Silver Star for holding back an insurgent attack just North of Basra. They were cherry-picking the best of the best right out of the veteran units that had just returned from Iraq. On my return I was approached to be short-listed for Super-S serum research.

JS: So you volunteered to be part of the experiment?
MA: Damn right! I was pulling $30,000 a year and there they were, waving five times that, just for making the short-list. You got to be some kind of fool to turn down an offer like that. Hell, they'd bankrolled some serious candidates, I didn't even think I would make it past the screening process; felt sure I would be kicked out after a few months and drafted back to HQ. But I just kept progressing on thru. The selectees dwindled until soon, there were only five of us. Then it became two. Then just me.

JS: What happened once you'd been selected?
MA: I tell you what happened – Major Action happened! They pumped me full of all sorts of good stuff; they made me faster, stronger, gave me the ability to fly. And my hands, man, they could melt through anything! All I needed to do was think about it and the heat generated from my palms alone was amazing. I was indestructible too; destroyed everything and anything they threw at me. And, boy, they tried – tanks, jets, rockets. I mean, everything. They tested me to limits I didn't even know I had but I came thru with flying colors. A weapon of the people to protect the people, Made in America, pumped full of Momma's home-cooked goodness. Forget the Boy Scouts, baby, The Major's in town!

JS: Were you a very expensive investment for the military?
MA: You betcha! And I'm worth every cent!

JS: Were there any plans to create more super-soldiers like you?
MA: Sure there were plans. I was to be the first of many. M.I. were planning on creating a whole unit and shipping us off to Iraq to finally clear up that goddam hell-hole.

JS: So what happened?
MA: The recession happened, bud! I heard it cost over a billion dollars just to get my gears working, let alone a squad of us bad-boys stomping the yard. And look at the whole situation over there now; it's gone all goddamn political-heavy. No place for the likes of me in those kind of negotiations. So, in an effort to recoup the investment to the taxpayer, I've been loaned out to New York for the foreseeable future as Protector of the City.

JS: So you won't be returning to Iraq in the near future?
MA: Not a chance. But hey, you never know; the time could soon be coming when America decides she has to send her Super-S abroad to tidy up the mess this world's in again. Whenever that is, man, I'm ready to step up.

JS: That could potentially create a great deal of tension between the U.S. and the international community.
MA: That's something M.I. and XoDOS are working on.

JS: XoDOS are involved?
MA: Of course! Amazing people! America owes those guys. Big time.

JS: Taking your first experience of your powers as a given, what's been your most memorable moment?
MA: That's a tricky one. There've been so many; pulling a broken-down ferry out of the East River was cool. I saved over three hundred people that day. I was given the keys to the City for that one. Then there was the tanker fire on Hwy 9A. I flew over the Hudson with the whole carcass on fire, spewing volatile liquid everywhere and praying the damn thing wouldn't explode on me before I reached a safe destination. But if I had to pick one moment, it would be the time I fought Abrasion. He was one hard son-of-a-bitch. Had to dig real deep to beat him. He had these mean rays he could shoot from his eyes, plus strength, regeneration, you name it. And a nifty anti-grav bike to boot. We fought from Liberty Island to Harlem, and all the way back again. That bastard just wouldn't stay down. Had to use all my military training to off the guy.

JS: How did you eventually defeat him?
MA: I led him down an alley, just off 12th Avenue. As he followed me, the alley became narrower and narrower. Eventually, he couldn't maneuver his anti-grav bike and, by the time he figured out what was happening, I had him off the bike and kicking air. It was sweet.

Once he was off the bike, I worked out how I could halt his regeneration. I reasoned that, if I ripped his limbs off then cauterized the stumps with my heat power, then they wouldn't regen back. Turns out, my hunch was right; it was like pulling legs off a spider. Just with a very pissed head and body left once I'd finished.

Major Action chuckles.

JS: Didn't that incident cause several million dollars worth of damage? I heard there were also quite a few bystander deaths from the result.

Major Action glowers at me.

MA: Look, buddy, I'm fighting a war here! On the streets, in the air, underground; fighting to keep the likes of Abrasion from enslaving goody-goody people like you and your kids; fighting so the pencil-pushers at City Hall can sleep easy at night. If a few citizens get in the way, then so be it. Boom! Casualties of war. Always had 'em, always will.

JS: So you're saying that we should accept a certain level of collateral damage for the greater good?
MA: Accept and expect. That's the thing about war, man, there's always going to be casualties. Last time, it was civilian. Hell, I ain't happy about it, I know for sure the Mayor in City Hall ain't happy about it. No one is, least of all the ones that are left picking up the pieces. But this is war. Shit happens. Just get on and deal with it.

JS: By the way, what rank did you reach in the Army?
MA: Private First Class. Why?

JS: Just curious.

Artwork: Liam Sharp - Major Action

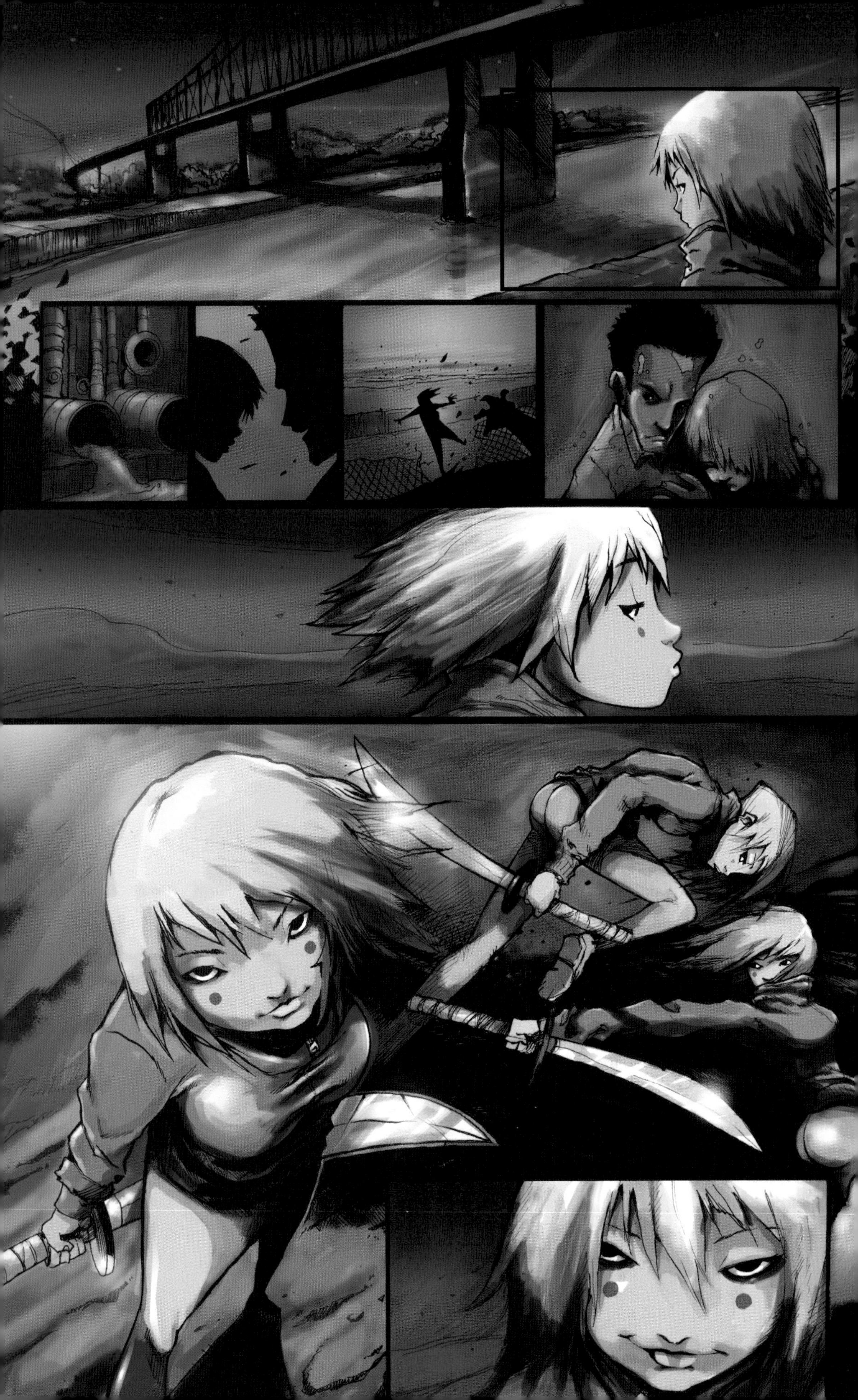

Ali Bailey, a twenty-five year-old woman from Louisiana, became a 2nd Degree after a river accident. She operates under the name of LunarBlade and she watches over the city of Baton Rouge.

We're standing on wasteland by the Mississippi River. Ali was insistent that the interview be conducted at this particular location.

JS: Hello, Ali. Thank you for agreeing to meet me.
LB: Ah'd appreciate you callin' me LunarBlade, please.

JS: I'm sorry. LunarBlade.

LunarBlade turns and looks out, over the river. The glow of the moon highlights the faint, silver sheen of her skin. She doesn't seem to notice the drastic drop in temperature on this cold November night.

LB Tha's ok. Ah wanted to meet you here, 'cos this is the spot. This is where it all started; where I was *reborn*, so to speak. Ah ain't angling for a hard luck story or nothin'. This is jus' the way it went down; a white, workin'-class girl, foolin' around with her boyfriend one night by the old chemical plant. Fell in way over there, by that outlet.

She points to a fence next to a pipe outlet.

LB: 'Course, it's a bit different 'round here now. Things have changed. The plant's gone for one; shut down and demolished after the incident. An' they went an' filled in all the waste outlets with concrete, too.

JS: The incident? The one that gave you your powers?
LB: Yeah. They'd been pumpin' all kinds o' weird crap into the river, an' no-one knew. Nothin'. Bastards got away with it for years an' years. They'd probably still be doin' it to this day if it wasn't for mah accident. Just bad luck on them that ah happened to fall in where ah did.

JS: Are you ok to talk about that night?
LB: Sure ah am. Ain't much more harm it can do now, is there? Well, Josh was mah boyfriend at the time. We were goofing around by that fence over there when the riverbank just clean broke away an' ah tumbled straight into the water. Right underneath that pipe. Ah became covered in this nasty, heavy, metallic liquid; so heavy ah went under two, three times. Fourth time, ah didn't come back up. That's when Josh jumped in after me and pulled me out. He saved ma life.

JS: Was he affected by the chemicals as well?
LB: Sure he was. Took over his whole goddamn body in the space of two weeks; cancer of the lungs, liver, colon an' pretty much anywhere else you care to think of. It rotted him away from the inside-out. He died a few weeks later.

JS: I'm so sorry.
LB: Don't be. Ain't your pollutants that were bein' pumped into the water.

JS: How did you manage to survive, whereas Josh didn't?
LB: Turns out ah was a *One-in-Five*.

JS: A One-in-Five?
LB: Yeah. A one-in-five million chance that the chemicals in the water that night would react with mah molecular structure the way they did. Rather than killing me, like Josh, they changed me into *this*. It seems someone up there decided that it weren't ma time to leave this earth.

The doctors, they ran all kinds of tests.; S.o.B's kept me hospitalized right until Fall. Told mah daddy that ah should be dead. But as you can see, ah pulled through. Y'know, mah whole life ah ain't been that lucky. Some kinda quirky luck, huh?

She holds out her arms. Her skin is covered in glistening flecks of silver.

JS: What about others that would have come into contact with the water further down-stream, or for that matter, the fish and other wildlife?
LB: You can bet those boys at the plant were on the case pretty sharp after they'd pulled me out and taken me away. A cordon was immediately placed around the entire area an' they prodded, cut an' fingered pretty much everythin' that crawled, walked or breathed within a half-mile radius.

They discovered that the chemical's properties broke down as soon as they came into contact with water. It had hardly contaminated this section of the river at all. If ah'd fallen just a few inches further along the bank, ah may not have been affected; an' Josh probably wouldn't be dead. As for the wildlife, ah can't say ah heard anyone mention catching acrobatic, silver fish with a panache for swords before.

LunarBlade pulls out a crescent-shaped sword. She twirls and catches it as if it were a natural extension of her body. It's breathtaking to watch.

JS: What happened to the chemical plant?
LB: Ah told you it was demolished, right? Too right it was. As soon as ah had the use of mah legs back, ah walked right in and ripped the whole damn place apart. No way ah was gonna let them get away with what they did to mah Josh.

Sure, they tried to defend themselves, but folks tend to underestimate a skinny eighteen year-old girl, all silver-like and swinging a sword. Plant security tried to stop me, but ah sliced through them as easily as an over-steamed crawfish shell. They tried to shoot me an', hell, ah out-dodged those suckers an' in a heartbeat, ah was behind them. They didn't live long enough to face their one, true maker, let alone the one exacting great vengeance upon their ass. And neither did them scientists.

The cold November night feels like it just became a lot colder.

JS: How did you feel, once you'd taken your revenge?
LB: Get one thing clear – ah don't do revenge. Not mah thing; that was Ali's revenge, pure and simple. How could ah kill them when they made me what ah am today? LunarBlade is grateful to them for her existence.

JS: How did the authorities react?
LB: They sent a whole bunch of State Troopers after me and tried to bring me into custody. Didn't want to take 'em out but they weren't going to let me go easy. By then ah was big-time news. They jus' couldn't catch me. Troopers don't fare too well 'gainst little girls who can see in the dark as well as they can see in daylight, know what ah'm saying? An' this silver sheen ain't jus' for show; it helps me survive in the coldest of climates. Baton Rouge ain't exactly a winter wonderland so ah figured ah'd head North, use the weather to my advantage.

Ah was on the run for over two years, Canada mostly, Alaska too, until some important folk became interested in me. They'd been tracking me since ah destroyed the plant in Mississippi. Don't ask me how. They offered me a chance to make all the attention go away, a new start. Well, ah was tired of living like a bum, so ah accepted their proposal. Actually, Ali Bailey did. A year later and her name was no more; it was LunarBlade that returned home, together with her real purty sword; a gift from those kind folk over at the organization she now worked for.

Y'see, even after ah'd completed mah training, there were a few personal demons needing exorcising, chemical plant owners that hadn't been brought to justice. Let's jus' say that sword came in *real* handy during hunting season.

JS: Would this organization have anything to do with XoDOS?

LunarBlade flashes me a wicked smile.

LB: Ah could tell ya. But then ah'd have to kill ya.

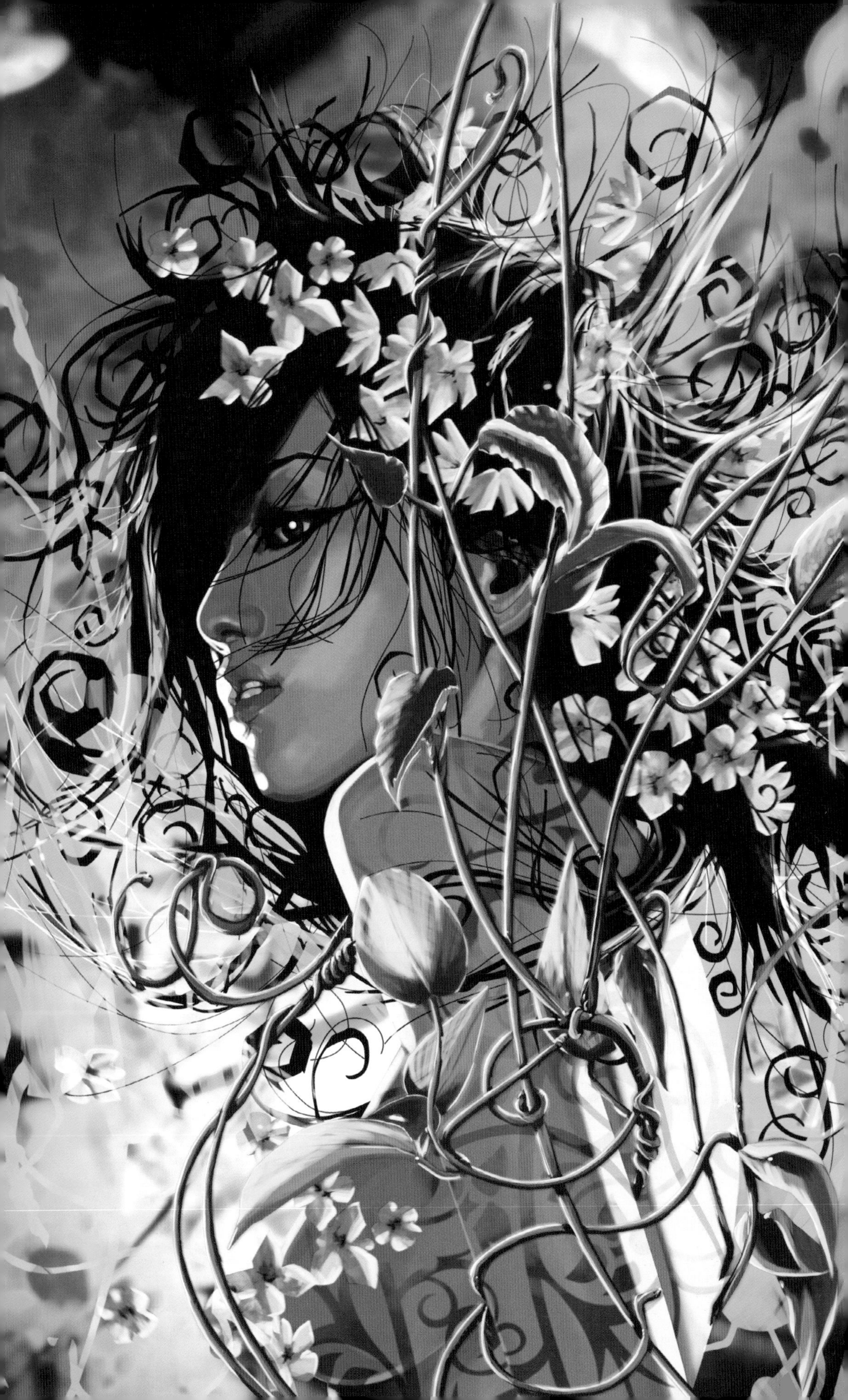

Katrin Dupuis is a pretty twenty-seven year-old woman. She lives in Lyon, France. She goes by the superhero name *L'Ange de Rose*, or The Rose Angel.

I am in a typically-French apartment. Francis Cabrael is playing softly in the background and a welcoming spread of coffee and pastries sits between myself and Katrin.

JS: Katrin, why are you known as The Rose Angel?
KD: Is quite simple. I 'ave the ability to, I think your word is, "manipulate" flowers an' plants.

JS: *Control*, maybe?
KD: Control? Yes! 'Excusez-moi. That is the word I am looking for.

JS: You can control flowers and plants?
KD: Control, change, an' charm, too. Do not think of it just as pretty flowers moving, like dancing in the wind. It is more than that; I 'ave an empathy with all flora. With my love an' attention they grow very strong, very quickly. I can command a single seed to grow into a thick vine and 'ave it tower the highest building in seconds! All the plants listen to my songs an' do what I bid of them.

JS: I didn't know you sang to them.
KD: Of course! They love to be sung to. You should always sing in your garden. You 'ave a garden, Mr. Stanley?

JS: Well, I'm not sure if you could call my neglected patch of earth a garden, but I'll try to look after it better when I return to England, I promise!

Katrin laughs.

KD: We should always look after the flowers and plants, Mr Stanley, an' they in turn will look after us. They are our natural friends.

JS: So you were born a Super-S?
KD: Yes. I was born in Guillotiere an' grew up there as a child. My father works for La Poste; the Post Office. My mother is a gardener. When I was old enough, she would take me with her to work. I so loved exploring peoples' gardens; I would play in wonderful places amongst beautiful flowers. J'aime des fleurs!

JS: Do you think there is some relevance in your mother having an aptitude for horticulture and the fact that you have an empathy with flowers and vegetation?
KD: It is not clear exactly 'ow I came to 'ave such abilities, but we believe that her talents 'ave manifested themselves to the extreme in me. I know she is proud of *L'Ange de Rose*. I was a lucky child, brought up in a house of happiness, but I 'ave heard of many situations where the parents turn against their Super-S children. That is very sad and very wrong. I was a very lucky child. Now, I care for all the flowers in Lyon. They are *my* children. I see that no harm comes to our parks, our fields, our forests.

JS: I must say, it's a beautiful city. Your parents chose for you to be schooled from home. Do you think they made the right decision?
KD: I 'ad a gift which most people do not understand, so it was the most sensible thing to do. My mother knows everything there is about flowers an' plants but she also taught me History, English, Maths, Biology and Sociology. She is a very intelligent woman. I 'ave no regrets; her plants were my school-friends an' her garden was my crèche.

A knock at the door interrupts us.

KD: Excusez-moi.

Katrin walks to the door and opens it. I can see a handsome man standing in the doorway, looking over Katrin's shoulder at me.

KD: Peux-tu revenir un petit peu plus tard s'il te plait ? Tout va bien, ce n'est qu'une entrevue. Nous allons boire un pot dans une heure,

d'accord ? Je t'aime.

She kisses him on the lips and returns to her seat, a smile on her face and a slight blush on her cheeks.

KD: Sorry.

JS: It's fine. Your boyfriend?
KD: Yes, 'is name is Antoine. He works as a warden in the Parc de la Tête d'Or. He is a Norman. We met one day when I was walking around the grounds; I like to visit there on the weekends. He asked me out an' we started dating a few months ago. He is a beautiful man.

JS: You think he might be the one for you?
KD: I don't know. I 'ope so. It's too early. He's nice. I like him. He loves plants. I think that's a good sign, no? We get along very well, but I am in no rush, we have all the time in the world.

JS: How does he feel about your powers?
KD: I 'ave not told him yet. We 'ave not been together long. When I feel it is right, I will tell him everything, but only when I feel the time is right. I believe it is a revelation Norman's do not take too well, especially him being a French male!

She laughs.

KD: His pride might be 'urt, but he is a good man, a gentle man. I think he will be understanding. Like I said, he is a park warden; he loves his plants very much so how can he not love me?

JS: Hypothetically-speaking; let's say we're ten years from now. You're married to Antoine. Any children?

She smiles.

KD: Anything is possible! Children, as well as the flowers, are very important to me.

JS: How many do you see?
KD: Two. A boy and a girl.

JS: How would you feel if one child developed powers but the other was a Norman?
KD: Super-S or Norman? It would not matter to me. They would be my children and I would love them both, equally. Of course, a Super-S child would need different care to that of a Norman child, but not at the expense of the other. I 'ope that I can nurture my future children in the same way I nurture my current ones.

She motions to the plants and flowers that adorn the room.

JS: Do you worry that your children could become targets of your success?
KD: Mon dieu! I am not famous! I am barely known outside Lyon. But I know what you mean. Hmmm... It is a dangerous world outside that window. It must be so 'ard for the Norman mothers to protect their young. I may 'ave more enemies than most, but I 'ave the means to deal with them. Norman mothers 'ave no special powers, other than those that Mère Nature gifts them. I am no hero. They are the real heroes. Of course, I would worry, but I would do everything and anything to protect my children.

JS: What's next for The Rose Angel?
KD: I 'ave been approached by SoulScreamer, you know of him?

JS: Doesn't he work for the United Nations?
KD: Exactement! He 'ad 'eard of my abilities an' wanted me to work with him under the jurisdiction of the U.N. I am going to be working in famine-struck areas of the world, coaxing the flowers and plants to breath life back into the land again, to dance in the wind, like they do in Lyon. I 'ope I can make a real difference. I want to do something that will make my mother proud.

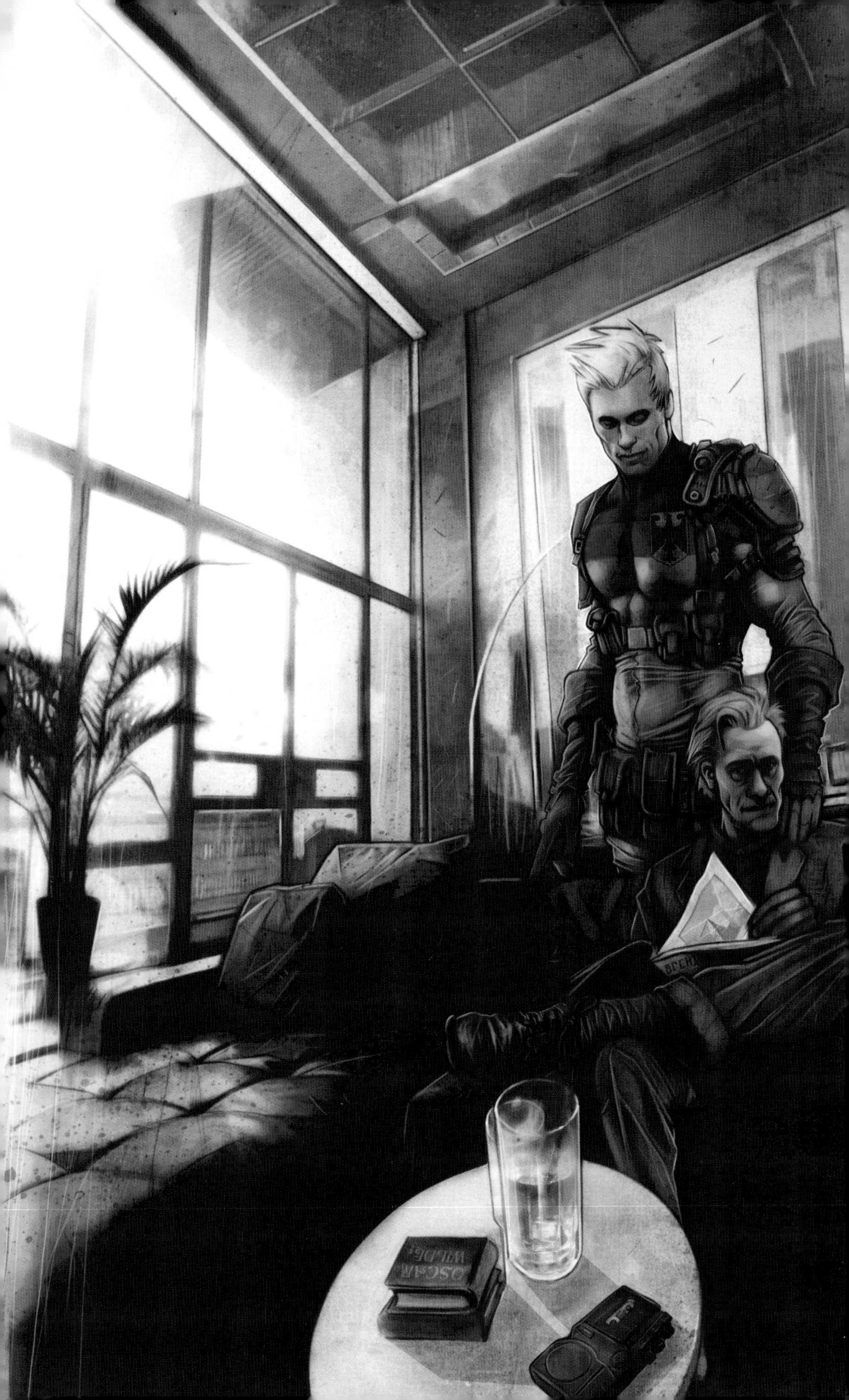
OSCAR WILDE

Twenty-eight year-old **Militär** is your quintessential German stereotype: blond, toned, and with an air of efficiency and superiority. He lives in, and protects the people of, Berlin, Germany. For reasons that will become clear during this interview, he has brought with him a Norman called Klaus.

The living room is funky and contemporary. The entire apartment evokes style and functionality. I can sense an air of trepidation emanating from Militär and Klaus.

JS: This is quite a place you have here, Militär.
M: Actually, it's Klaus's place, I just live here. Klaus is an interior designer. He's worked on several projects around Berlin. At the moment he's redesigning the American Embassy. You know the one? Near to the Brandenburg Tor?

JS: I saw they were building something next to the gate, but didn't realise it was the American Embassy. That's pretty remarkable.
K: Thank you. It's my most ambitious project to date, so I'm very excited about it. It should be finished some time early 2010.

JS: Militär, why have you chosen to live with a Norman? I've found a few examples of Super-S's and 2nd Degrees co-habiting with Normans but generally, it's because they are a spouse or a dependant.
M: I guess that's no different for us. I... I mean we... wanted you to be the first to know.

Militär takes Klaus's hand.

K: You see, we heard that you have been interviewing superheroes and Militär and I have been talking about making some kind of announcement to the media. We wanted to let the world know that we are more than just close friends, that we are in a relationship. Physically, I mean. We felt that your interview would be the perfect opportunity for us.

JS: Well, thank you for that consideration – I've never encountered open homosexuality amongst the Super-S community before. How did you both meet?
M: It was a bar called the 'House of a Hundred Beers', just off Potsdamer Platz. You know it?

JS: I can't say I do.
K: You must go! They have a hundred different beers from all around the world. Everything you can imagine. Being English, I thought this would be a dream come true for you!

JS: I'm glad to say that I fail to live up to the archetypal Englishman! I rarely drink these days.
K: That's a shame. You would have loved the place. Anyway, that is where I met Militär; obviously not as Militär, but in his Norman disguise. He was on his own, in a corner of the bar, reading a book and drinking beer. I can't remember which beer.

M: Köstritzer Schwarzbier. I remember seeing you across the bar. You were with friends. I wouldn't normally stare at people – being who I am, I like to blend in as much as possible – but I knew there was something about Klaus the moment I set eyes on him.

K: And I knew there was something about him, something exciting. I could tell. But I didn't realise *how* exciting!

JS: How did you cope in the early days of your relationship? Klaus, what did you do when you found out who Militär really was?
K: Of course, he didn't tell me straight away; being both gay and a Super-S is not something you openly publicise, but I knew there was something more than just his concerns about his sexuality. For one, our relationship was a scheduling nightmare. For a German, that's unheard of!

Militär laughs.

M: I would be out at different times of the day and night, or

sometimes I would simply disappear, right in the middle of a date. Do you remember, in the Paris-Moskau? I left before the main course arrived.

K: I was so mad at you for that!

M: That was the point I realised that I had to take a leap of faith if I wanted Klaus to be a part of my life. I knew I had to come clean and confess.

JS: So how did you break the news?

It's Klaus's turn to laugh.

K: Where else, but in the bedroom! He appeared, dressed in his costume. I thought he was... how do you English say...?

JS: Role-playing?
K: Yes! That's it. Role-playing! He looked fabulous dressed as Militär. I was laughing so loud. And then when he said he really was Militär, I laughed even harder. That's when I told him that I'd had an inkling all along. You could see the burden lift from his shoulders. Then, he levitated off the ground towards me and he held me in his arms. I was speechless. Here I was, a simple Norman, dating Militär, the Super-S. Me – of all the people he could have had– he picked me. I cried in his arms.

M: He's the emotional one of the two of us.

JS: Why did you choose this interview to "come out"?
M: We wanted to make an announcement to the world and not be hounded by the media through speculation. We felt the honesty that your book was portraying allowed us to do so in an appropriate way. We can't help who we fall in love with, all we can do is realise that it doesn't change who you are. I'm still Militär, I still want to do what's right for Berlin, for us. I have the right to happiness just as much as the next person. In Klaus, I have found that happiness.

JS: How do you think the public will react to a gay superhero?
M: I expect there to be some negative reaction from the public but not from the media. After all, they have been supportive of homosexual rights for many years now, so why should their opinion change, simply because one superhero has proclaimed his sexuality? No, it will be the older generation who will find it hard to understand, especially as I have done so much for this country.

K: I always thought there was something gay about comicbook superheroes anyway.

M: You just like the tight costumes and vibrant colours!

JS: Once the news breaks, how do you plan to conduct your relationship in public?
M: As opposed to what? Being closet'ed gay? Just because we are gay doesn't mean we will openly flaunt our sexuality in the public eye. I assume by the ring on your finger that you are married? Do you feel it necessary to make any more of a declaration than that?

JS: I'm sorry, I didn't mean to offend. You misinterpreted the question. Let me rephrase; the public know you as a superhero but they don't know your secret identity. How will you handle your relationship, having two personas? How will Klaus cope, effectively dating two separate people?
M: Now I understand what you are asking. Well, when this book is published people will easily work out both of my identities. However, Klaus and I have agreed that where possible, for the sake of our relationship, we will only appear publicly together with me in my Norman identity. Militär will be saved for the times when I would like to do something more personal, more... special. You know; sweeping low over the Caspian Sea at midnight, or drinking champagne at the top of the Eiffel Tower. A magical moment will be perfectly acceptable. Given the circumstances.

K: Militär, that is so romantic! I can't wait for the world to know!

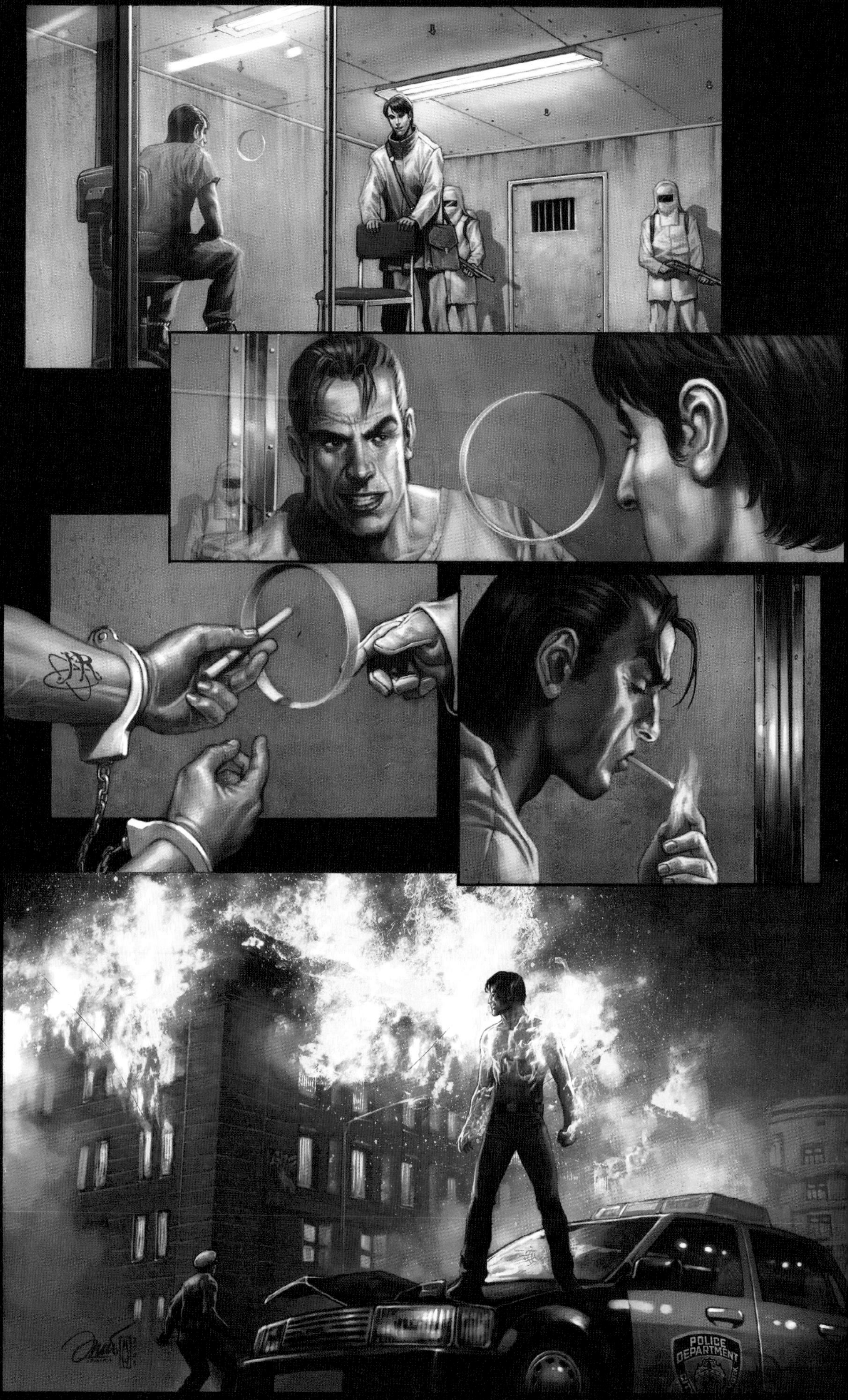
POLICE
DEPARTMENT

For the past eight years, Jack Redden has been incarcerated in the El Reno Penitentiary, Oklahoma. He's now thirty years-old.

I sit opposite Jack in a small interview room. He's dressed in orange overalls and his wrists are handcuffed together. He appears irritated. There are two, heavily-armed guards behind us wearing insulated clothing. I have been requested to wear the same. Jack himself is separated from me by a glass, fire-proof chamber. He is a 2nd Degree – a former Super-S heart-throb called Firetrail.

JS: Thank you for seeing me.
FT: Not as if I had much choice in the matter, is there? Nothing better going on around here anyway.

JS: How did you end up here?
FT: You read the files on me. Why do *you* think, pencil-neck?

JS: That's why I'm here. I'd like to hear your side of the story.
FT: Arson. Amongst other things. Burnt down a Police station, didn't I? Roasted a lot of pigs that day. I just love the smell of bacon.

Firetrail laughs.

JS: You're a *Flambo* then?
FT: Usually what Flambo means, don't it? Shit, where'd they dig you up from?

JS: Why did you go Vader? As Firetrail, you were idolised, you had an amazing reputation. Where did it all go wrong?
FT: You got a cigarette?

I look over to the guard, who nods. I produce a packet of cigarettes out of my pocket and pass one through the air hole in the glass. Jack places the cigarette in his mouth and ignites the tip with a flame he has generated from his finger. Firetrail smirks as I watch, nervously. He exhales the smoke.

Kinda jumpy, ain't ya? You don't work for *them*, I can tell.

JS: Who?

He motions for me to come closer.

FT: Who d'ya think?

He sits back in his chair, smiling. I decide to try a different tactic.

JS: How did you become Firetrail?
FT: It started with a small ad in a local newspaper. Can you believe it? A thousand dollars for a simple drug test. I was out of work, needed a break. At the end of the day, I was just thinking about the money; I wasn't too bothered about what they planned to pump into my body. It would all be monitored, right? Seems the drugs liked me more than the other applicants. Took to me straight away. It was like – pop – two pills, then a few minutes later, all hell broke loose. The room was on fire, and so was the cute nurse that had administered the drugs. I ain't kidding when I say she was smokin'.

'Course, the docs were elated. First time they'd had *any* reaction, let alone one so explosive. They kept me in for a month. Paid me another five thousand dollars for the privilege. Thought my number had come up.

JS: How did you cope with your newfound ability?
FT: Like a duck to water. After the month was up, I was a fully-fledged recruit.

JS: Recruited? By XoDOS?
FT: I was to be the next big American hope, or so they promised. Wanted me to be their weapon in the fight against terrorism, evil, all that crap. "An offer you can't refuse," they said.

JS: What did you say?
FT: I said no. Wasn't interested. The thing is, XoDOS don't take too kindly to being told "no", especially as they were backing the experiments in the first place. Eventually, they 'persuaded' me.

JS: More money?
FT: Women, more like. Or one woman – The Lotus.

Firetrail looks off, wistfully.

Awesome. I would have walked 'cross hot coals for that one, y'know what I mean? She managed to get right under my skin. Her pillow-talk had me convinced working for XoDOS was the way to go. Said she'd even sign up with me, pretend we were fighting side-by-side for freedom, justice an' the American dream but not let on who we were really working for; red tape, profile, all that jazz. Keep up the pretense of protecting the regular, hard-working Joe. I said yes. It didn't take long for people to take notice of us. We had our own legion of fans; signings, guest-appearances, everything.

JS: So what went wrong?
FT: I started believing my own hype, passed up XoDOS priority missions for ones of my own. I wasn't too enamored with being branded a tool, it gets to you after a while. I guess I said no once too often. Once you bite the hand that feeds you, you can't go back looking for a pat on the head, know what I'm saying? Woke up one morning and it was all over the papers; don't make out you don't know what I'm talking about.

JS: Could you clarify for my records?
FT: It started with me being accused of hanging around kindergartens. Worse was to follow. Pictures appeared across the media; me with kids, doing stuff to 'em. Lies, all fucking lies! All fake! That shit was fucked up!

JS: Why didn't you try to clear your name?
FT: What did you think I tried to do? That ain't the kinda crap I was gonna take lying down. But when *They* want that shit to stick, it sticks, 'specially here in America. I was brought in for questioning, then questions turned into charges until finally, I wound up in court. Had a top ball-breaker in my corner ready to knock the allegation outta sight, but there was a further twist of the knife; *She* testified against me. Said she saw me doing stuff but didn't know what to do, on account of her being abused by her parents as a child. Bullshit! She didn't even know her parents, she was brought up by HomeLight. I know! But the jury bought her story, hook, line and sinker. My reputation was in tatters. They made damn sure I weren't getting outta here anytime soon. Once I was here the guards thought it would be funny to dish out a little justice of their own, didn't you, boys?

Firetrail looks over at the guards and sneers.

Don't worry, I gave those bastards a burning they'll never forget. Teach them to play with fire.

JS: How do your fellow cons feel about you?
FT: I don't care. If they deal with me, I deal with them. An' they know which one of us holds the ace up his sleeve. The system ain't ever going to release me, even though I'm innocent. Everyone knows me now as a Pedo, not a Flambo, an' *They* made sure there ain't no way I can clear my name now. So I guess I'll just sit tight an' bide my time.

Do you know how many Super-S's or 2nd Degrees are in here with me? I'll tell you. None. I'm the only one. That makes me special. I got my own fan base again. Sure, they're rapists, murderers and thieves... but they love me. Who knows, maybe one day I'll tire of all this and bust my way outta here with my own goddamn army behind me and put paid to those that lied about me, including that two-faced, back-stabbin' bitch.

One of the guards indicates that our time is up. Firetrail winks at me.

FT: Thanks again for the smoke. Be seeing you around.

Artwork: Admira Wijaya - Firetrail

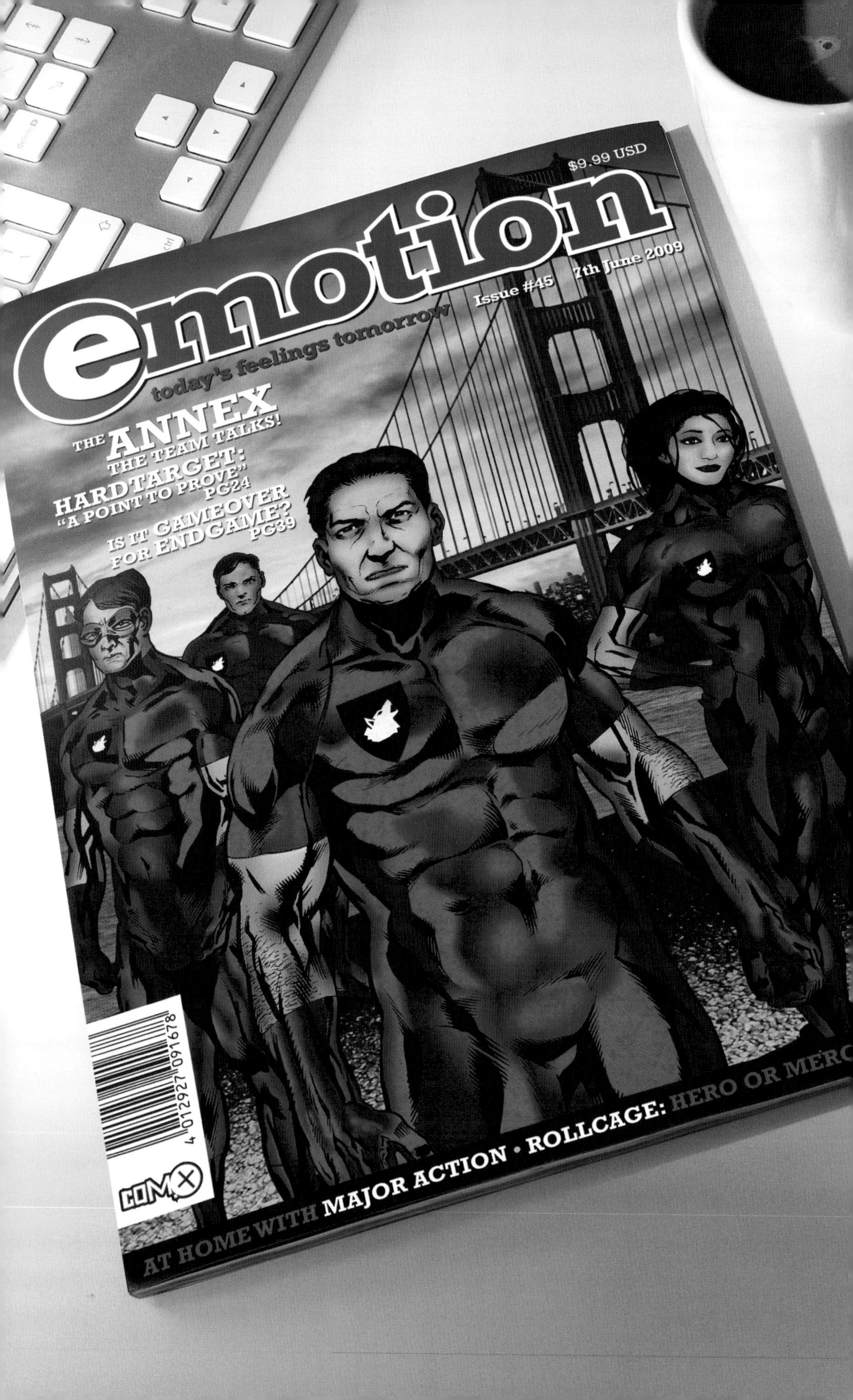
$9.99 USD
emotion
today's feelings tomorrow
Issue #45
7th June 2009
THE ANNEX
THE TEAM TALKS!
HARDTARGET:
"A POINT TO PROVE"
PG24
IS IT GAMEOVER
FOR ENDGAME?
PG39
4 012927 091678
AT HOME WITH MAJOR ACTION • ROLLCAGE: HERO OR MER

Thirty-one year-old Trojan is leader of The ANNEX, a Super-S team that graduated together from the San Francisco Academy of Higher Development fifteen years ago. At just over seven-feet tall, he makes quite an impression when you are stood next to him.

We are in a secret location, somewhere on the outskirts of San Francisco. I am in a large briefing room. On the wall sits a plasma screen with a schematic showing all the continents across the world.

JS: Thank you for meeting me. For the record, could you list the members of The ANNEX and the team's mantra please?
T: No problem. There are four of us: HardTarget, EndGame, Quicksteed and myself. Our mantra is a simple one: *Protect the Innocent.*

JS: Are you supported by the US Government?

Trojan seems momentarily taken aback.

T: What are you implying?

JS: Well, I've been led to believe you have Presidential authorisation that allows you to intervene in unstable countries.
T: Let me clarify. We aren't some kind of government-sponsored, global police force. We abide by international law; we obey rules and local protocol and respect cultures. We're not the sort of team that would, say, simply walk into a Middle Eastern country back in 2003 and impose our authority over them, just because we were ordered to. Even though there were those of us in the team that felt we should have participated, we stayed completely neutral.

We only intervene when we are asked to, and only through the correct political channels. The United Nations are often in contact asking The ANNEX to appropriate in affairs. Even if we arrive at an incident ahead of the local authorities, we always seek permission before getting involved. There are no third-party interests or concerns when it comes to us saving lives.

JS: The people of Iraq asked you for help liberating them from their oppressive regime, why did you refuse them?
T: We do not fight international wars. We're not XoDOS.

JS: XoDOS?
T: You seem surprised? Do you know what the phrase *Shock and Awe* refers to?

JS: Isn't it defined as, a swift opening strike in a war, designed to beat an army into a quick submission with a show of strength?
T: Wrong. *Shock and Awe* were a Super-S duo who wreaked havoc over Baghdad in the second night of hostilities in Iraq. And you know the level of damage that was inflicted that night. Goddamn disgusting.

JS: Did XoDOS ask The ANNEX to assist?
T: There are plenty of Super-S and Vaders out there who are prepared to do anothers' bidding. When it came to Iraq, it was our decision and ours alone to help distribute aid; we played our small part as a show of solidarity to highlight the suffering to the world, but that's all.

JS: I hear you also hunt Vaders. How many do you face on a regular basis?
T: There's no real pattern to the numbers, except we find it's busier in the capital cities around summertime. Guess the good weather brings them out. See this HD display behind me? It's connected to every ruling leader of the civilized world, regardless of their religion or political stance. It's a live, open feed, updating and reporting back any and all Vader disturbances. If there's any whiff of activity, we're the first to know about it.

JS: What about in the last month then?
T: Four Vaders. Two of those were working together. All of them were dealt with appropriately; three are now pending conviction.

JS: What happened to the fourth?
T: Unfortunately, he was killed during the struggle. Sometimes we are left with no alternative. It's a last resort, and a decision I'm always reluctant to make, but when the fate of thousands of people rests on your shoulders, you have to make the choice.

JS: So, how does the group dynamic work? Do you see each other socially? It must be hard working together in such intense conditions on a daily basis.
T: It's no different to working for any other emergency service; you watch each other's back, no matter what. But I'd be lying if I said it was all plain-sailing. We're close, but even the greatest of friends can have their run-ins.

JS: How do you resolve internal disputes?
T: We'll talk it out. If that doesn't work we might have to take it a step further to get it out of our system. The training room is good for that, it offers up a chance for some restrained combat – *restrained* being the optimum word!

JS: Does anyone get hurt?
T: To some degree, but we don't push it too far. Just because you fall out with someone doesn't mean you want to maim them. It's just a good excuse for a bout of 'hard' sparring; sharpens the edge a little.

JS: Does sparring really resolve issues?
T: It works for us. We're very physical people, so an intense session is very therapeutic for ironing out our differences. If that doesn't work, then I'll intervene and act as mediator. I'm the designated leader of The ANNEX, so the others will look to me to make the final decisions if there are any upsets.

JS: You certainly have the physical presence of a leader.
T: The ANNEX was my idea. The others may bring their own, unique qualities, but the leadership of the group ultimately falls to me. We work well as a team. I like to think I'm not too overbearing and we always discuss things first. I might have the strength of a demigod but we are a democracy and I am fully aware that I don't have all the answers.

JS: So what other powers do The ANNEX possess?
T: Quicksteed has been gifted with lightning speed; HardTarget is nigh-on invulnerable, and EndGame can paralyze with a single touch. All our powers are pretty basic, but very effective when honed as a team.

JS: Has your relationship with EndGame interfered with the group dynamic?
T: Relationship?

Trojan looks agitated.

JS: I'm sorry, I thought it was general knowledge, I didn't mean to-
T: It's okay. I guess it had to get out eventually. Yes, we're an item. It's hard not to become involved when you're around someone as much as we two are. EndGame and I just... happened. Ultimately, we're still human, albeit ones imbued with super-powers. She's an extraordinary woman: determined, strong-willed. We're a great fit.

JS: Is it serious between you?
T: Well, we've been seeing each other for about six months. I'd like to think it's pretty serious.

JS: Has the relationship altered the dynamics within The ANNEX?
T: I don't think so. The guys seem fine with it. I think any issues would have surfaced by now.

JS: If the relationship were to become too complex for the team?
T: Without hesitating, I'd put The ANNEX first. Of course, it would be a tough decision to make but I can't say it would be the first time. It certainly wouldn't be the last. That's what it means to be team-leader, to be the one that people can rely on, whatever the situation.

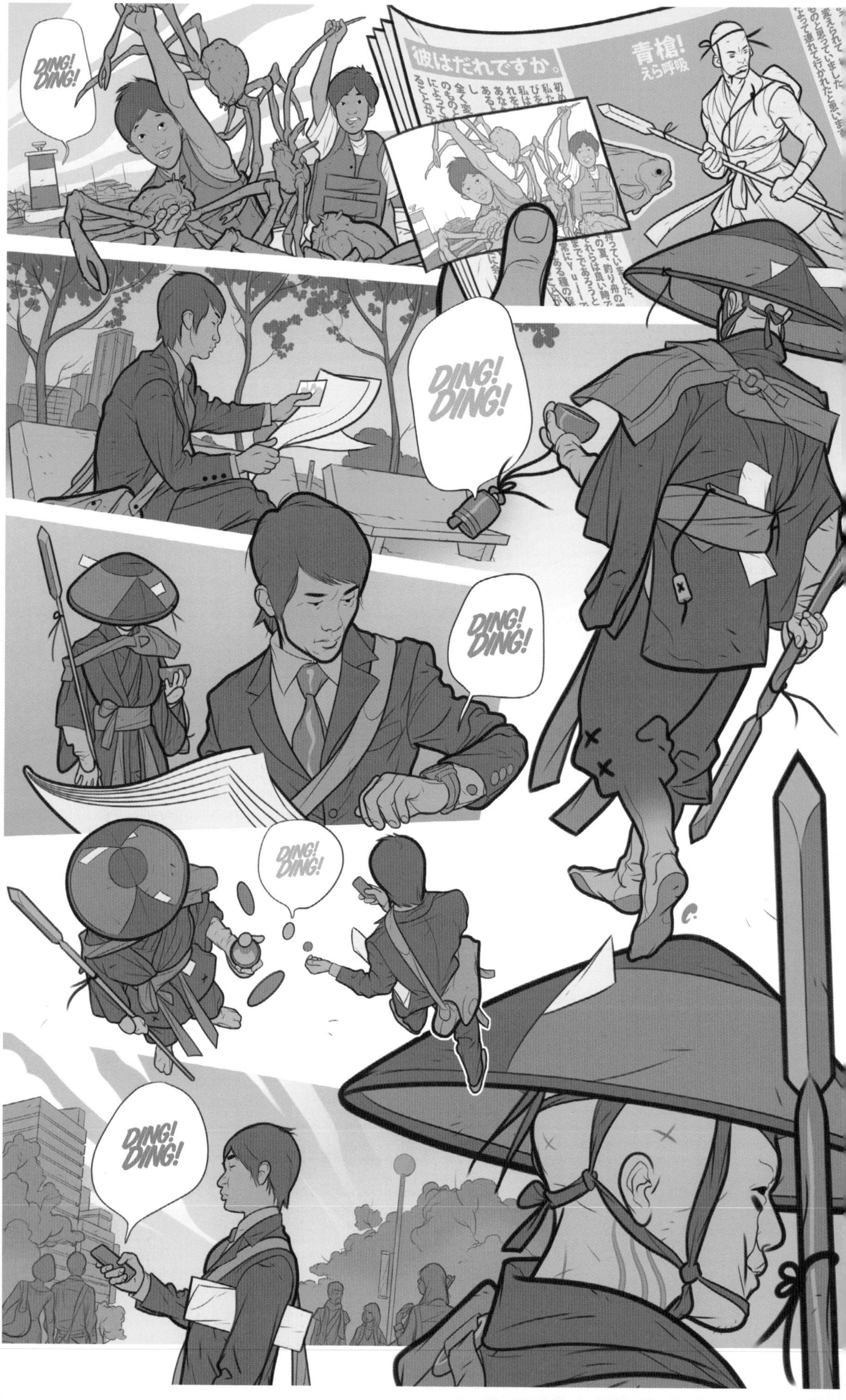
DING! DING!
彼はだれですか。
青槍！
えら呼吸
DING! DING!
DING! DING!
DING! DING!
DING! DING!

At thirty-two years-old, Akira Tomikawa is the younger brother to Yuji Tomikawa – the legendary BlueSpear – a superhero that walks the neon streets of Shinjuku in Tokyo. Akira is a Norman. He works for a large petroleum company.

I'm in a tenth-floor office, looking out of a window, over the hustle and bustle of a Tuesday afternoon in Tokyo. Akira is sitting at his desk waiting for me to begin the interview. My attention is drawn to a photograph of Akira and Yuji, 'hanging out' together as children.

JS: Let's start at the beginning. You're the younger brother of Yuji-san. How was your childhood together?
AT: In the early days we had a wonderful relationship. We enjoyed many a summer in Funakoshi Bay, playing amongst the fishing boats. They were good times. I was always getting into mischief and Yuji was always there to put things right. Even from a young age he was a guardian, of sorts.

JS: Yuji wasn't born a Super-S, was he? He's a 2nd Degree. How did that happen?
AT: I am embarrassed to tell you that it was my fault.

Akira's answer takes me a little by surprise.

JS: Your fault?
AT: I was twelve years-old. We were on a weekend break away from the city. I had convinced Yuji to take a small fishing boat out into the harbour. I wanted to fish for crabs, just under the sea wall. Yuji said he didn't like the idea; there was a lot of traffic on the water and it was dangerous. I was selfish, I didn't really give him a choice – I was going, with or without him. I remember him sighing as we pushed the boat out. We had been fishing for ten or fifteen minutes when my line became snagged on something. I tried to pull it free but it wouldn't budge. Yuji was a stronger swimmer than I and, like the dutiful brother, he offered to dive in and untangle it for me.

He jumped over the side of the boat and disappeared under the surface. One minute became two, then two became ten. I shouted his name, but he did not resurface. I dived in to try and find him but ended up in difficulty. Two fishermen rowed over and pulled me out. When I explained that my brother had disappeared they tried to find him also, but to no avail. The emergency services were called. Hours passed. It wasn't until the next day that they found his body, washed up twenty-three miles along the coastline.

JS: Was he alive when they found him?
AT: Yes, but not in the normal sense of the word. The sea had taken him and claimed him as one of her own. He was changed, utterly changed. Many say he was consumed by the Yurei, by the ghosts. His eyes glowed like pearls, he had developed gills and his hands and feet were webbed; he was no longer of this world. He stayed in a coma for thirty-two days.

JS: Was he ever able to explain what happened?
AT: Not really. He was incoherent most of the time, even after he was discharged from the hospital. He spoke in mumbled, broken sentences; of pale, shimmering lights under the water, and a quest to locate a blue spear.

Our family presumed it was a result of his near-death experience, or the medication the doctors had placed him on. But he was only home a matter of days before he disappeared from the house, during a particularly heavy rainstorm. We alerted the authorities; the police, ambulance, coast-guard. We had no idea where he had gone.

Seven days went by and still we had heard nothing. Nobody had seen him, there had been no reports of a body turning up or a person admitted to hospital. And then suddenly, as quickly as he left, he returned. Just turned up at the family home, with the [now legendary] blue spear in his possession. That was the beginning of the hero, BlueSpear.

JS: Did he ever tell you where he went during his disappearance?
AT: No. Personally, I think he returned to the sea, but he never spoke about it. It didn't seem to bother Yuji that he had put the family through so much anguish. He looked so different, behaved so strangely. The doctors and their hospital tests seemed to say otherwise, but to us he was far from human, far removed from the brother I once knew.

My parents found it all too much. They became scared of him. Eventually, my father couldn't cope with the shame and left us. Then, my mother had a breakdown. It was a hard time for us all. We continued living with my mother and her immediate family for four more years. I never saw her embrace Yuji once during that time, although she continued to feed and clothe both of us. She took her own life when I was eighteen.

JS: How were you affected by such a traumatic childhood?
AT: You have to understand that I felt responsible for the change in my brother and the trauma it caused my family. I will never forgive myself. After my mother's death, I stayed to look after Yuji. I worked hard to strengthen my relationship with him. I thought I could bring the old Yuji back, but I was wrong; he grew ever more distant. He was twenty-one, his powers were still developing but he was rapidly becoming recognized as the phenomenon we all know as BlueSpear. I came back to the apartment after work one day and he was gone, all he left was a note saying he would be in touch. I guess he'd decided that he didn't need me in his life anymore.

JS: Have you seen him since?
AT: No. He's called me a few times since he left but we don't talk for long. In fact, I read more about him in the newspapers and on the internet than he divulges when we are on the phone. I think he just wants to hear a familiar voice. He never tells me where he is calling from. We have become very disconnected.

The situation has become increasingly worse for me these last few weeks. Somehow, my father has managed to reacquaint himself with my brother and Yuji has accepted him. They are becoming very close. My father has succeeded with Yuji where I failed. I can't believe it.

JS: Why do you think your father wanted to communicate with your brother again?
AT: I really don't know why or what has brought my father back. Maybe it is my brother's fame. After all, BlueSpear is adored by people. But I do not understand why Yuji has embraced my father's return so.

JS: How do you feel about Yuji's decision?
AT: Emotionally, it hurts. The pain goes deeper than the sharpest blade ever could. I try to temper my heartache by convincing myself that I lost my real brother the day the water took him.

Tokyo embraces BlueSpear with all their hearts; he is the icon of our generation. After he single-handedly fought and defeated N-NRA and O-RYO, two supervillains that were threatening to level the entire Midtown Complex, he became a national hero. Organizations began featuring his likeness on packets of sweets, cans of drink, action figures, manga – there is even a computer game in development! He also has a fan-club that dress like him. We call them *Spearos*.

Akira stares out across the city.

Do you know what it's like to walk down the street and see your brother's image everywhere, staring back at you? Wherever I look, wherever I go, he is there, flirting with my conscience, a permanent reminder of my selfishness.

JS: That must be unbearable.
AT: I would give anything to turn back time and change that fateful day at sea. I pray to the Gods that somewhere, deep inside the hero that is BlueSpear, my real brother is waiting, ready to return home.

Artwork: Calum Alexander Watt – BlueSpear

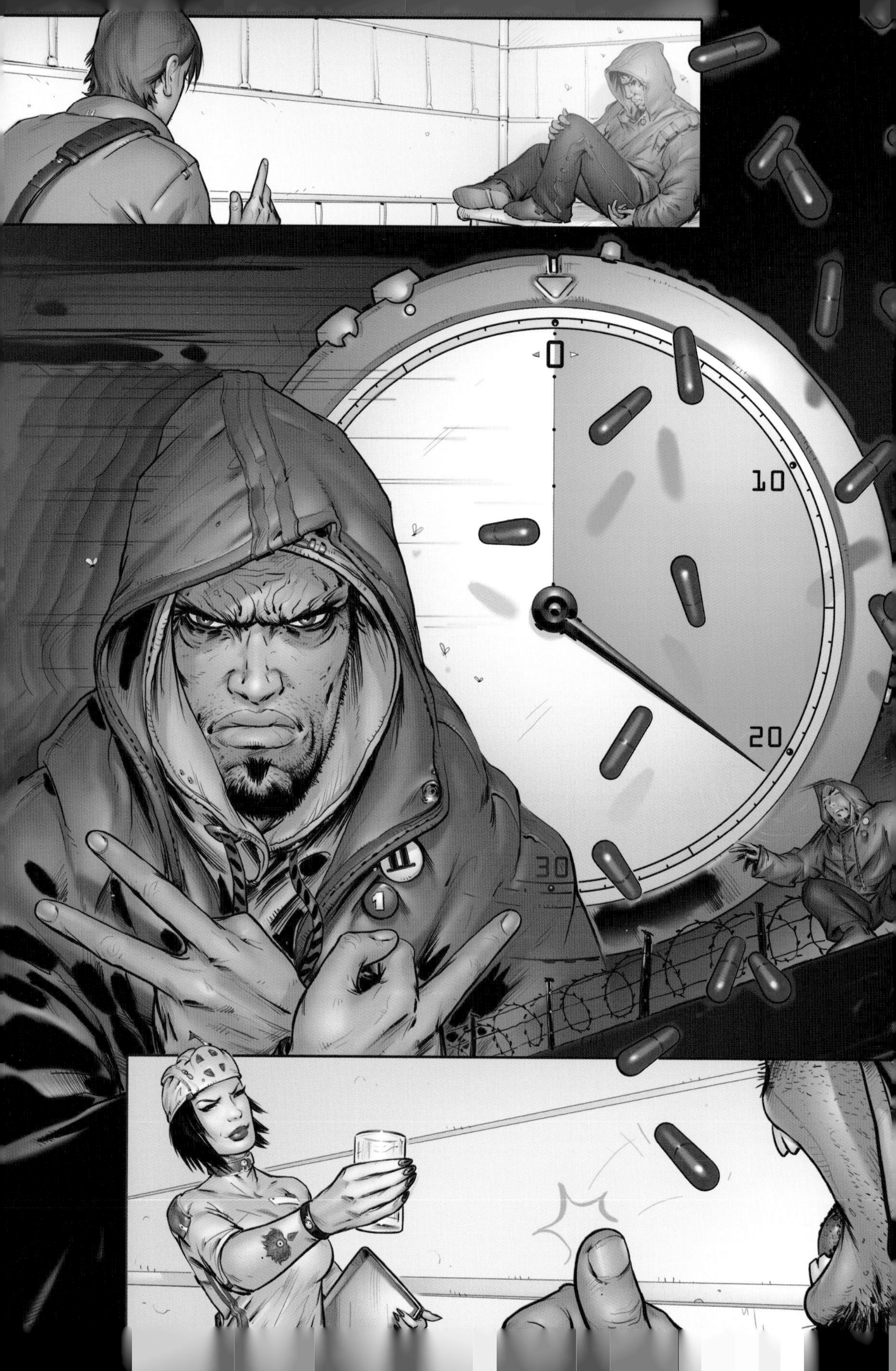
0
10
20
30

Black'Jak'd is a thirty-six year-old 2nd Degree, residing in Boston. He is dependent upon the drugs that give him his trademark power: the ability to see twenty-one seconds into the future. In a last, desperate bid to control his habit, Black'Jak'd has booked himself into a S.T.A.R.T. program.

We are in a white room. Black'Jak'd is curled up on a medical bed. He's somewhat shaky, but insists we continue with the interview.

JS: I didn't expect to be interviewing you in a rehab clinic, let alone one specially designed for Super-S – are you sure you're in the right frame of mind to talk to me today?
B: Yeah, yeah, yeah. S'okay, man. I know it looks a little fucked up right now but seriously, s'all cool with me. Ask your questions, interview man, ask away.

JS: Let's start with an easy one, why-
B: -'Cos I got a problem, man. Big problem. The drugs I need to do the things I do, man, the bastards fucked up! Made them so fucking addictive. Can't work without 'em. Every day I wake up, I jus' gotta pop one. Get to 'bout eleven and I get the shakes bad, so I take another that sees me thru 'til about two, then another, you get my drift? Fuckin' meds. Fuckin' XoDOS.

JS: How did-
B: -Sorry, old habits die hard. Twenty-one seconds into the future, remember. I already know what your next question is. I'll try not to do that again, though I'm a bit fucked up right now so I might forget.

JS: You mentioned XoDOS-
B: You bet your ass I did! Fuckers stole my life! Made me into someone else – this fuckin' Black'Jak'd dude. That's why I wanted to see you. You need to warn others about them. The shit they're dabblin' in is gonna start a war, I'm telling you! The Middle East? Man, that's just a taster of things to come.

JS: What have you heard?
B: Not heard, man; seen. With my own fuckin' mind's eye. That's how it works. They always talk about war. You would have thought they'd learn to keep quiet around me, when they're walkin' away after briefings. You don't think twenty-one seconds is long enough to see much? I tell you, man, it's enough. Twenty-fuckin'-one. You know, it starts to drive you a little nuts, seeing what's gonna happen. An' it always does; never stops, never wrong. The meds help control it.

JS: Control it? I thought the meds helped you maintain your power? That's why you use them.
B: See! Fucked up! That'd be too logical, man. That's how I would think, too. But these meds, they're what stop me goin' into full meltdown. If I don't take them I start seeing longer into the future. The further forwards I go, the harder it is to return. You dig? No meds? I end up a vegetable; suckin' soup thru a straw, like a 'tard. Fucking-A! They never told me that when they signed me up to their 'special' programme, no sir.

JS: What's it like being able to see into the future?
B: It's like watchin' two channels of MTV at once. On the left sits the present day, the world as it is. On the right, it's almost the same fuckin' thing, just slightly ahead of the other. Issue is – you gotta work out which one is real-time an' which one is the 'jump', or that shit jus' fucks you up, y'know what I'm sayin'?

JS: How do you endure it? It must be a huge struggle maintaining your focus on which one is present day.
B: Why the fuck do you think I'm like this? Gotta keep on top of it all the time. Never friggin' stops. Even when I dream I'm seeing dual images. It's either that or a one-way trip to the nut-farm. And I ain't no lob-job.

JS: What's the farthest you've seen into the future?
B: Thirty-seven seconds. Any longer and I'd have been gone for good. Fuckin' bastards! Stuck their needles in me, operated on me for days. Told me I'd be some big-shot American hero, protecting my own kind. Bullshit, man, they just wanted their own early-warnin' system, jus' so they would know everything before anyone else. Had to get out of there, man.

JS: How did you manage to detcah yourself from the organisation?
B: It's not as hard as you think when you know what's 'round the corner.

Black'Jak'd grins.

They shouldn't have fucked me over.

JS: What happens if your medication runs out? Will you need to go back to them?
B: I managed to snag me a big batch when I escaped. I also got me some dudes on the inside; there are plenty of anti-XoDOS types out there, plenty with a grudge that are all too willing to support the likes of me. I'm grateful for the help, but I really don't care about the deeper cause – I just gotta make sure I get my gear, else it's good night, Vienna. Ain't no way I'd go back to them with my ass on a plate.

JS: That's a big risk, especially considering your condition. What if they cut-off your supply contacts?
B: Then I got me a plan B; twenty-one seconds is long enough for me to get in and out of where I need to be in order to obtain my stuff. Fuck, they wouldn't even know I was there. Wait up, here it comes again. Sugar-time. She's coming. I don't wanna talk when the nurse is here.

The door opens. An attractive, dark-haired nurse walks in carrying a tray. On it sits a pill and a cup of water.

Time for the good stuff.

Black'Jak'd swallows the pill and washes it down with the water. The nurse smiles as he relaxes and waits for the tablet to take effect. He hands her back the empty cup and she leaves.

Yessiree, like candy to a kid. Fuck, yeah. That's what I'm talking about. I'd swear that nurse is takin' longer each time she does her rounds.

JS: So why have you admitted yourself to this private hospital? Aren't you worried about XoDOS tracking you down?
B: S.T.A.R.T. is a different type of clinic. It's part of HomeLight and it's for Super-S and 2nd Degrees only. They're anti-XoDOS, big-time, so no way these cats'll sell me out; they wouldn't let one leg of a suit step foot thru that door.

All I wanted was to go back to being Norman, so I just kept poppin' the pills, hoping my powers would go away. Not a chance. So I turned up here. My body was totally slammed, shutting down for good. I was [this] close to going under, way out of control. Best move I ever made. They saved my life, said they'd help find a cure for me. I'm down with that. I got nothin' to lose 'cept the future.

JS: I hope you can maintain your anonymity here.
B: If I don't then I'm prepared for them – they gotta have every option covered if they wanna capture my ass again. I'm prepared for those fuckers this time – they ain't catching Black'Jak'd off guard.

JS: How did you feel about handing your meds over to S.T.A.R.T?
B: Hardest thing I ever done, but it was cool, once I understood what they were offering me. They also got some cool docs here trying to simulate my meds, so that I don't need to go hunting when my stash runs out. Deal is, I come and go as I please within the complex, but they get to control my habit. They're hoping I can eventually come off 'em altogether, but we're takin' it one step at a time. For me, that's enough for now; I don't wanna see any further than that, y'know what I'm sayin'? Don't get me wrong, I got me some future plans, but I ain't showing my hand just yet. This is one hombre that ain't ready to fold just yet.

Artwork: Boo Cook - Black'Jak'd

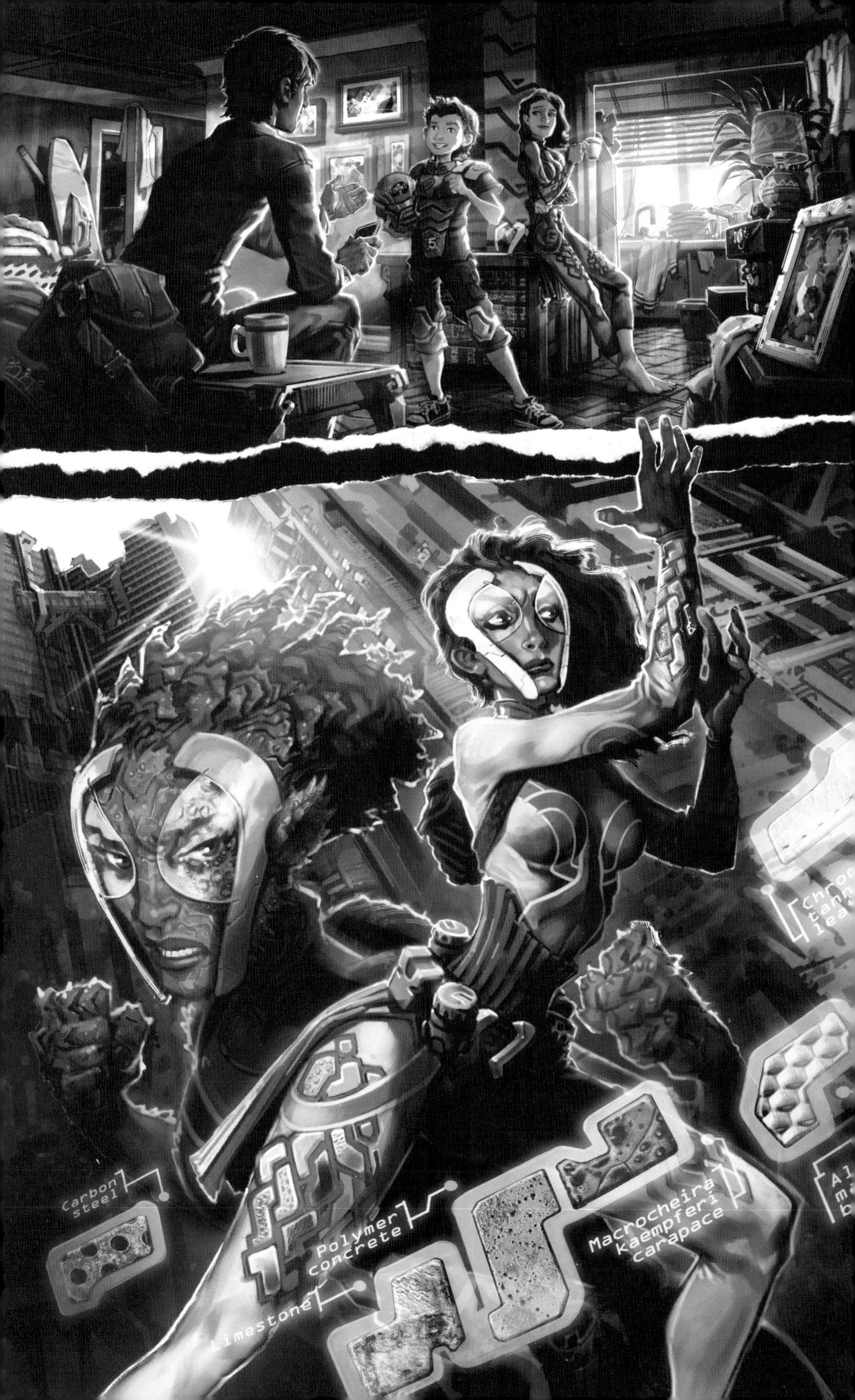

Carbon steel
Polymer concrete
Limestone
Macrocheira kaempferi Carapace

Grace Cassidy* is a thirty-seven year-old Super-S struggling to cope with the demands of her eight year-old Norman son, Rocky. Together with her Norman husband, they live in an apartment in Brooklyn, New York.

The apartment is large, yet still manages to feel claustrophobic. Washing hangs on the doors and dirty plates are stacked high in the sink. Grace, dressed as her alter ego Material Girl, sits opposite me. She appears slightly nervous.

JS: I thought Lou, your husband, might be with us for this interview?
MG: Sorry, sugar, he got called away last minute. Work. Just the way it goes in our household, I'm afraid. He was pretty upset about missing you though, but he sends his regards.

JS: How often is he away from home?
MG: Well, he's in the haulage business – a longshoreman over in Port Elizabeth. They sometimes need a few of the guys to work extra hours at night when large shipments come in. We need the extra money, so he takes what he can get. After all, Super-S pay is non-existent; saving civilians doesn't pay the bills!

JS: How do you cope when Lou has to work shifts and you're called away on duty?
MG: We're fortunate that we have understanding neighbors. Mr and Mrs Sands are awesome; they're more than happy to take Rocky at a moments notice. They treat him like a grandson.

JS: The name 'Material Girl' conjures up a lot of possibilities, so for the record, what's your superpower?
MG: My gift is that I can augment my body with the attributes of any surface that I touch; it means I can assume numerous physical properties. I can become as hard as steel or as light as paper. You can't ignore a gift like that. I made an oath very early on in my career to use my power for the good of society, so sacrifices have to be made, whether I'm predisposed or not. Lou respects that. I hope Rocky will too, when he's older.

Just then, Rocky runs into the room. He's dressed in a familiar superhero costume.

R: Ta da ta da!

Rocky sings the theme tune to the RollCage cartoon series. His mother smiles and winks at me.

MG: Hey there, RollCage. Who ya saving today?

She hugs him and he runs out of the room, back to his bedroom.

JS: How does Rocky react to having a Super-S mother and a Norman father? Does it have a negative effect on him?
MG: Not really. Rocky is old enough to appreciate what we do and why we do it. We try and make it an adventure for him, reminding him that he's playing an important role in keeping New York safe for other kids to grow up in.

JS: What does he say about that?
MG: He gets a real kick out of it. He loves the idea that he's helping to protect his school friends. You saw his costume; he keeps asking when he's going to be allowed to go on missions with me. It would totally make his day if they made a cartoon about his Mom. When I arrive home he's always full of questions; who did I save? Who did I defeat? Which other heroes did I meet?

His room is full of newspaper articles and magazines about Super-S. He's always keeping track of who's new, though I can't say I approve of his latest favorite-of-the-month, RollCage.

JS: Isn't RollCage a well-respected superhero?
MG: The only thing RollCage respects is money. I completely disagree with his mercenary approach to being a Super-S. I swear, he only saves people if the price is right.

JS: At least there's no danger of Rocky following in your footsteps, what with being a Norman.

A look of sadness appears on Material Girl's face. Suddenly, I understand.

JS: Rocky thinks he's going to be a superhero when he's older, doesn't he?

Material Girl nods, holding back the tears.

JS: Does Rocky know that he'll never have superpowers?
MG: We haven't told him. Not yet, anyway. You've seen him in his sweet, little costume; he's superhero mad. He keeps on asking when he's going to be a Super-S, like his Mom. I've discussed it with Lou and we really don't know what to say to him yet. Every time he asks us when he's going to get his powers, we give him the same answer, "Maybe in a year or two, honey, just be patient".

I see the poor thing, becoming more and more frustrated at not being able to do Super-S things. I caught him last week, hanging out of the apartment window. He said he wanted to get used to looking at the people far below, just in case he acquires the ability to fly. We're fifteen floors up! If Lou knew, he'd kill me.

Rocky's already told his friends he's going to be a Super-S when he grows up. I've seen them, laughing behind his back; they have an inkling for the truth. We'll have to break the news to him soon, but he's at such an important stage of his development that it may do more harm than good. I don't want to take away his dreams and aspirations. It's like, do you go ahead and tell your child that Santa Claus doesn't exist or do you just wait for them to realize it for themselves?

JS: It's certainly a difficult situation.
MG: I hope and pray it's just a phase he's going thru and that he'll cotton on soon that he isn't going to develop powers. Maybe I should stop being Material Girl and concentrate on my role as a mother so that he doesn't just see me as this super role-model. Sometimes I think I should give it all up so that we can lead a normal life, but I'm just not ready for that. I do work a few hours a week as a Norman; nothing heavy, just a bit of admin for an investment banker. It's not very taxing, but it means I get to bring in a little cash and it's a chance to work away from Material Girl one day a week. I could do that full-time, I guess.

JS: When you're Material Girl, how often does Lou get called away at the same time as you?
MG: Two, maybe three times a week. It's certainly not ideal, but when I'm here, I try hard to be a good mother. Rocky's a happy kid. I hope I'm doing the right thing.

Rocky calls out from his bedroom.

R: Can I come in now? Does the man want to interview me yet?

Material Girl looks at me.

MG: Yes, you can come in now, sweetheart.

Rocky rushes in, still in costume.

JS: Hello, I'm James Stanley. What's your name?
R: I'm RollCage!

JS: So, RollCage, what's your superpower?
R: I'm an Exo-S. I can fly way up into the sky an' I can fire missiles an' deflect bullets an' beat the baddies. Watch!

Rocky proceeds to charge around the room, lost in his superhero world. I smile at Material Girl.

JS: You're doing the right thing – I'm sure Lou would agree.
MG: No matter what happens, both of them will always be the inspiration in my life.

Artwork: Ross Dearsley - Material Girl

*Interviewee name has been changed

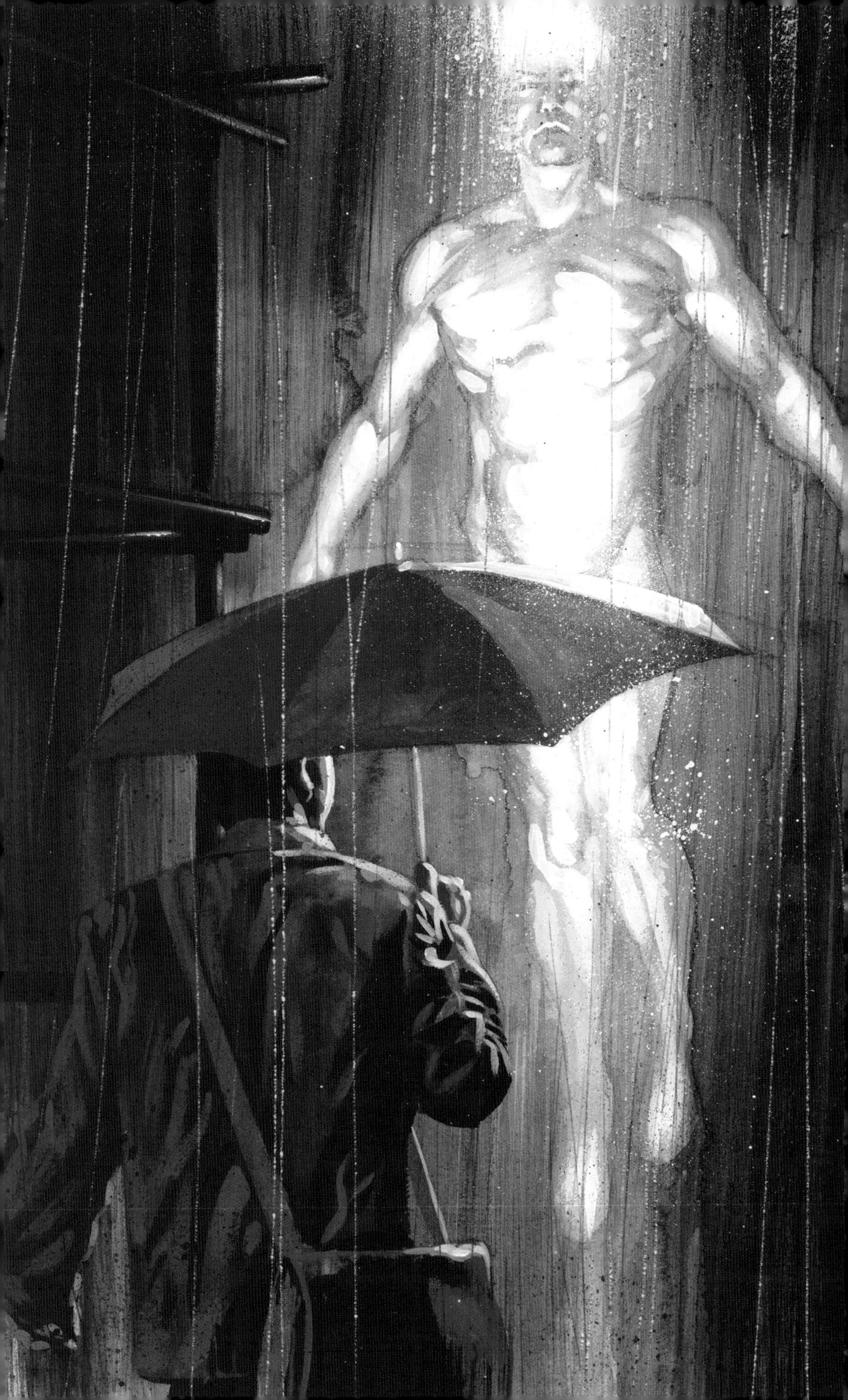

The time is 01:47am. It's raining hard. I have a pre-arranged meeting with Auroron (aged thirty-eight), an 'import' from The United States. He left the East Coast twelve years ago and established his home, here in England.

Upon his unusual request I've agreed to meet Auroron at this ungodly hour in a quiet street off Chancery Lane, Central London. The rain hammers at my umbrella and, for the first time since beginning my research, I find myself wishing I were home with my wife, tucked up in our warm bed. I check my watch; Auroron is late. Just as I feel the rain invading the soles of my shoes, I hear a voice.

A: You Brits sure have a thing for punctuality.

I look up to see Auroron descending through the rain towards me.

JS: Do you mind if we find somewhere with a bit more shelter? My umbrella's struggling to keep me dry, and you must be cold.

I motion to a building with scaffolding erected around it. Auroron shrugs his shoulders, nonchalantly.

JS: Not exactly the place I had in mind for our interview but...
A: That'll be your fucking British weather for you!

JS: So, how did you come to be in London in the first place?
A: What's the matter? Don't like the idea of us Yanks coming over and stealing your women? Man alive, you Brits are all the same. Shoulda been left to the Krauts; you'd be goose-stepping your asses off if it wasn't for us.

JS: If you're not that fond of this country, why are you here?
A: Well, I ain't here for the weather or the chicks, if that's what you're getting at. But I don't have much choice in the matter; things were just too fucking dangerous at home to stick around, too many Vaders with grudges, for my liking. There was always at least one badass mutha ready to kick off. That shit got all too real on a weekly basis, even for me! Plus, I had XoDOS blowing smoke up my ass, trying to recruit me. You say "no" too many times and they get a bit too forceful with their offers.

So, I certainly ain't here of my own, free will. Sheesh! You don't seriously think you guys have anything to offer me, do you? I've been here, what, ten fucking years or more? Man, that's way too long in my book. But I don't have an alternative. And that just sucks, big time.

JS: I heard that you were caught in bed with another Super-S' wife and that's why you had to flee your country? Can you confirm or deny the rumour?
A: Better be careful with those rumors, boy. They can introduce you to a whole new world of hurt. For the record, I *chose* to leave America. And hey, I didn't fucking "flee", I just decided my help was needed elsewhere.

JS: Right... so you chose England?
A: Only decent English-speaking country out there, wasn't it? There ain't that many options.

JS: What about Canada? Or Australia?
A: Canada? You're fucking kidding me, right?! And where the fuck's Australia?

JS: Nevermind. Try "Googling" it sometime. So is there something you *do* like about England?
A: Like what? Apart from the fact that protecting your skies is like a stroll down Easy Street, your coffee tastes like crap, your TV shows are lame and you ain't got an ounce of pride left in your sorry asses. There's another thing that sucks, and that's your women. But I don't mean that in the *right* way.

Yeah, yeah, I can tell by that look on your face that you think I'm being totally disrespectful. OK, your girls ain't that bad. I've had my good times, if you get my drift, got to sow a few oats. They can be real grateful when they discover you're an out-of-town Super-S, here to protect their precious nation. Mind you, I've had to use a bit of artistic license with my powers on a few occasions, just in case they went screaming to the papers; you know, what with me being a super-celebrity and all.

JS: What do you mean by that?
A: You've done your research, right? You know how I can influence people? Manipulate their memories? Had to do that to a few of them, just to be on the safe side. There was one in particular; kinda cute, nice rack, with a bit of an attitude but then, I like the feisty ones. Nothing serious as far as I was concerned, but she just got way too heavy on me. Turns out she wanted more than just a good time. I mean, who the hell did she think she was? They know at the beginning there are no strings attached; I'm a Super-S, she was just a fucking Norman whore. But no, she wasn't having any of that, so I had to condition her.

JS: What do you mean by that?
A: Let's just say I put a little suggestion out there – made her think I'd taken a working trip somewhere in the Caribbean and was never coming back. Nothing too extreme; just a bit of creative cerebral manipulation to get the bitch off my back. Don't get me wrong, I could have gone real hard on the woman; wiped her entire mind and erased all knowledge of myself and our relationship but hey, she was just a fucking Norman, right? Why bother using my full power on her when she wasn't worth the effort? Only downer with what I did to her is that she don't ever get to fully remember bumping hips with the awesome Auroron.

JS: What was her name?
A: That don't matter.

JS: It might.
A: Ermm... Jenny, alright? Sheesh! Can't remember her last name, can't say I care. *She* sure as hell don't remember much about *me*, that much I can promise you.

JS: What if this Jenny, or one of the other female "Normans", had a child by you?
A: Not a chance. Wouldn't happen.

JS: Ok, hypothetically speaking, what if someone did have a child by you and that child was a Super-S?
A: Can't say I've thought about it, but I'll play along. What would I do? That's a tough one. To be honest, I dunno. I do know there's no fucking way I'd leave a Super-S kid of mine with a Norman woman, that much is for sure! You sound like you know something I don't?

JS: No, it's just a hypothetical question. As you said, you, "got to sow a few oats". In ten years or so I would guess you'd have to expect a bit of reaping in return?
A: Jesus, now you put it like that I've gotta be a bit more careful. I don't want a fucking load of bastard Brit-kids crawling out of the woodwork looking for me. No fucking way!

JS: Do you think you'd make a good father?
A: Me? I'd be the fucking best, man! I mean, what kid wouldn't be in awe of me? Fuck it, I'd even consider going back to the 'States when it was old enough. You know, set up a little family team, and all that. No mother-fucker would dare step out of line knowing they would have to go head-to-head with us. Man, I could say goodbye to you moaning, limey bastards and this Goddamn country for good.

JS: But children aren't programmed like that. They develop their own traits and personalities. They might not approve of yours.
A: I'm fucking AURORON, man! I can fucking make them believe I'm a GOD if I want to! Fuck it. Want me to prove it? I'd condition you right now if it wasn't for the fact I can't be bothered to use my powers. You haven't been listening to shit I've been saying, have you? I'm bored now. You're wasting my time.

I watch as Auroron disappears into the rain-filled sky.

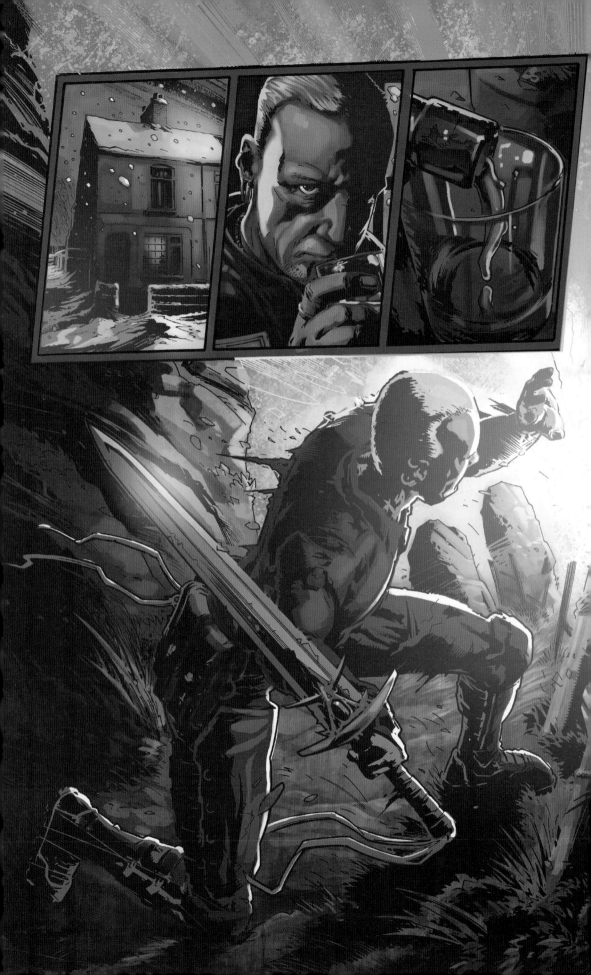

Roger Wilson lives in Glasgow, Scotland. He is a well-built man with eyes seemingly older than his thirty-nine years. His superhero name is Bearach.

I am sitting in the living room of a small, suburban house. His legendary weapon, a claymore, hangs proudly above the fireplace. By contrast, numerous empty whisky bottles are scattered about the floor.

BH: Ah cannae start ma story without a drink in hand. Will ye not join me in a wee dram?

JS: Well, it's a little early in the day, but I'll make an exception.
B: Grand!

Bearach pulls out two tumblers and takes a bottle of whisky off the sideboard. He pours two generous measures and hands one of the glasses to me.

JS: Cheers.
B: Aye, Slainte Mhath!

Bearach takes a hearty gulp to my one, tentative sip.

JS: Where would you like to begin?
B: Let me see... Aye, let's start with a tale of two Super-S pals, both native Scots, eager to do right by their homeland, both working together for the benefit of the people.

JS: That's a good place to start as any.
B: Aye, but these lads are more than just team mates. One is learning from the other. They are mentor and student – Nay, more than that, they're like father and son, ye getting me? They were *that* close. That is, until one, fateful day when everything changed for the worse.

JS: The much-publicised death of The Flying Scotsman?
B: Aye, Stuart Mackintosh. The Flying Scotsman. The one-and-only. God rest his soul.

Bearach raises his glass and downs the remains, then proceeds to refill it again.

15th January 1997. Ah remember as if it were yesterday. It was bitterly cold. Most of Scotland was under three-feet of snow. We were independently working the M8, helping stricken drivers trapped in their cars, when we met somewhere around Junction 6. He proposed, taking into account the circumstances, that two Super-S working together would be better than one. Now, you see, here was the chance to collaborate with Scotland's finest – The Flying Scotsman. How could ah refuse? So we spend the next three hours rescuing the drivers and clearing snow drifts. Once we'd finished, he turns 'round to me and asks if ah fancy teaming up.

Let me tell ye, it was like a dream come true! I'd been a Solo for just over a year. Small-time stuff; rescuing cats, house fires, stuff like that, and here was the famous Flying Scotsman offering to be ma stablemate! Greatest moment of ma life! The Flying Scotsman's sidekick? Get in there! See, Stuart was fifteen years older than me with far more hands-on experience, so ah absolutely jumped at the chance of working with him. From that point on ah watched, studied and learned as much as ah could; things were going absolutely grand. That is, until we came up against the Dunwood Invasion. Ye heard of it?

JS: Wasn't that when the billionaire Scottish entrepreneur, William Dunwood, sought to wrestle control from English Parliament with his Drone Army?
B: Aye, ye've done ye homework. That bampot, Dunwood, dispatched a legion of Drones over London. It was going to be a bloody massacre; thousands of peoples' lives at threat. Stuart and meself decided to head South, for a barnie with the Drones. When we arrived, it took twenty minutes for us to neutralise the entire assault. But something just was'nae right. It was almost too easy, ye know what I'm saying?

JS: It was a decoy?
B: Too right. It was a plan Dunwood never meant to succeed. We were being drawn away from the real objective.

JS: The Strathclyde nuclear explosion?
B: We only discovered his real agenda after Stuart hacked intae one of the disabled Drones and deciphered Dunwood's core directive; a nuclear reactor meltdown at Strathclyde. We had to get back to Scotland as fast as we could; we were on the cusp of the worst nuclear atrocity since Chernobyl. Hundreds of thousands of people's lives were at risk, never mind the possible radiation fall-out for years afterwards. Problem was, we did'nae have the time to apprehend Dunwood and prevent the reactor from exploding.

JS: What did you do?

Bearach finishes his drink and pours another.

B: We came to a decision. Ah say we – Stuart did. He told me ah should go after Dunwood, while he would head to Strathclyde to try and stop the meltdown. Ah disagreed. Ah thought we should both try for the power plant, then we might have a better chance of stopping it. We could deal with the search for Dunwood once we knew the public were safe.

JS: There was a lot of publicity following Stuart's death. You came in for a lot of criticism.

I can see the sorrow in his eyes. Tears roll down Bearach's face.

B: Bloody fool! Ah bloody told him that, if we worked together, we could stop it in time. Ah knew we could. He would'nae have it. Told me to remember that day and if things didnae work out right, to tell his wife, Megan, that he loved her and to give his children a kiss from him. Bloody fool!

JS: Did you try to stop him?
B: Ah tried to stop him from going alone. We fought, briefly. He screamed at me to let him go and threw me to the ground. He was way too strong that lad; ah could'nae stop him. Ah watched as he disappeared towards the horizon.

Bearach looks at the claymore.

Ye know how it ends. Ah never saw him again. Ah like to think he did'nae suffer, but he was a tough one. Ah blame meself. Maybe if ah had'nae tried to stop him, he might have made it in time.

JS: What did you do whilst he tried to tackle the blast?
B: Ahh did what ah was supposed to do.

JS: You went to his family?
B: Nah, laddie. Unfinished business with William Dunwood.

JS: Did you find him?
B: By the time I'd infiltrated his fortified estate he'd vanished, never to be heard from again. Ah spent years after Stuart's death hunting that bastard down, but every lead turned cold. The Flying Scotsman was dead because of me and ah had failed the one task that he had entrusted to me. Eventually, ah discarded ma persona and swore never again to take to the skies.

JS: Did you ever visit his wife and children?
B: How could ah face that wonderful man's family knowing that I'd failed to avenge his death? The guilt was just too much to bear. I'd lost a friend, a teacher; ah loved that man like a father! And that bastard, Dunwood, is still out there, somewhere, probably laughing his bloody socks off. Not a day goes by that ah don't sit here, playing those events back in ma head, replaying that fateful moment he and ah fought, over and over again. Megan... the kids... they never knew what really happened. Just that, one day, their daddy did'nae come home. If only we had'nae fought. If only I'd taken his place... Can ye turn off the recorder, please? I'm so sorry, Stuart... so very sorry...

Artwork: Simon Coleby / Colours: Alex Owens - Bearach

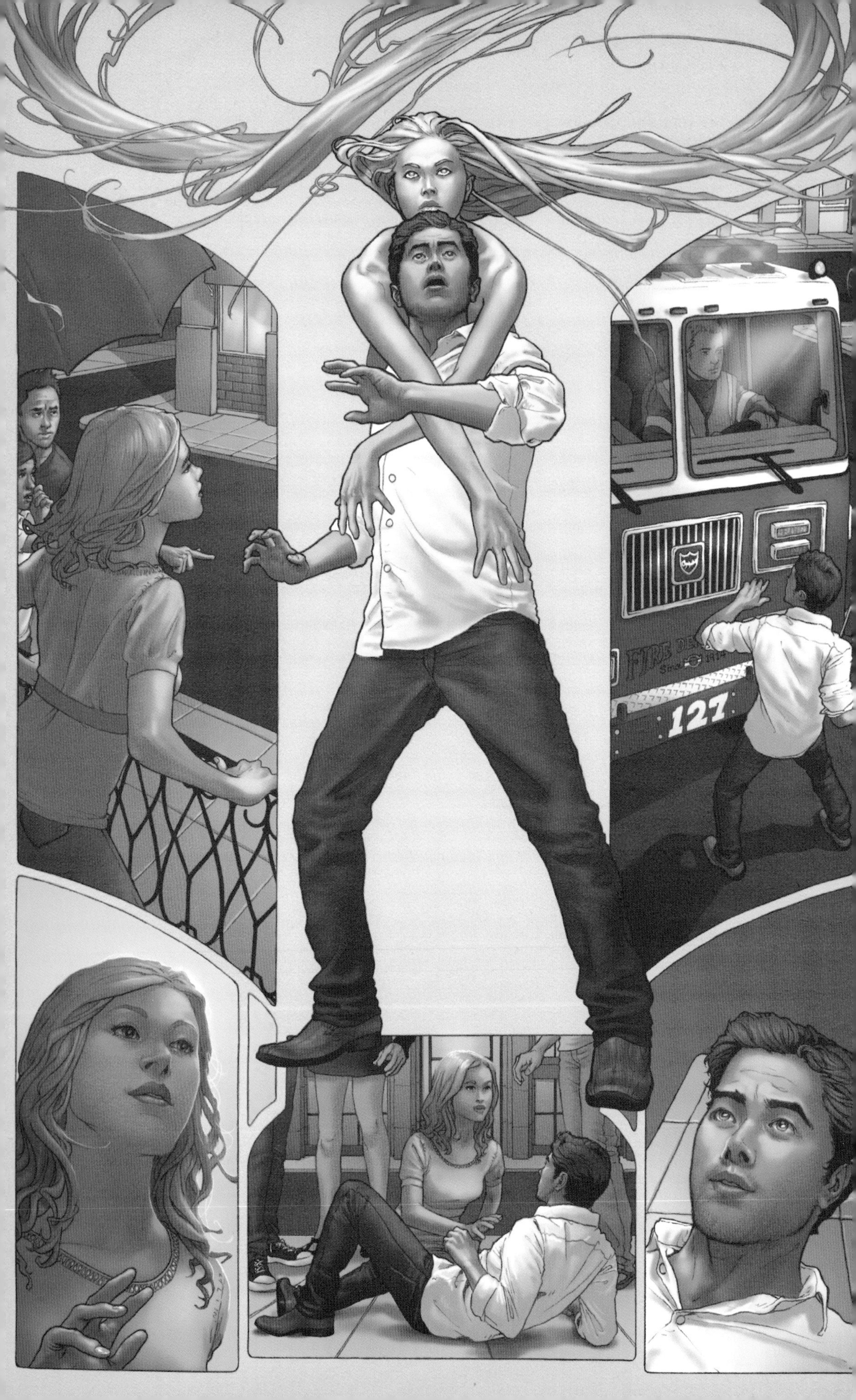
127

Elaine Howard* is forty years-old today. She's preparing for her milestone birthday party. She's known to the world as Residence and lives in West Portal, San Francisco with her husband, Kane.

I'm watching Elaine apply her make-up. With her curler-filled hair and towling dressing gown, she could easily pass as a regular, Norman wife.

JS: Congratulations on reaching the big 'four-o'.
R: Thank you. It seems like only yesterday I was single and in my twenties. I certainly never saw myself as the marrying-type, let alone married to a Norman and turning forty!

JS: How do you feel?
R: Mixed emotions, really. But I'm happy my relationship has made it this far. It's not easy being involved in an Inter-Meta relationship. Even though I'm a Super-S, that doesn't necessarily make me immortal; I still have to consider the likelihood that I could die at any given moment whenever I'm in a dangerous situation. I have to be constantly aware that I have a personal life and a partner to take into consideration. You'll have to excuse me. I can be a little morbid at times.

JS: I imagine that risking your life must be quite a burden for you and your husband to share.
R: Kane is a wonderful man. I don't think I could have made it this far without his support. It must be unbearable for him sometimes, not knowing if I'll walk through the door at the end of the day.

JS: How did you meet?
R: I saved his life.

JS: That's pretty amazing. I only met my wife at work.
R: Well, if you think about it, so did I.

JS: So, what happened?
R: I saw this man crossing the street. Well, technically he was jaywalking, but it wasn't until later that I found out he'd just arrived here on a twelve-month business visa, from England, and wasn't familiar with the way things work here. I guess he miscalculated, stepped out at the wrong time and literally froze when he saw a firetruck speeding around a corner towards him.

I was having coffee in a café across the street, watching the whole thing like it was in slow motion. I knew he wasn't going to get out of the way in time; his mind had acknowledged what was about to happen but his body just wasn't responding. He was paralyzed to the spot. So, I took over.

JS: Took over?
R: Yes. My ability is body-jacking – I can phase into an individual and assume control of their actions – I can see what they see, feel what they feel. It's like being two people at once, but only one of them having control. Well, in an instant, I was inside Kane and I was able to respond; I made his body roll clear of the firetruck. Once I knew he was safe, I 'detached'.

JS: Did he know it was you that saved him?
R: No. When I'm in control of someone, it's a subconscious possession. They still believe they are in control, albeit their body is physically doing strange things that belie their thoughts and intentions, but in reality they are complicit passengers. It means I can pretty much slip in and out of people unnoticed.

Once I was back in my own body again, I ran from the café, to Kane's side. He seemed quite shaken by the incident, so we went back over to the café and sat together while he re-composed himself. Well, when he looked at me with those big blue eyes of his, I simply melted. What can I say? It was fate! We started talking and, before we realized it, we'd been there for two hours. I so wanted to see him again, but I wanted him to get to know me as Elaine, not Residence. He was very shy, so I made the first move and ask him out. He said "yes". And by that, I mean he said "yes" of his own free-will, there wasn't any manipulation on my part!

JS: And how did things progress between you?
R: We started dating. As he worked during the day, I could comfortably juggle my official 'work' with my alter-ego's persona; I just had to stop the evening patrols. We'd stay up all night talking about anything and everything. We began to fall for each other in a big way and I knew the day was coming when I would have to reveal my true identity to him. I needed to tell him the truth if the relationship were to survive. And I so wanted it to.

Eventually, I revealed Residence to him, abilities and all. He was hesitant at first; he sat there in silence for quite some time before asking if I had ever body-jacked him.

JS: What did you say?
R: I told him the truth. Just the once, when I saved his life.

JS: How did he react to that revelation?
R: He was shocked, but once he'd grasped the gravity of the situation he hugged me. He was so sweet. He said it was just one more reason why he was so grateful for having me in his life.

JS: You must have been relieved.
R: I was! It was the one obstacle that had stood between us and it had been removed. Now, everything was out in the open and Residence began to take a back seat in the relationship. Elaine became the dominant force. I know it sounds ironic but, whenever Residence was removed from the equation, it made me feel... complete. Like a whole person! It's hard to explain, but being a Super-S means you're a friend to everyone and no-one at the same time. It can be the loneliest job in the world. When Kane and I were out together and I was Elaine, I was treated as a member of the public, the same as everyone else. I fitted in.

Kane proposed to me six-months later. I hesitated at first. He was taking a huge risk on me with his future but I knew I had found someone that I wanted to spend the rest of my life with and who wouldn't judge me for who I was, whether it be Elaine or Residence. So I accepted.

Elaine applies some rouge lipstick.

JS: What are your plans, now that you've reached a landmark birthday?
R: Well, firstly I'm going to have one hell of a party and enjoy being with close friends and family. You're only forty once, so why not make the most of it?

JS: And what then for Mr and Mrs Howard?

Elaine looks flushed. She can barely contain her glee.

R: I'm pregnant! I just finished my first trimester! Kane doesn't know, I'm going to tell him and the rest of the family tonight. I can't wait. We've been trying for so long, I wondered if it would ever happen. You start to replay all those scenarios over in your mind like; should I have fought Krysis? *(Krysis; a Radioactive villain that clashed with Residence on numerous occasions).* Could he, inadvertently, have damaged me somehow? Stupid stuff like that. I guess I can put those fears to rest now.

JS: Congratulations! My wife is expecting our first, too. What does this mean for Residence?
R: I guess this means early retirement. I can't be thwarting the despots of evil looking like a beached whale now, can I? I have to put the baby and my family first. The world will survive without Residence. At least, for the foreseeable future.

JS: That could bring its own dangers. Might your enemies look to exploit that vulnerability?
R: If they discovered my secret identity, of course they would, but if that happened I'd do whatever it takes to protect my family. WHATEVER. IT. TAKES. If the life of my child were endangered, I wouldn't hesitate in permanently erasing that threat.

Artwork: Rodin Esquejo - Residence

*Interviewee name has been changed

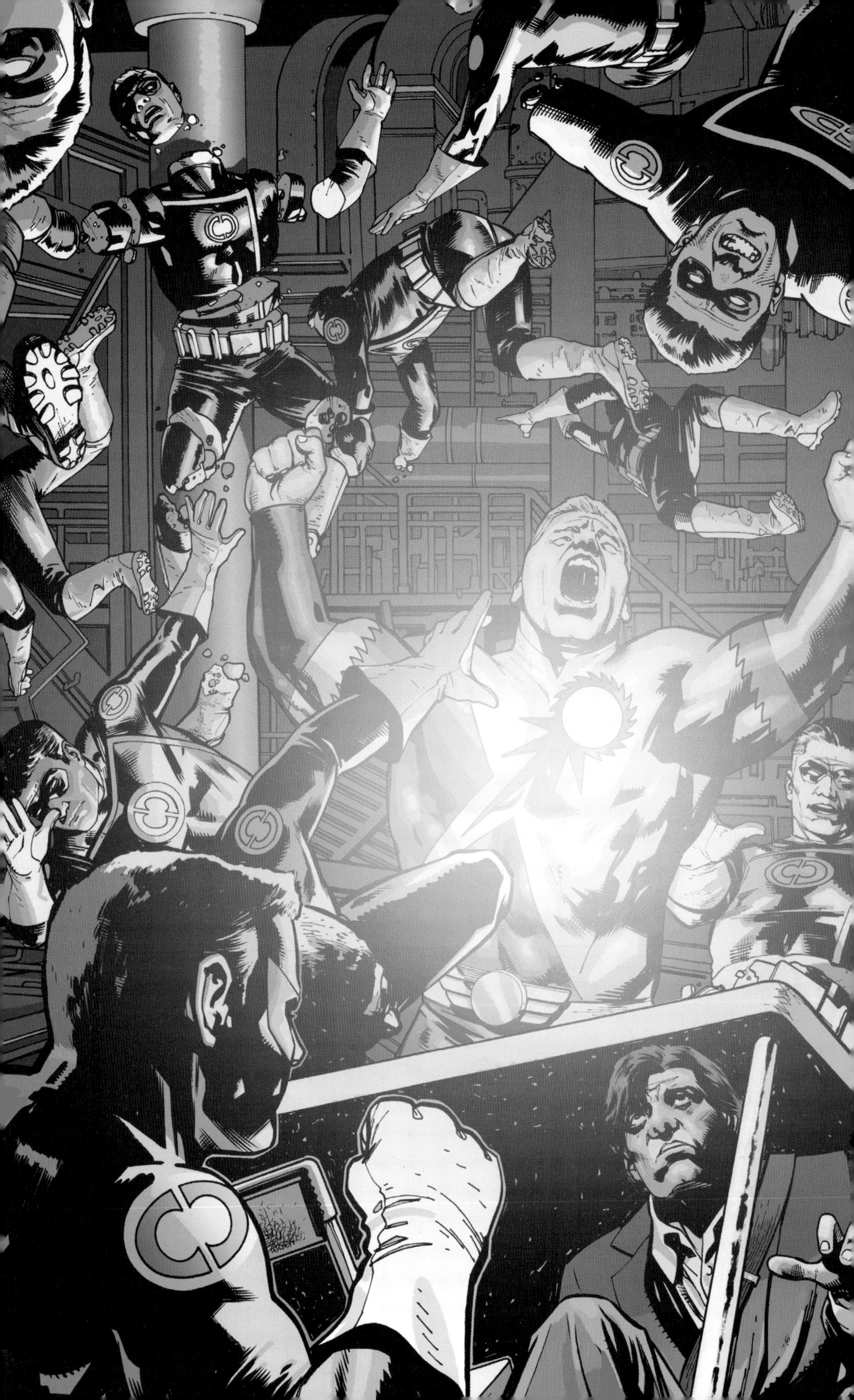

SolarFlare (41) and his crime-fighting sidekick CarbonCopy (24) have been working the city of Miami, Florida, together for just under two years. Having faced a number of supervillains in quick succession, they have suddenly found themselves in the glare of the media spotlight.

I'm in a secret base, deep in the heart of the Miami Metropolitan Area. SolarFlare sits opposite me; he's a foreboding figure dressed neck-to-toe in a golden suit – I can see why he's recently been voted Miami's #1 Super-S. CarbonCopy sits to my left.

JS: SolarFlare, let me start by congratulating you; Miami's #1 Super-S? That's an impressive accolade. The press have been very complimentary.
SF: I'm honored the people of Miami chose me as their favorite hero. To be given this award by such an auspicious city is one of the highlights of my career.

CC: Though, when they voted for SolarFlare they were also voting for me, CarbonCopy. We're a team, a unit. Can't have one without the other.

SF: Yes, CarbonCopy's correct... up to a point. I know he came in fourth, but really, it's a first place I willingly share with him.

CC: Right on.

JS: CarbonCopy, can I ask; what's it like working with SolarFlare? You must have learnt a lot from him.
CC: Yeah, you could say I've learned from his successes, but I've also learnt from his mistakes, too. I am just as good as SolarFlare; just because I don't harness the sun's power doesn't mean I lack the necessary chutzpah to make a valued contribution-

SF: -what I think you're trying to ask if I'm correct, Mr. Stanley, is if CarbonCopy minds being perceived as my sidekick by the media?

CC: I'm not *your* sidekick-

SF: -please, let me finish. Yes, you're seen as my sidekick but of course, you're much more than that. And you do enjoy learning from me.

CC: If I can ever get a word in edgeways.

JS: SolarFlare, you're a Super-S and CarbonCopy is a 2nd Degree. Does that affect the partnership in any way?
SF: It's not CarbonCopy's fault he's a 2nd Degree. He was an accident. Despite that, he's still a good Super-S.

CC: Not my fault? Accident? Still a good Super-S? What the f-

SF: -hey, mind your language, buddy. Remember, our fans will be reading this. They will be reading this, won't they? Can I post it on my... sorry... our blog when it's finished? We have quite a following.

JS: So, do you feel partnerships are harder than being Solo?
SF: Oh, they're perfectly fine. Nothing a vigorous workout won't solve if things get heated, eh?

CC: You're the one that needs the extra exercise – after all, you're carrying the extra weight of your Super-Ego!

SF: Look, I've had enough of this-

CC: -so the fuck have I! For two years I've had to eat your bullsh-

SF: -I don't think that's-

CC: -I've had enough of standing in the wings, listening to you go on about how great you are, how you're the voice of experience that speaks for the both of us. Man, you talk to me like you're my mother. "Do this, do that, don't do this, don't do that, I'd do it like this, if I were you..." Well, I've had enough of it! It's about time I stepped into the limelight. You know, it wouldn't take much for you to talk about me for a change, rather than massage your own fucking dick and balls!

SF: Listen to yourself. Perfect example; if you act like a petulant kid all the time, then you deserve to be treated like one! So you can create copies of yourself, all made from Carbon Graphite? Woohoo! Big deal! Let's compare that to, say, the power of the sun. How's it stack up? Ooo, not good! Did I gripe like a sissy when I was a sidekick? No, I didn't. I kept my mouth shut and listened. I expect the same respect from you. If you hate working with me that much, why not leave the real work to me and go make pencils or something. Or maybe you just haven't got the wood?

I become nervous as the two team mates size each other up.

CC: Why, you...! Well, I've got news for you, old chum. I'm moving on. Onwards and upwards.

SF: What are you talking about?

JS: Erm, are you planning on going Solo, CarbonCopy?
CC: No. Something much cooler than that. I've been approached by XoDOS.

SF: Give me strength! Haven't you listened to a single word I've told you about them?

CC: Clearly not. And lucky for me, because it appears that you were talking out of your ass anyway. I saw their facilities for myself. Very impressive.

SF: You really are a gullible fool.

CC: You're the fool. You know, they told me you'd react like this, once you found out. I didn't want to believe them, but they were right, you're nothing but a control freak. SolarFlare? You're *SoloFlare* now. Time I stepped out of that huge shadow of an ego you have and do my own thing.

SF: What lies did they spin? What promises did they seduce you with? Cash? Pensions? Medical cover?

CC: All that, and then some. They're going to let me lead my own Super-S team. The Lotus said-

SF: -that bitch! Fuck, you really are as stupid as you look.

JS: Gentleman, this is obviously an awkward time. I'm happy to return at a later date and interview you separately.
SF: No, you stay right where you are. I'm not letting some snot-nosed punk with delusions of grandeur ruin this interview. Carry on, Mr. Stanley. Please.

CC: I didn't want it to come to this but XoDOS said there'd be no other way...

CarbonCopy shimmers, as hardened, grey duplicates of himself separate from his body, rushing towards SolarFlare, smashing him to the ground. Blow upon blow rains down upon him.

CC: It's time I eclipsed you, SolarFlare!

A searing heat fills through the room, shattering the duplicates of CarbonCopy. Undeterred, he generates more. SolarFlare's eyes glow an intense yellow. He fires a concentrated beam of light from them, which decapitates the new batch of copies. I dive for cover under the table. This isn't where I need to be right now.

SF: Okay, kiddo. Let's dance!

The room becomes a battleground as 'Copy duplicates himself a small army and 'Flare recharges. Whilst they are both occupied mid-fight, I take the opportunity to grab my bag and recorder and run for the door.

Artwork: Stephen Thompson – SolarFlare & CarbonCopy

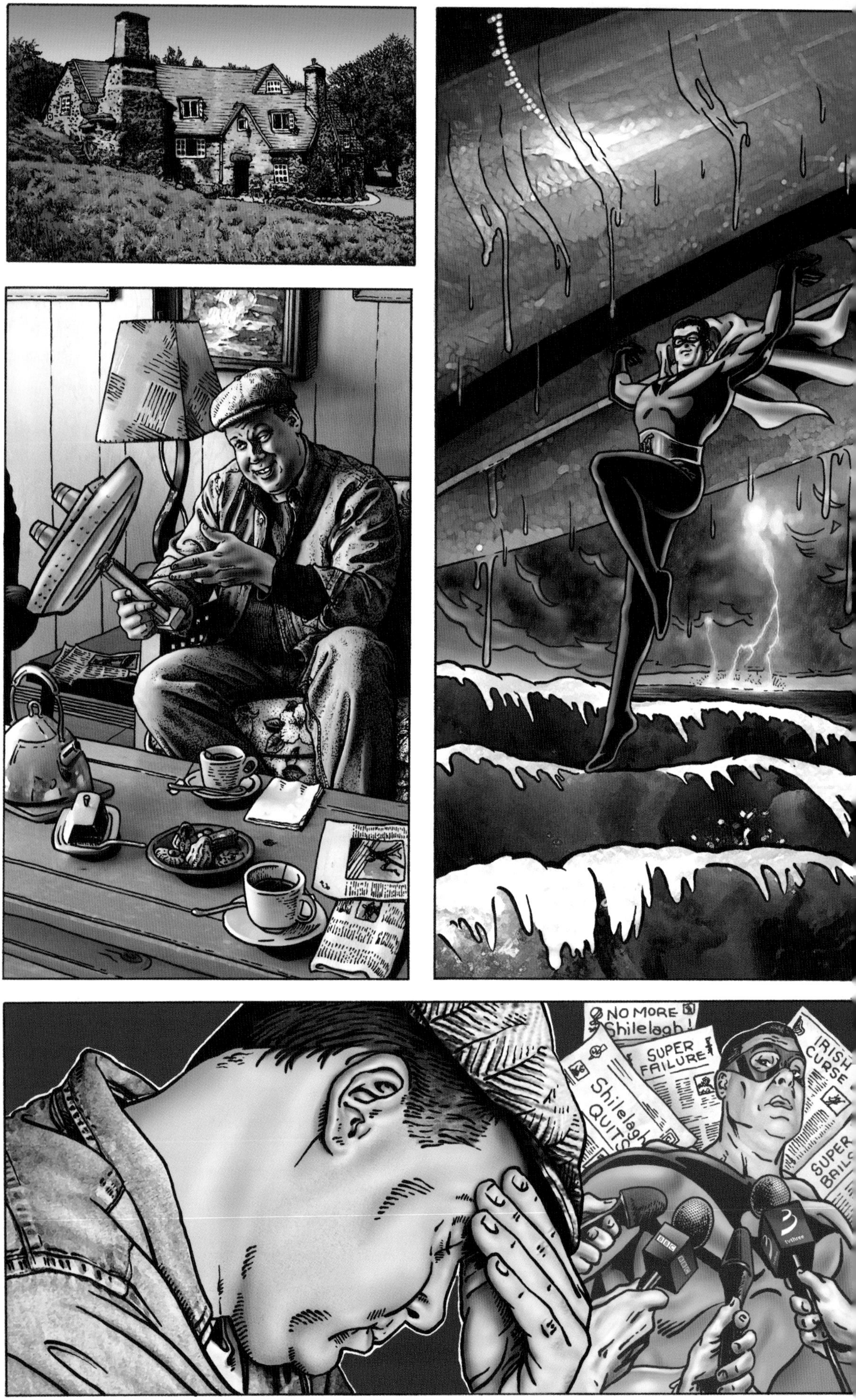
NO MORE
Shilelagh!
SUPER
FAILURE
IRISH
CURSE
Shilelagh
BBC

Dermot O'Donnell* is Ireland's best-known Super-S, The Shilelagh. He is forty-two years-old and has been protecting the 'Emerald Isle' for just over twenty years.

Dermot greets me at the front door to his country cottage. He is a well-defined man. We shake hands and he motions for me to go into the living room. The walls are adorned with news-clippings, trophies and various other memorabilia.

JS: Wonderful collection you have here. It's great to see so many of your achievements on display.
DO: Thank you! I've been collecting these snippets ever since I took to the skies. It's a job-and-a-half trying to keep up with every event I've been involved in. In the end, I gave up trying to collect them all – it was becoming impossible!

JS: What's your favourite piece?
DO: Ooh, that's a tough one. If I had to choose, it probably would be that one over there.

Dermot points to a framed clipping behind me. The headline "FREESPIRIT RESCUE!" is splashed across the front page of the Irish Times. Below the headline is a picture of The Shilelagh, in full Super-S guise, hovering alongside the docked cruise-liner in question.

I was a bit slimmer back then! That was my first official interview – saved over six-hundred lives that day, after the FreeSpirit encountered problems on her maiden voyage, three miles from Rosslare Harbour in the Irish sea. They gave me an award for that.

Dermot picks an impressive golden replica of the ship off a cabinet shelf and hands it to me. It's incredibly heavy.

Sorry, I forget it's solid gold! You wouldn't believe the problems I have sometimes; pulling doors off cupboards, crushing crockery whilst washing up. I've had to reinforce all the hinges on the doors in the house and I've lost count of the times I've called a plumber out because I've twisted the taps off the bath! I'm becoming more clumsy, the older I get. I had a lot more control back in those days!

Dermot pauses, smiling. He seems lost in thought.

JS: You were big news back then. I remember covering your exploits when I was working for one of the nationals in England.
DO: The newspapers were filled with stories and rumours about me; where had I come from? What were my abilities? My political views? What religion did I follow? Was I married? Heterosexual? Where did I live? Was I going to be Ireland's next entry in the Eurovision song contest? The next Prime Minister? The gossip just wouldn't stop!

JS: I can understand the pressure the media exposure must put on someone when they're so prominent in the public eye.
DO: You don't know the half of it. It was making me physically sick. Me, a 140Kg, flying power-house, throwing my guts up from the sheer pressure of wondering what tomorrow's headline would bring! That was when I decided that I had to go on record to clarify the facts, to help quell the media frenzy whipping up around me. So that's why I did the interview. It was the first time I officially went on record about myself; I thought I wouldn't care what they wrote about me after that – I'd said my piece and made my peace. I was wrong. Turns out, it would be my last.

JS: Did you feel that excommunicating yourself from the media after that first interview was a mistake? There were still a lot of unanswered questions.
DO: Ironic, eh? A Super-S, with a secret identity, and he's expected to answer all the questions the hacks throw at him – you'd think my previous candor would be enough for most, but you journalists just wouldn't let it lie, it was an obsession with you.

JS: Could you blame them? You'd just conducted the most candid interview a Super-S had ever partaken in and moments later, you were turning your back on them.
DO: That's true, but I just wished they'd respected my decision and honoured my request for anonymity.

JS: That's the media for you; they answer to their superiors and are driven by the public's desire to know more.
DO: That's what I realised. I misjudged them. Their desire to satiate the public's thirst for gossip, for glorification. They're not content with you simply saving lives and protecting them from the bad guys. No – they treat you like a nasty scab; rather than leaving it alone to do its healing, they pick at it, digging deeper, making it worse, just because it's unusual and it's there. So they keep on picking and picking away, until it bleeds. And you know what happens after that? It leaves a scar. A permanent one.

JS: So the media had that much of a negative effect on you?
DO: Little by little, month by month, I noticed how their perception of me altered. They became overly analytical and critical of my actions. It was shocking; from being Ireland's green-eyed super-saviour, I was suddenly a target for abuse, a failure if people succumbed on my watch, under my protection. What were they thinking? I didn't have super-speed! I couldn't save everybody! Impossible! A trawler capsizes off the west coast, there's a fire in a school in Galloway, a building collapses in Dublin – who do you save first? That's when the animosity builds. When loved ones die, the first thing people do is point the finger at the person that couldn't save them, not at the cause of the death.

JS: Did the situation change your attitude towards the public and their perception of you as Ireland's "Great Green Hope"?
DO: Of course it did. I questioned my motives, my action, my words. Every single decision I made felt like it was the wrong one. It all became too much to bear and I began doubting myself. I even pinned up the negative press on my walls here.

JS: I can't see any bad press. There's nothing but praise and gratitude.
DO: Now there is, yes. But back then it wasn't my accolades that consumed me, it was my failures. The place was a patchwork quilt of blame and guilt, with the headlines of my accusers screaming down at me. I went into psychological meltdown.

JS: Did you seek help?
DO: Who was going to listen to me without contemplating selling out to the media for a fast buck?

The Shilelagh takes off his cap and massages his head.

There was no-one else to turn to, I had to get through it on my own, and the only way I felt I could do that was to distance myself from The Shilelagh. I worked on the house, tried to live a Norman life. It was incredibly dull. It was perfect.

JS: Was it hard letting go?
DO: I had to discipline myself, shut myself off. I ignored the television, the radio, newspapers, anything that would potentially wind me up. Anything that would highlight the fact that, despite the selfishness and antagonism towards me, I was still needed. I took things slowly; I rebuilt this house, I built a shed. It was all about rebuilding. Internally and externally. And those clippings on the walls? The bad press? Gradually, they all came down, one article at a time. Took just over a year before my guilt was wiped clean – and it took another year to restore all the good stuff to its rightful place. Including my passion for doing what's right; saving lives.

JS: Were two years away from the public eye long enough to recover from your experience? When you returned as The Shilelagh the media didn't exactly welcome you back with open arms. How did you feel about that?
DO: I made the choice to return and when to return, to make a difference once again. It wasn't for them and their column inches; it was for the good of the people. I can't save everyone and I know now that I shouldn't carry the guilt for those that I fail, no matter what the papers print. Saving one life is better than saving none, even if that one person turns out to be yourself.

Artwork: Dave Ryan - The Shilelagh

*Interviewee name has been changed

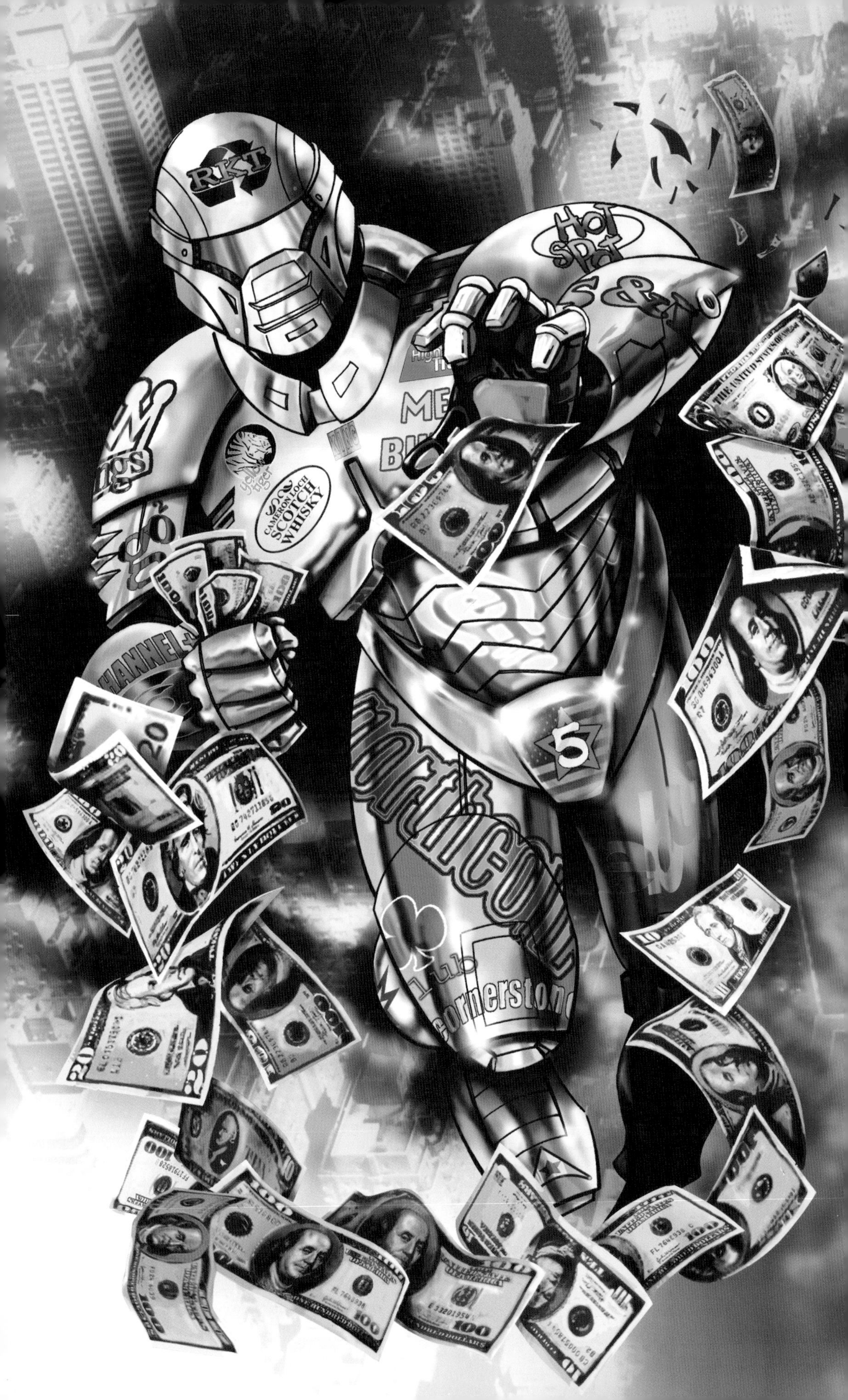
RKT
CAMERON LOCH
SCOTCH
WHISKY
5

Forty-three year-old RollCage is signing at a New York bookstore, just off Fifth Avenue. As an Exo-S, RollCage doesn't have natural or 2nd Degree abilities; instead, he wears a highly-advanced combat suit which his personal team of scientists are constantly updating.

It's raining – a typical October in the Big Apple. The weather does little to dampen the spirits of the screaming fans queuing outside, waiting for the entrance doors to open. RollCage sits in the store surrounded by his entourage of P.A.'s and other media types.

JS: Thank you for seeing me today.
RC: No problem. Saw your email a few weeks ago and told Agatha to contact you. So, you're writing an editorial on Super-S – I couldn't let that get published without one of the heavy-hitters gracing its pages, right? So how do you want to do this?

JS: How long do you have?
RC: Well, not long. Doors open at nine-thirty, then it's a total free-for-all. Not even I would be able to save you from "The Mob"!

He laughs. His entourage follows suit.

JS: Well, I'll try to be as brief as possible. You're an Exo-S – how do you feel you compare to say, a Super-S or a 2nd Degree?
RC: Well, I consider myself superior to a Super-S, simply because I have the option of choice. They, on the other hand, are the unfortunate participants in a genetic lottery, where they're born with restrictions and a social outcome that has been predetermined for them. They're either a winner or a loser and – trust me on this one, bud – most are losers. Me? I become the legendary RollCage out of choice, combined with a mean slice of cutting-edge engineering and science. When I hang up my costume at the end of the day, I'm a Norman, plain and simple; I'm not stuck with my powers while I'm out at a charity function or scrutinizing the housekeeper's diligence 'round the shower edges, you know what I'm saying? That's something a Super-S will never be able to experience. Takes a genius to create a god that you can switch on and switch off. I guess I'm that genius!

JS: And how do you feel about 2nd Degrees?
RC: Feel? To be honest, I don't feel anything. Poor things are 'super-wannabes' with the misguided aspiration of being something they never were and never can be. A hapless attempt to outshine Mother Nature, or an unfortunate victim of circumstance, willing to endure torture and experimentation in the hope it will offer them the semblance of a better life? Sorry, that doesn't sound like a person who's mentally stable enough to cope with the pressures of being a Super-S, if you ask me.

His entourage nod in agreement.

You need more than a quirky name, trendy costume and a fancy power to last in this business. And believe me when I say – it *is* a business. It's bottled and sold to those that want and need it. So why not be the one supplying the resources for the demand? I have bills to pay, mouths to feed, like any other decent, hard-working American. Do these lovely people here work for free? No, they do not. I am responsible for these people, for making sure they put food on their families tables.

JS: Some say you can be a little mercenary in your approach to your profession.
RC: Well, you can't have it both ways. You can't be one of the most prolific heroes of the 21st century *and* operate on the bread line. The two simply don't mix. I need funding if I'm going to protect the people; I have upgrades of weapons and technology to take into consideration, new alloy enhancements to make the suit more durable. For example, have you seen the advances the Japanese are making in lightweight amalgams? You can pretty much fold the stuff without the aid of hinges! That's what I'm talking about – staying ahead of the competition. The public aren't fools, they realize that in the end, everyone pays one way or another. This way, everyone stays happy. The kids outside get to wear the T-shirts, buy the toys or watch the TV series and that, in turn, enables me to protect them in the style they've become accustomed to.

JS: I recently heard that you've been approached by several companies to advertise their products. Can you expand on that?
RC: Sure, there are a few deals that are being punted around. Let's just say a well-known cigarette company has offered a substantial financial return for my involvement in promoting their product. I can't say more than that; contracts still haven't been signed.

JS: Promotion?
RC: On the Exo-suit. It could open doors to a lot more sponsorship and advertising opportunities and really change the way Super-S are portrayed publicly. Just imagine; Captain Mountain Dew, or Finger-Lickin' Good Girl – now that's one lady I could really get my teeth into! The marketing potential is endless. I'll go down in history as the man who gave Super-S real value. They'll be making movies about me next!

JS: Don't you think you're giving out the wrong message to your fans? What about the saying, "*Virtue is its own reward*"?
RC: Of course not! Where was virtue when those bastards ridiculed my Grandfather's blueprints for his first Exo-Suit? Where was virtue when he died in poverty during the depression? The legacy of his work lives on through my actions and mine alone. I've always said; I'm someone that gets the job done and is rewarded for putting life and limb on the line. That isn't some misguided ethos I'm inflicting on the masses – unlike some I could mention – no, my fans are shrewd enough to understand what I stand for.

JS: Don't you think that's a touch mercenary?
RC: I'm just an ordinary guy who's looking to earn a crust, like my poor Grandfather all those years ago. You don't see me pushing governments around or aspiring to change the world; I just want to do my job, get paid and go home.

JS: Don't you think children need more noble role models? Someone who teaches them moral values?
RC: Firstly, I'm not a teacher. Secondly, are they my kids? Preaching right and wrong isn't my responsibility. It's the parents. Think about it, would you want a Super-S telling YOU how to bring up your kid?

JS: Won't that attitude alienate a lot of the older people, especially if they see the younger generation influenced by your money-driven ethic? Won't that put them off?
RC: It doesn't really affect me. My team have done their market research; there's not much mileage in the 'gray' dollar anymore, they're way too practical. We're in the middle of a global recession and they're simply not spending the way they used to, unless where their precious little kids are concerned. So, we've developed a new strategy to build upon my current success.

JS: The children?
RC: You got it! The kids hold the purse strings! And they, in turn, will be the hard-working and well-paid adults of tomorrow. Never ignore your future market. Look out that window, what do you see?

JS: A queue of RollCage fans?
RC: Yeah, well most short-sighted people would. You know what I see? Dollar bills. Three thousand autographs at ten dollars apiece. That's thirty-thousand, right there. And that's before they've bought the toy, read the comic, listened to the music compilation or signed up to the fanclub. Can you imagine the possibilities in the next ten years? Who needs a Super-S when you have a world-class marketing team like mine? Which reminds me, Agatha did negotiate my fee for this meeting, didn't she? Four-thousand, plus residuals on the book sales?

JS: Well, I spoke to Agatha and explained this interview was research for my book. She said it would be okay to talk to you for free. She even gave me a copy of your book.
RC: She said WHAT?! Gave you WHAT? Gratis, my ass. Okay, interview stops right there. I don't care what Agatha said. Time is money, pal. AGATHA! WHERE ARE YOU?! Get your sorry, soon-to-be-fired ass over here, NOW!

Artwork: Jeff Anderson – RollCage

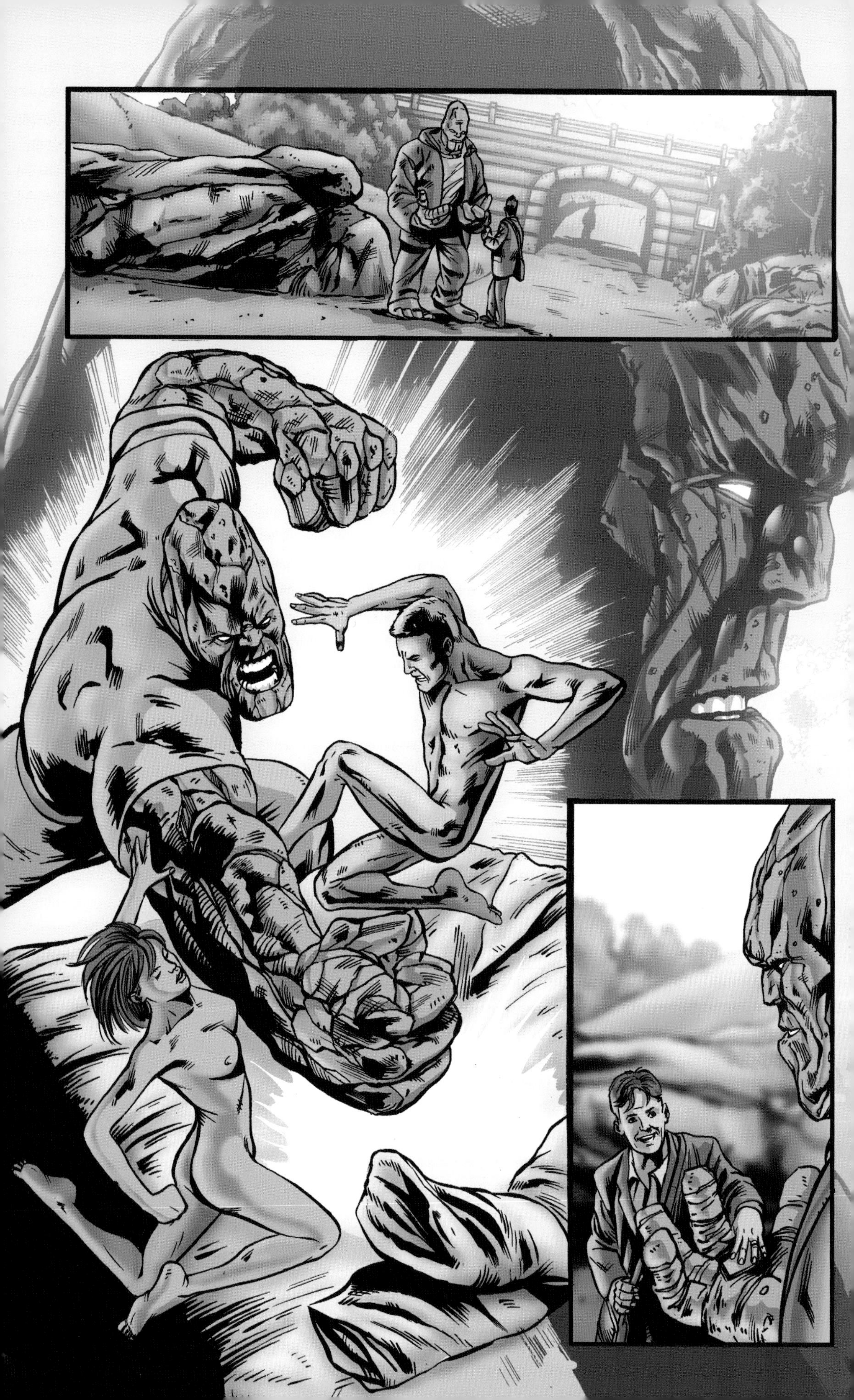

Forty-four year-old Stronghold is an extreme mutation of a Super-S, more commonly known as a "Super-M". In fact, he was one of the first cases of a Super-S 'morphing' beyond normal development parameters in the recorded history of Super-S evolution. He acquired the name Stronghold because of his granite-like skin condition.

I am on a park bench in Central Park. Stronghold sits beside me, dressed in worn-out, casual clothes. I look closely at his skin; despite living out his days deep in the park, along with the other tramps and vagabonds, he appears to be in excellent physical condition. He's something of a celebrity in the belly of the forgotten: a superhero for society's fallen.

JS: Can I ask why you choose to hide yourself away, here in Central Park, along with the homeless?
SH: I guess you could say I feel comfortable around them. All my life I've been looked upon as some kind of freak. These guys are just like me; scorned, rejected, running from a fight they don't have the stomach for anymore.

JS: Do you have any family or friends?
SH: My parents gave me away when I was born. The moment they were told what I had wasn't curable, they passed on me. I grew up not knowing what a real family upbringing was like. I was in and out of care up until the age of sixteen. In some ways, I guess I'm thankful; had to grow up quickly and it taught me a heavy lesson in survival. I'd had enough by the time I turned seventeen. I reasoned that, if no one else was bothering to look out for me, then I had to look out for myself.

JS: Did you ever imagine you'd be using your abilities to survive living rough on the streets?
SH: No. When I was growing up, I always thought my destiny was to be a Super-S – sorry – Super-M. Never got used to using that label for my condition. How was I to know that one of the very people I rescued would end up destroying my life? I thought my powers would be used for saving others, not trying to save myself. Ironically, even though my heart and emotions are vulnerable to pain, my rock hide's impervious to extreme cold and heat; perfect for a reject's life on the streets of NYC, don't ya think?

JS: But you were the one who turned your back on being a Super-S. Why did you choose to do that?
SH: Didn't start out that way. At first, I was filled with good intentions. It was an ambition of mine to be a superhero. At the height of my fame I was a regular feature, springing into action at a moment's notice. Folks appreciated me back when I was helping the people of the City. Those were good days, albeit short lived.

JS: What happened?
SH: What usually happens to naive, young heroes that succumb to the fame? I fell in love with someone I rescued. A rookie error of judgement. It was a whirlwind romance, we married soon after. Even at the time I knew it was a mistake. But that's the thing about love, you ignore the warning signs and happily stumble into it. We tried to work it out but to no avail; it all ended in a messy divorce.

JS: What caused the marriage to break down?
SH: Sex. Or the lack of it. I mean, look at me, it's impossible to have a physical relationship when you look like this. Impossible. She said it didn't matter but it didn't take long before it did. She became more and more bitter about it, and I became more and more frustrated. In the end, I spent all my spare time working late, looking for any excuse not to go home. Eventually, it happened; I came home one day and found them together, in our bed. I snapped. I still remember her screams as I rained blow upon blow down on him. Turns out, he was also a Super-S, otherwise I would have killed him with my first few punches. I guess he could offer her the one thing I couldn't.

JS: Did you know this Super-S?
SH: I knew *of* him. He tried to use his powers to stop me pummeling him but I guess he didn't take into consideration my immunity to mental attacks. If it wasn't for my ex, he wouldn't be here now; she threw herself over his bloodied body in order to protect him. She chose HIM over me! Lucky bastard barely escaped with his life.

JS: Who was it?
SH: His name's not worthy enough to pass my lips. You're a reporter, find the answer yourself.

JS: And your wife?
SH: The hatred and fear in her eyes that day told me all I needed to know. I was served divorce papers twenty-four hours after.

JS: How did you cope with the divorce proceedings?
SH: The relationship between us became a helluva lot nastier. I tell you, man, those lawyers are more evil than any Vader I've fought in the past! Those bastards made sure she was awarded the house, on account of her being a Norman, and they figured that, what with my powers, I'd be regularly employable, so I also got lumbered with maintenance payments. Lover-boy also sued for assault and she sold her story to the rag-mags. To rub further salt into the wounds, I found out that she'd trademarked my name without my knowledge and had licensed my image to a comic publisher for an on-going series! Where was I going to find the kind of bucks I needed to fight my case? Talk about hitting a man when he's down. I might have skin made of impervious rock but she managed to cut right through it – straight into my heart. I fell deeper into despair. Found I couldn't concentrate on doing what was right when everything in my personal life was going so wrong. What with all the negative press, people lost respect for me and would make comments, in the street, to my face! I mean right in my face, as if I was crap on their shoe. I couldn't take it, after all I'd done for them. I turned and never looked back.

JS: So Central Park is your home – how are you coping?
SH: I'm not proud of it, but no-one really bothers me anymore. I have genuine friends I hang out with and I'm not judged for what I am – we're all in the same boat; brothers brought together under similar, unfortunate circumstances, all here to forget – to blend into the background. There are other 'Supers' here, you know, I've seen them, living amongst the rest of the downtrodden. Where else can they go when it all goes wrong? Here, I'm still a legend, a hero; I look out for the guys and they, in turn, look after me. They're my boys; the family I never had.

Stronghold sighs.

JS: Have you had many run-ins that you've had to deal with?
SH: A few, but they don't last long, not when they realize who they're messing with. They steam in with their big egos and they leave without them, simple as that. And maybe a broken rib, or two. I always make sure they depart with a better appreciation for their fellow man. There's a lot of victimization of the down-and-outs by Normans. For some reason, they think we're an easy target. They don't understand that we have enough personal problems of our own to deal with; starvation, abuse, drug and alcohol addictions, not to mention the memories of what brought us here. They forget we used to be like them.

JS: You have an exceptional gift, yet you now choose to hide it from society. Doesn't the world need someone like you?
SH: The world doesn't even acknowledge I exist anymore. As far as I'm concerned, the milk of human kindness soured a long time ago. Beyond looking out for my brothers and sisters on the streets, all I care about these days is where the next meal is coming from and where I'm going to sleep. Simple. Uncomplicated. Speaking of which, if you'll excuse me, it's time I was going. Sister Petuna runs a volunteer soup kitchen on Thursdays and it tends to get mighty busy if you don't turn up early. Good luck with the rest of your research, I hope I've been of some help.

Stronghold heads towards his friends, who are congregating near the underpass.

JS: Hey! Hold on a second... It's not much but it's all I have on me...
SH: Hey... thanks. Appreciate it. I owe you, bud.

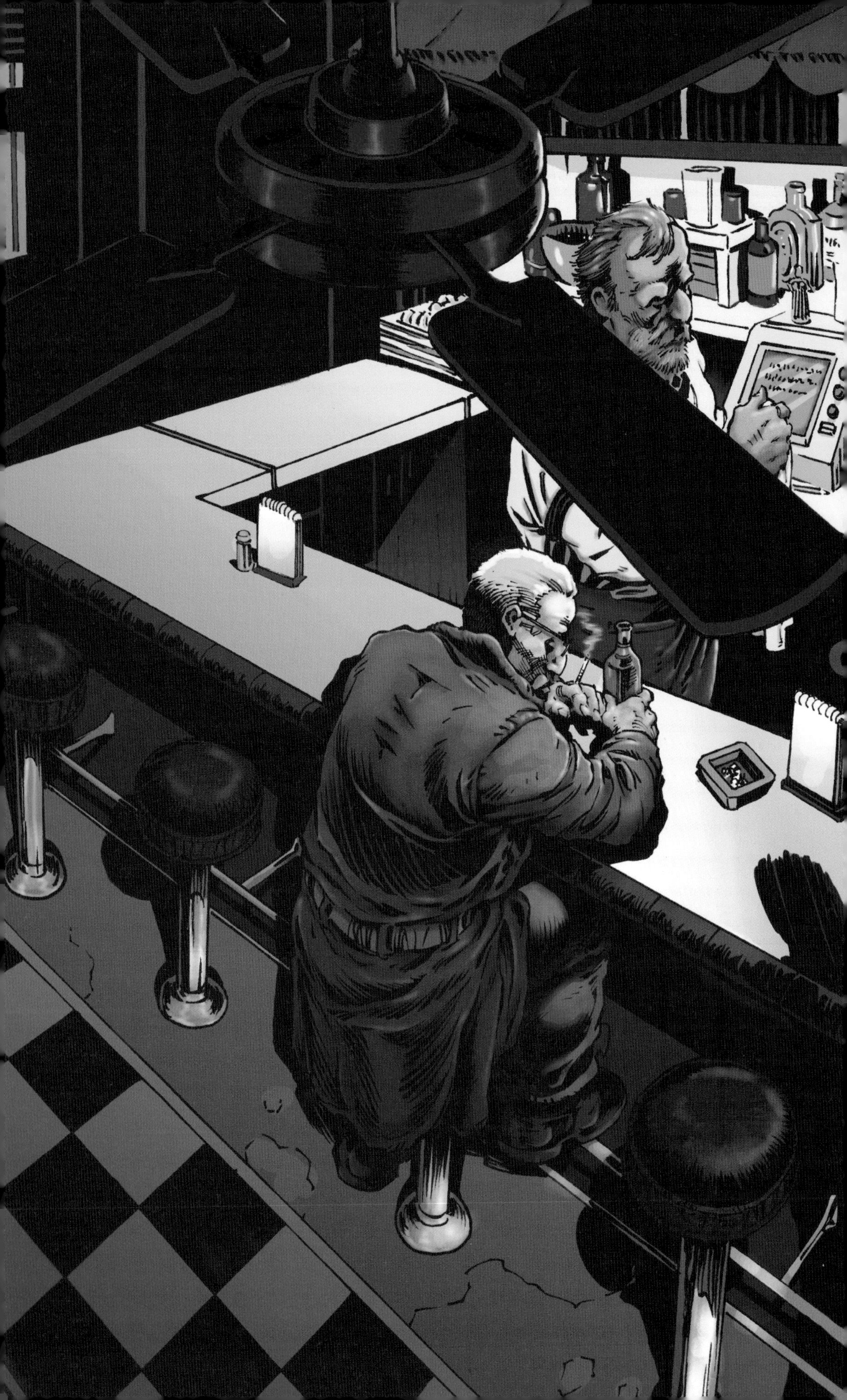

I'm sitting in a quiet bar in Atlanta, Georgia, next to forty-five year-old X, a former operative of XoDOS. X shocked the organisation by resigning unexpectedly after a failed mission. He has been in hiding ever since. I was unaware of him or his involvement in XoDOS prior to this meeting; he contacted me for an interview after he heard I was compiling this book.

A bartender places two Rolling Rocks on the bar in front of us. X waits for me to pay before taking a swig from his bottle.

X: First thing's first, I want to make it clear to you that I tell you what I want to tell you and nothing more. You do not push me for more information than I am prepared to divulge. And I will leave this interview when I choose to leave. Capiche?
JS: Yes, I understand.

X: Good. Let's get down to it then.

JS: How long did you work for XoDOS?
X: About thirty years, off and on. I was recruited through the usual channels. You've probably heard how they scout for potential candidates; through the orphanages, foster homes, private education facilities and the like. I was one of the "lucky" orphans assigned to their protection. It was a lot easier to get hold of kids back in those days – no red tape, no questions asked if the odd one was taken into special care.

JS: Didn't the orphanage question why an organisation such as XoDOS was interested in you?
X: You've got to get out of today's mind-set and go back to the Sixties way of dealing with issues; orphanages back then had no idea how to cope with those of us with abilities. No idea. They had no experience in caring for kids like me. And most foster parents were scared of anyone displaying abnormal skills. Kids were either dismissed entirely when it came to fostering or adoption, or they were returned real quick if they activated whilst in foster care. The orphanages were relieved if anyone showed the slightest interest in taking us off their hands. That's where people like XoDOS stepped in, with their financial and educational support. They were the perfect win-win solution; money changed hands, paperwork was lost in the system, and so were we.

JS: What happened when they took you away?
X: I was relocated to a nice family. I say family, what I really mean by that is two agents trained in the art of monitoring, tutoring and training Super-S kids. There was no parental bonding going on there. Kindness, but not a lot of love. Just endless drilling and preparation. I was schooled with other Super-S and 2nd Degree kids at big, private facilities. They did weird shit to us, lots of fucked-up-messing-with-your-head kind of stuff. They pumped us with experimental drugs to see how our bodies would cope or react – got no idea what kind of shit was going in. Every day, there seemed to be another needle. Some 2nd Degrees ended up with serious addiction problems as a consequence.

JS: Just the 2nd Degrees? Not the Super-S?
X: Yeah, spooky, huh? Something to do with genetic make-up. Take a Super-S, born and bred with raw, natural power. In normal circumstances, the body would naturally develop to accommodate its owner's ability, even during its gestation period in the womb. Those type of kids could adapt quickly to the drugs, absorb and process the foreign toxins in the body, like you would alcohol. 2nd Degrees, on the other hand, reacted exactly the opposite. Their bodies couldn't cope. You introduce a foreign substance into a 2nd Degree and you've got some seriously deadly side-effects; paranoia, delusion, aggression, schizophrenia.

And then, they went and put these guys into active duty alongside the rest of us. I've been involved in some fucked-up operations; I've seen 2nd Degrees go postal on their own team, go Vader right in the middle of a mission. Not a pretty sight. One group lost three Super-S to a 2nd – a supposed team-mate. I ended up mopping up what was left of them and retiring the son-of-a-bitch. I begrudged taking on missions with them after that.

JS: Have you retired many people?
X: Too many to mention, yeah. Retired, killed, eliminated, whatever we want to call it. For the so-called "Cause" that I'd been educated into believing in. We were taught never to question the organization's practises or why a specific individual was brought under their scrutiny, just that we should do our job and do it to the best of our ability. The only lines you crossed were the ones XoDOS drew up themselves.

JS: Can you enlighten me further on who those individuals were?

X looks around before speaking.

X: Diplomats. Political enemies. Businessmen, with dubious links to foreign nationals. Terrorists. High ranking government officials. Generals. Renegades. A few Vaders, of course. Not all were retirement jobs; I've been involved in several AFVs.

JS: AFVs?
X: Bungles. Botches. Super-S that XoDOS feel need to be rescued when they're in awkward predicaments. Basically, those that have fucked up. Mostly, they were third-world country ops but we covered North Korea, Russia, Japan, even Somalia. Not all AFVs were abroad. Had to deal with a few back home, too.

JS: But, interfering in the international arena is a policy that XoDOS vehemently denies, isn't it?
X: Oh yeah, that's right, what the hell was I thinking? Guess I must have just made that shit up.

X grins, sarcastically.

JS: What is your ability?
X: I'm a Phaser. I can travel through objects; concrete, steel, you name it. Nothing can hold me when I'm transient. In. Job done. Out. I'm fast too, three times faster than a Norman. That means I'm on my target before he/she knows I'm there. If I'm in a particularly nasty mood, I'll pull my target into the wall with me and phase him back out. But only halfway. Very messy. So what do you know about XoDOS?

JS: Not much. I've heard good and bad things about them. Some people look forward to working with them, some are glad to have left their employ. They're funded by the U.S. government, aren't they?
X: Oh, they're legit, alright. Totally legit. No flies on them! Do you know the poem 'Antigonish' by William Hughes Mearns?

JS: Very well. I studied it on my English literature course. "As I was going up the stair. I saw a man who wasn't there. He wasn't there again today. I wish, I wish, he'd stay away... "
X: Yeah, well, XoDOS is that man on the stair. A word of advice. Tread carefully. You've gotten to know a lot more than is good for you, James Stanley. If I wasn't an ex-employee, you'd be the kind of guy they'd have me retiring right now. In fact, I wouldn't be surprised if *she* isn't on your trail already, keeping tabs on your movements.

JS: Who's that?
X: The Lotus.

JS: Who's The Lotus?
X: XoDOS's most experienced and persuasive agent. She's almost caught up with me several times this year already. She put paid to Redden, saw to it that he wouldn't be a nuisance anymore, and she's done it to plenty since. That's the thing about XoDOS; once you're a team player, they don't like you changing sides. Are you a team player, James? An asset or a threat to their cause? I'm not here to help you understand what it's like to exist as a Super-S, I'm here to make sure you understand, period. Watch your back, Mr Stanley, because you can't just disappear if things get too hot for you to handle. Or at least, not of your own choosing...

X appears to drop through his seat, into the floor, and vanishes.

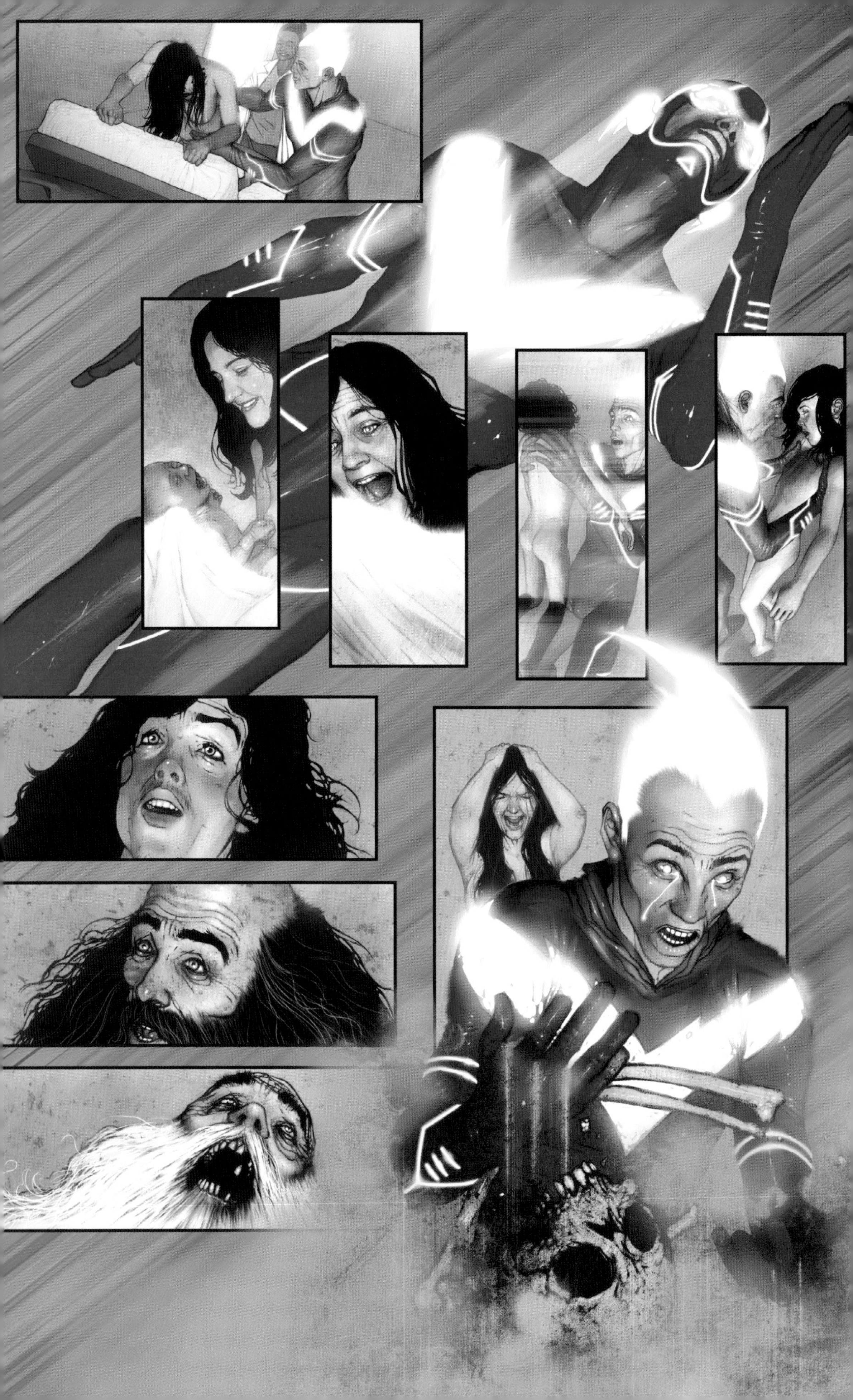

Zip is a forty-seven year-old Super-S who possesses the gift of incredible speed and stamina. He's married to Kate, a Norman, who is thirteen years his junior. After receiving a positive result in their HALE-CRITERION test, they have invited me to witness the birth of their first child. It will be a great experience for me to see the birthing process of a Super-S child first-hand.

We're in a private labouring room in an undisclosed location. I'm sitting next to an anxious Zip, who is helping Kate through her contractions.

JS: I'm very grateful that you've invited me along for this momentous occasion.
Z: No problem at all. To be honest, it's Kate you should thank. As you're aware, we planned to hold this interview with you a few weeks before Zip Junior was due to be born, but it looks like the little devil had other plans!

K: Well, I can't say I'm enthralled about having another person in attendance with us, but I'm hoping it will be beneficial for you and your project and, you never know, it might help take my mind off the contractions. Speaking of which, here... comes... another one...

Kate spasms and takes long, deep breaths. An efficient-looking nurse enters the room.

Midwife: Okay, Kate, let's have a look at you.

K: This fucking hurts! Zip, get me some water!

Midwife: You're doing well. Almost there.

Zip feeds Kate some water through a straw.

JS: You took the Super-S test and it came back positive. Why did you choose to know?
Z: Considering my background, we both agreed that it was better to be prepared for any eventuality. It seems we made the right decision; the tests came back confirming the baby would be a full Super-S, just like his dad! I can't wait to meet him.

K: Her! I told you already, I think it's a girl. F...uck!

Z: Sure, babes. It's a girl. Now relax. Breathe. Controlled... slow.

K: Who are you to tell me to take it slow? And I'll tell you to fucking breathe in a minute!

Z: She didn't mean that.

K: You wanna bet?

JS: Any plans to tutor the child for a career as a Super-S? Maybe a father and son, I mean daughter, team?
Z: Yep, that's the plan. What a cool, crime-fighting duo we'll be!

K: We've discussed this before – she's not working with you until she's eighteen. Ah, rub my back!

Zip rubs Kate's lower back.

K: Harder... I said, harder!!

Z: Sorry, babes. There, I'm doing it, ok? I've promised Kate, I'll be with her – or him – all the way.

K: I've changed my mind! Fuck!

Midwife: Just a few more and you'll be there. Wait a moment... Don't push, whatever you do!

K: I WANT to push! I want this baby OUT! I will not be going through this again! You can forget it, buddy, that's the last time I let YOU anywhere near ME!

JS: So how many children do you hope to have?
Z: Oh, three or four. That way, I could start my own Super-team!

K: One – including this one. Fuck!

Midwife: That's it! Now you can push, Kate.

Kate screams. It's all becoming rather personal so I decide to leave the room to allow them some privacy. I go and get myself a coffee. When I return, Kate's screams have been replaced by those of a baby's. Zip puts his head 'round the door.

Z: You can come back in now! I knew it! It's a boy!

I enter the room to see Kate holding a tiny shape, wrapped in a white, cotton blanket. She is gently caressing the baby's head.

K: Hello, handsome.

JS: Congratulations to you both! Any names yet?
Z: Zip Junior.

K: We're not calling him Zip Junior. I want a Norman name. Benjamin. I like Benjamin.

Midwife: Kate, you should try to feed him, I'll be back in a minute to check how you're both getting on. Kate?

K: Zip?

Kate is staring at the baby, a puzzled expression forming on her face. She looks up anxiously at Zip, who rushes to her side and takes the baby from her. His eyes widen in shock. Something appears to be wrong.

Z: Someonegetadoctor,QUICK!

The midwife removes the blanket to look at the child.

Midwife: Oh my God! I'll... I'll be right back!

Z: Someone,help.Pleasehelp!

I can see the baby now. Or what was a baby. The child now appears to be about three years-old. I watch, incredulous, as within a matter of seconds it matures rapidly through the various stages of it's life cycle until Zip is left cradling a frightened teenage boy. Zip's muscles strain against the sudden weight-gain of his child.

K: Do something, Zip!

Z: Idon'tunderstandwhat'sgoingon.Help!Nurse!Helpmestopit!

The boy in Zip's arms continues to develop. He's now a young man.

Z: Ohmygod,myboy...myboy!Please,son.Makeitstop!

Benjamin tries to speak but cannot; his vocal cords are far too immature to have developed yet. All he can do is look at his father, the fear and confusion apparent in his eyes. I watch, helplessly, as he ages at an alarmingly accelerated rate; through his twenties, thirties, forties, and onwards until, the doctors finally arrive, only to find Zip nursing a frail, elderly man. Benjamin utters a feeble groan and then breathes no more. Still, his body continues to age; his flesh rots and his bones crumble, until there is nothing left but dust, trickling through Zip's clenched fists. Kate is screaming hysterically on the bed. Zip can do nothing but stare at the remains of what was, mere seconds ago, his new-born baby boy. The medical team are in chaos.

Z: NoNoNo...

At this point, I am ushered out of the room by the midwife. There is nothing I can possibly do to help here. I leave Zip and his wife to their grieving. To outlive your children is something no father and mother should ever have to experience. Especially not like this.

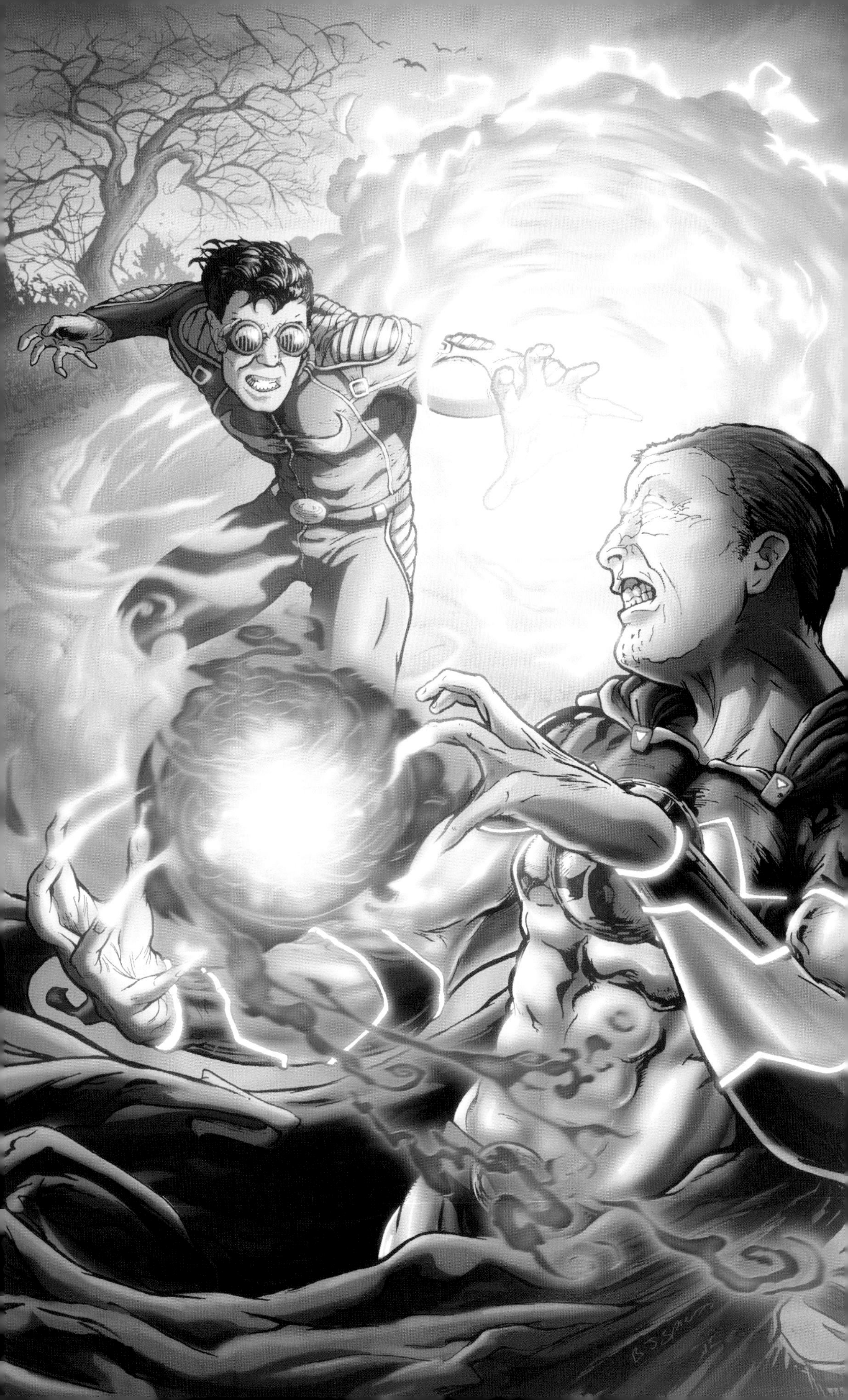

I've been granted an unusual interview with two Super-S. Unusual because these two heroes – DarkMatter (49) and Twister (26) – have an extreme dislike for each other. They have agreed to the interview on the understanding that I will act as mediator for them, in the hope they may be able to resolve their differences. I'm hoping it will be less explosive than my encounter with SolarFlare and CarbonCopy.

I've chosen what I would loosely term 'neutral ground' on which to hold this meeting: Hampstead Heath, overlooking London. DarkMatter has already arrived. Twister has not shown up yet.

JS: Thank you for agreeing to be interviewed here, with Twister. I know it's not exactly the kind of interview you had in mind.
DM: No problem. I've been looking forward to this. You never know, some good might actually come of it. I wouldn't put money on him turning up though, he's not exactly reliable.

JS: Since you are here, perhaps you could tell me about yourself?
DM: Certainly. Well, it began back in the 70's, when I discovered I had the ability to manipulate negative energy. I refined my skills to the point where I was able to create miniature black holes and reverse gravity.

JS: That sounds extremely dangerous.
DM: Only if you get in the way of one; they'll literally tear you apart if they're powerful enough or, depending on the size of the hole I generate, they can simply just root you to the spot. I rarely need to generate anything larger than a golf ball to settle most encounters.

London was a very different city when I was young. Back then, organised crime was anything but organised; there were a lot more hair-brained schemes concocted on the off-chance and a lot of opportunists that really had no idea what they were doing. And, of course, there were less guns on the streets. It was a lot more, shall we say, easy-going? Almost... fun. Not like crooks today. Trouble is, things change, don't they? As the world became more violent and aggressive, so did the criminals. Even the odd Super-S or two were lured to the dark side of crime, whereas others just became reckless and lazy. A bit like our absent friend-

T: Talking about people behind their backs again, DarkMatter?

A tremendous wind whips the air as Twister touches down on the grass beside us. I'm almost knocked clean off my feet by the force. Twister's abilities are certainly synonymous with his name.

DM: Surprise, surprise. Late again. But then, I wouldn't expect any less from you.

T: Nice to see you, too. James, is it? Sorry I'm late; had a coach full of schoolgirls to save – you understand. So, you're here to do a piece about London's greatest Super-S, are you?

DM: "London's greatest"? Pah. You have no idea what a detriment you are to this city, do you?

T: "Detriment"? Sounds to me like you're jealous, old man. Anyway, what do you care? I heard you'd retired months ago. Couldn't handle the pace...

DM: Why, you-

JS: Sorry, gentlemen. Could we get back to the questions? It's clear that there's animosity between you; why is that? Why the hostilities? Surely, you should be saving that kind of aggression for the villains? There have even been several confrontations between you both where you've put public lives at risk.
DM: You can't blame me; I was assisting after part of the Embankment collapsed in the City. I was in full concentration mode, generating a black hole underneath the damaged structure to support the underpass. It was only when Twister turned up that the entire operation went awry.

T: How many times do I have to listen to this same, old drivel! I was helping the emergency services tend to the public!

DM: Well, they didn't need your help! And nor did I! It was all under control. Your interference cost lives that day and I'm the one who had to deal with the criticism afterwards.

T: The way I saw it, you were struggling to keep everything together. Those people's deaths should be on your conscience, old man, not mine.

DM: HOW DARE YOU! *He's been like this since the first day we met.*

I'm growing increasingly uncomfortable with how this interview is proceeding.

JS: Twister, you're a relative newcomer. Do you feel you could learn something from DarkMatter? You have to admit, he has an established reputation with the people of London.
T: Credit where credit's due, he was great... once upon a time. I won't deny it. But, as they say, every dog has its day. And that's true for Super-S, too. He should think about hanging up his cape rather than trying to keep up with today's generation. Life's moving faster than he is. With all due respect, he should have the decency to bow out now, whilst he's got some dignity left. We're on the cusp of a new dawn of Super-S, you know? I deserve my time. No offence, DM, but you've had yours.

DM: I'm not ready for retirement just yet, young man. London still needs me. There are still a few tricks left in this old dog.

As if to prove his point, DarkMatter executes the splits, then jumps back to his feet again.

T: The only thing you have to offer is the superhero equivalent of helping old ladies across the road. You're a glorified Lollipop Lady. You have no concept of the new dangers that threaten the world. That's why the government have appointed me to represent my city at the European conference on supervillains in Berlin next month.

DM: You? You can't even turn up to an interview on time. How can they rely upon the likes of you? They deserve someone they can trust. Someone that won't fail them. Someone like me.

T: You're failing them every time you put that cape on, old timer. I'd rather turn up a few minutes late than jeopardise an entire mission with my incompetence. You just don't get it, do you?

JS: Surely, the capital is big enough for the both of you? I would have thought you both have integral roles to play in helping society. Hasn't the Mayor of London considered dividing the city into different jurisdictions for you?
DM: Well, it has been mooted, but even if they did agree to it, that wouldn't stop *him* turning up, trying to steal my thunder.

T: The only reason I'd turn up is to undo the errors that your disruptive ability causes. Face it, you just can't control yourself anymore. You create more problems than you solve.

DM: Rubbish. I have complete control over my powers. Always have and always will.

DarkMatter gesticulates and accidentally omits a flash of black and purple energy from his fingers, which streaks past me and hits Twister square in the chest, driving him into the ground. Twister breaks free and jumps to his feet. I feel the air around me compress.

T: Why, you... you did that on purpose! You're going to regret that, old man. You've had this coming for a long time...

Before DarkMatter can apologise, he's encircled by a mini whirlwind. Lightning arcs around Twister as he levitates off the ground. It's time for me to beat a hasty retreat. I guess I'll read all about the outcome of this conflict in tomorrow's headlines.

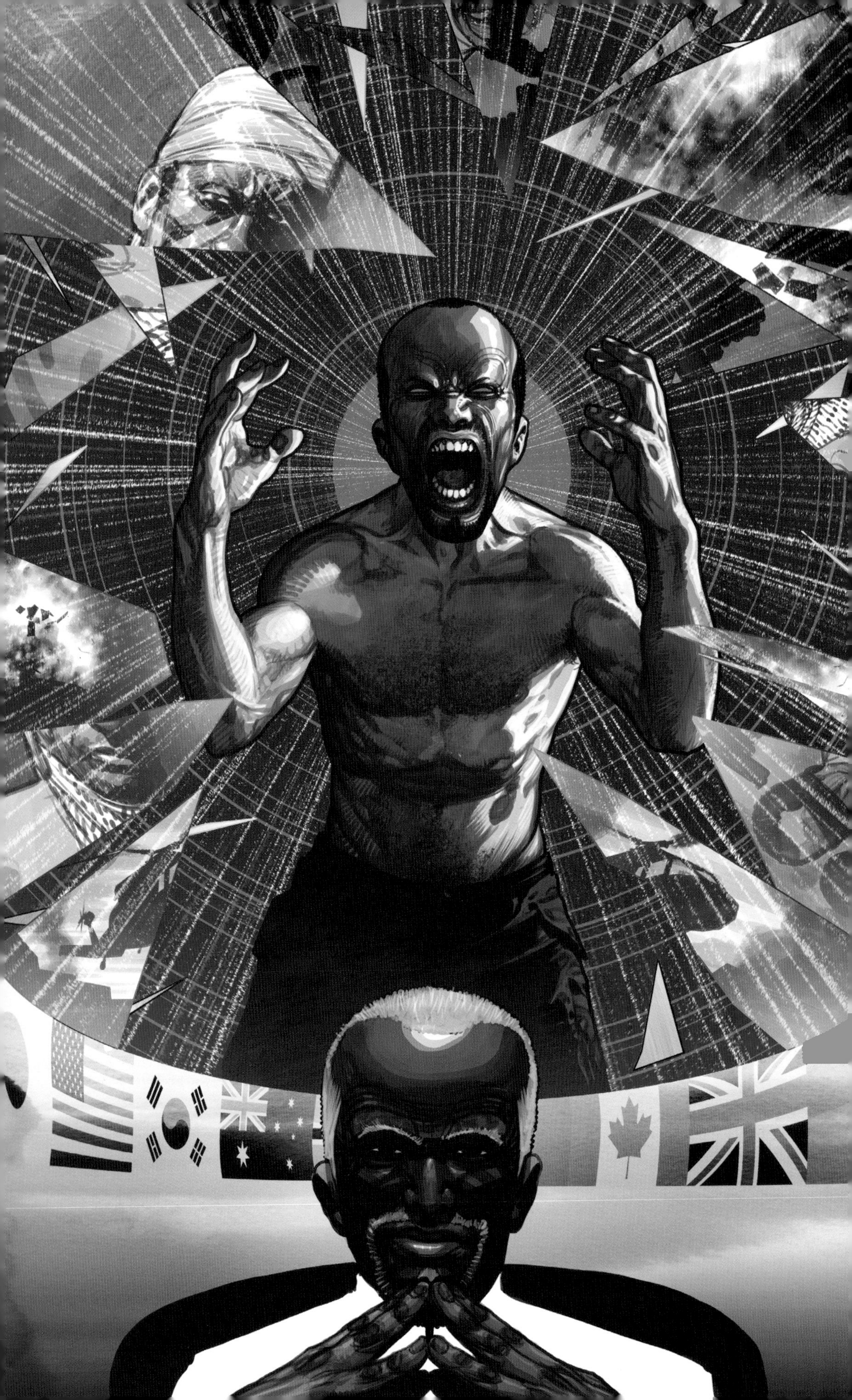

Still very much active for a fifty year-old Super-S, Asad Nadif Ghedi has found a new role in life as a humanitarian aid ambassador for the United Nations. His Super-S name is SoulScreamer and he has recently been involved in supporting victims of the Burmese Cyclone and the Chinese Earthquake.

We have arranged to meet at the UN headquarters in New York City. We are in the large auditorium where all nations assemble to discuss the current agendas.

JS: It's humbling, standing here in this room.
SS: Yes, it's truly breathtaking, isn't it? You can really feel its sense of purpose. All the countries are here because they want the same thing – for the world to be a better place; free from exploitation, war, death and starvation.

JS: What is your background?
SS: I was born and raised in Mogadishu, Somalia, the third son of Norman parents. I thought I was Norman too; I had no idea that an incredible power slept deep within my soul. The rebel invasion of 1990-1993 changed all that, when the streets were suddenly awash with gunfire, murder and starvation. I lost my wife and children in the bloodshed. It was at that moment, when I came across their mutilated, broken bodies, that my spirit awoke. At first, I cried, mourning the loss of my family, but as my anger grew, so did my voice, and I screamed like nothing on this earth. Bricks, mortar and glass disintegrated under my howl, the ground shook and buildings tumbled. That was the moment SoulScreamer was born.

JS: Didn't your parents suspect you were Super-S?
SS: If my parents knew I had abilities, they never told me. We are not like the West; my family lived in poverty, they struggled to put food on the table, let alone find money for education or medical care for their children. There is no Super-S test in my country, nothing to help people like me. I certainly didn't realise what I could do until it happened. Sometimes, it takes personal tragedy to discover you have been blessed with a miracle.

JS: What happened after you discovered your power?
SS: I buried the bodies of my dead family and pursued the rebels. I was driven by revenge. I guess that is where I made my error. I was a simple man, trained as a farmer. I had no military skills to speak of, I certainly wasn't trained to take on a rebel army. It was my anger which was fueling me, giving me the courage to hunt them down.

I attacked the first group I encountered. There was much bloodshed. As my newfound voice came in contact with their bodies it literally tore their flesh from their bones. But I was not tactically trained to cope with the situation and they quickly surrounded me. I became involved in the firefight from hell. They suppressed me, pinning me down behind a burning car. There was smoke and bullets everywhere. If I close my eyes I can still feel the heat on my skin. I used my voice, screaming in every direction; liquifying, maiming, destroying everything in my path. It was only when an RPG exploded on the other side of the car and it sent me spiralling through the air that I stopped. The next thing I remember was waking up in a dark room, gagged and bound, a prisoner of the rebels.

JS: Why did they capture you and take you alive?
SS: This particular rebel Warlord was a very shrewd man. He had witnessed over a dozen of his men destroyed by an unarmed civilian. He wanted to turn me into a weapon against my own people.

God turned His back on me that day. They tortured me, bent me to their will. They found my mother and brothers, they made me watch as my family were forced to kneel before me with guns pressed against their heads. They gave me the choice; work for the rebels or watch my family die. I became a caged animal, gagged and tethered until my masters chose to unleash me against their enemies. A weapon of their bidding. For three months I was forced to endure this nightmare.

JS: How did you eventually escape?
SS: I didn't. It wasn't possible for me to escape. I was saved. Do you remember the military incident "The Battle of the Black Sea"?

JS: Of course. They made it into a film.
SS: Well, forget what you've heard, my friend. *I* was the real reason the task force went in.

JS: How did they know you were there?
SS: XoDOS. It wasn't the U.S. on an extraction mission, as reported. It was XoDOS.

JS: I don't understand. Why XoDOS?
SS: Would *you* favor the idea of a Somalian Warlord having a Super-S as part of his arsenal? They were desperate to get me out, but something went wrong – the strike team got more than they bargained for. I think someone in their own team turned against them. Before they knew it, they were trapped, fighting the city. Even with a company of American Marines for support, it wasn't enough. They were losing. In the end, the United Nations intervened; with three armored divisions they retrieved what was left of the XoDOS extraction squad and pulled them out.

JS: And you?
SS: I was unleashed on the fleeing column of tanks. I destroyed the first two before I was nullified by one of the XoDOS team. He appeared out of nowhere and took me to the ground. I didn't resist him, I just wanted the nightmare to end.

JS: Did XoDOS take you?
SS: No, the U.N. took control of the situation. XoDOS did not have the authority to be involved and were told to leave immediately. I believe it was then that the U.N. realized for the first time that I could assist in evolving their cause; a Super-S in the ranks of the U.N. had been discussed, but was unheard of at that point. They weren't about to throw the opportunity away. I was invited to meet the Assembly and they presented their case to me and offered me a position as an ambassador. I accepted.

JS: Some would say you simply changed one set of masters for another. How would you respond to that?
SS: Those people have to open their minds to what the U.N. stands for and what they aspire to be. For years, people have perceived us as nothing more than an empty sabre rattle; a cat amongst lions. Not anymore. It is time for the cat to become the lion, to find its roar. And we are saving lives rather than taking them. Saving. Not hundreds, not thousands, but hundreds of thousands. I will do what it takes to earn the forgiveness of my people and my God.

JS: And what of your mother and brothers?
SS: I never saw them again. I have returned to Mogadishu on many occasions to look for them but I have never found them. We will meet again, if not in this world, then the next.

JS: Were you ever reapproached by XoDOS?
SS: No. I think once I was under the wing of the U.N. I became too prominent for them to take any further action to recruit me. That in itself is an indication that the U.N. should not be taken lightly. Although one day, I hope to meet the XoDOS operative that tackled me to the ground. I owe him my thanks, my freedom and my life.

JS: What is your current role in the U.N.?
SS: I have been involved in many missions, using my powers to clear minefields, or excavate wells. I have also been appointed to a new role which I am very excited about; I have been instructed to initiate an enlistment drive to recruit more superheroes to the cause. A number of Super-S volunteers have already offered to donate their time to assist in humanitarian aid to poverty-stricken areas. I want to show that the gifts we possess can be used for more than just fighting the villains and dictators of this world. But for those factions and governments that do choose to suppress their people, I represent a warning that they should not take the word of the Assembly lightly. Mark my words, when it comes to promoting World peace, our proclamation will always be heard.

Artwork: Frazer Irving – SoulScreamer

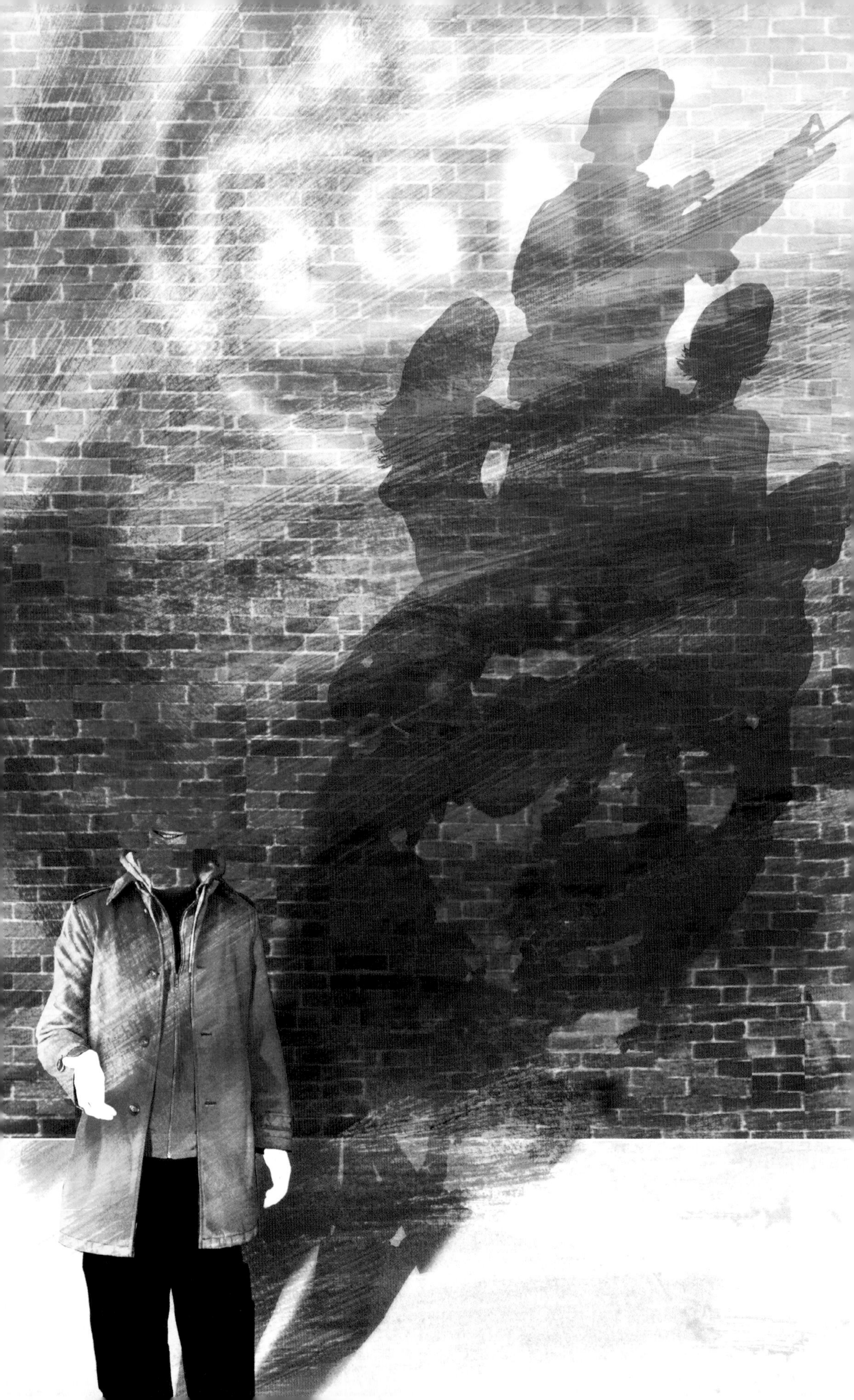

I'm a little wary of my next meeting because Turncoat is a very appropriate choice of name for the man sitting opposite me. At fifty-three years-old, he is somewhat of a late starter in the Super-S stakes. That's because Turncoat is a former Vader who chose to leave behind a life of crime to work on the "good" side.

I am at a restaurant in Las Vegas, Nevada, called The Top of the World, overlooking The Strip. The night is awash with gamblers and tourists, all searching for that one chance to make it big.

JS: If you don't mind, let's get the difficult question out of the way first; why did you abuse your power over others for personal gain?
TC: I didn't think the world needed a goody goody Super-S that couldn't teleport or fly. Couldn't get to the action quick enough and I didn't drive, so it would'a looked pretty lame if I'd turned up to save the day in the back of a yellow cab. An' being a shape-changer don't mean I get to acquire your powers or abilities as well. Best I can do is adopt your basic properties; height, weight, that kinda stuff. Strength-wise, I have trouble pulling the arm on the slots. That ain't much good when you're facing up to a 400-pound Rhino or saving orphaned kids from a burning building. Tell a lie. Did good by one person whilst I was Vader. Just the once. A suit. Got himself in a heap of trouble with a gang in the wrong part of town. That was a bit of an anti-climax. Saved the bum and he didn't even tip. Who the hell doesn't tip? We live in a society of tippers; waitresses, pizza boys, even hairdressers get some. Save a guy's life and what do you get? Gratitude. That ain't going to pay the bills. No, man, the good side wasn't gonna work for me back then.

JS: What happened, once you realised saving people wasn't for you?
TC: Took a long, hard look at myself, realized I wasn't gonna look good in unitards and had an epiphany; I evaluated my core skills and realized that there weren't too many Doppelganger Supers out there. Reckoned I could have some fun with that and make some cash at the same time.

JS: I hear that Doppelgangers are highly sought after by XoDOS. Did they approach you about working for them?
TC: Work for the big man in the White House? You gotta be kiddin'! I didn't vote him in. I might have been a sorry-ass, but there was no way I would put it on the line doing his dirty work.

JS: Did you become involved in organised crime?
TC: Didn't want to go that route, either. Didn't want eighty percent of my hard-earned cash contributing to some smooth-talkin' Italian's high-rollin' lifestyle. Not that they didn't approach me. No – down-the-line freelancer – that was the route to go; fraud, bank heists, mainly. I didn't even have to hold a place up – just walk in, meet-and-greet with the manager, a shake of the hand and away you go. Contact is the important bit. I can't replicate my target without skin-on-skin contact. Once I'd cased the joint out, I'd return a day or two later in the 'guise of said manager, access the vaults, take what I needed and then I was outta there. I'd usually leave in the form of a harmless ol' lady, a kid, something like that. The guards would even hold the door open for me as I walked out. Priceless! I had it all figured out.

Turncoat taps his temple.

I'd never hoodwink civilians, always corporations, always the money-men. Thinking about it now, I guess you could say I was destined to be a good guy; kinda like your Robin Hood...

JS: What made you change your ways?
TC: Well, it's Vegas, baby, Vegas; when you keep playing the house, the house is eventually gonna win, right? Turns out, an XoDOS team had been tracking me for several months – I'd been runnin' this great racket where I was impersonating major celebs and walkin' around like I was runnin' the joints. It was a piece of cake. You're one handshake away from being pretty much anybody in this town. Man, those fools were comp'ing me rooms, food, VIP tables, setting me up with markers, the works. Didn't matter if I lost, they thought I was good for it so they would just keep banking me. Anyway, I was turning over my fifth joint disguised as Samuel L. Jackson when I got caught. The casino bosses weren't too impressed. And the bastards that they are, the XoDOS team let them work me over some before taking me away.

JS: You robbed a casino as Samuel L. Jackson?
TC: Cool, huh? That shit still makes me smile. I just wish I got to use some of his cool lines. Especially the ones from Pulp Fiction. I love that shit.

There are a few gasps from other diners as Turncoat 'morphs' into the actor in question and quotes lines from scenes in Pulp Fiction. A range of celebrity transformations follow; Jerry Lee Lewis, Brad Pitt, Celine Dion, Nicholas Cage, Barbara Streisand, Bill Clinton. Moments later, he changes back into his real form (or at least, the form he has assumed whilst being interviewed by me).

Show's over people. Move along. Nothing else to see here.

JS: So, XoDOS finally got their man. How did they persuade you to join them?
TC: Let's just say, by the time they caught up with me, there were quite a few casino bosses who had a vested interest in my future; specifically, whether I had one or not. XoDOS gave me a choice – work for them or they'd hand my ass to the businessmen of Vegas for a very handsome donation to their worthy cause. Much as I stand by my political beliefs, I certainly wasn't going to risk my life for them.

JS: What kind of work did they assign you?
TC: Stuff I was comfortable with; socializing, partying, that kind of thing. I've met foreign dignitaries from the Middle East, Africa, Europe, Asia, a few Ruskies, too. Once you're mixing in those kind of circles everybody is so friendly, always willing to shake the hand of somebody as important as they are. The wives are charming, too.

Turncoat throws me a knowing wink.

You wanna see my John Holmes?

JS: No, thank you. How do you handle the pressure of juggling all the different identities?
TC: When you've been doing this as long as I have, it becomes second-nature; like bein' in my own movie and gettin' to play all the cool parts. I should win an Oscar for some of my performances and the way I've fucked with people's public personas. Remember Britney and the Kojak incident? Whoops, I did it... again.

JS: Have you been approached by any foreign powers or organisations, to work for them?
TC: 'Course I have, and XoDOS ain't stupid. They treat me right, make sure I'm financially comfortable and turn a blind eye to my social indiscretions when I feel like lettin' off some steam. As long as I'm on the other end of the phone when they call, they have no problem with me. We have an understanding. It pays to be loyal.

JS: So, how do you feel you compare in relation to those that are saving lives on a daily basis?
TC: Same shit, different heroics. You might not see my face plastered across the TV channels, but I'm there at ground level, doing my thing. In the time it takes a cape to rescue a cat from a tree, I could have signed a treaty in the 'guise of some diplomat and saved thousands of lives. Which reminds me, I've got an important meeting in twenty minutes with a senior ambassador at the Wynn. So forgive me if I cut and run. Nice meetin' you.

Turncoat holds out his hand for me to shake.

JS: Erm, I hope you won't be offended if I don't.
TC: Not at all. Anyway, gotta *roll*.

Turncoat grins and walks towards the restaurant door. Within the space of a few steps, he's transformed into a svelte, confident brunette whom I recognise as Agatha.

34

Artwork: Ben Oliver - Turncoat

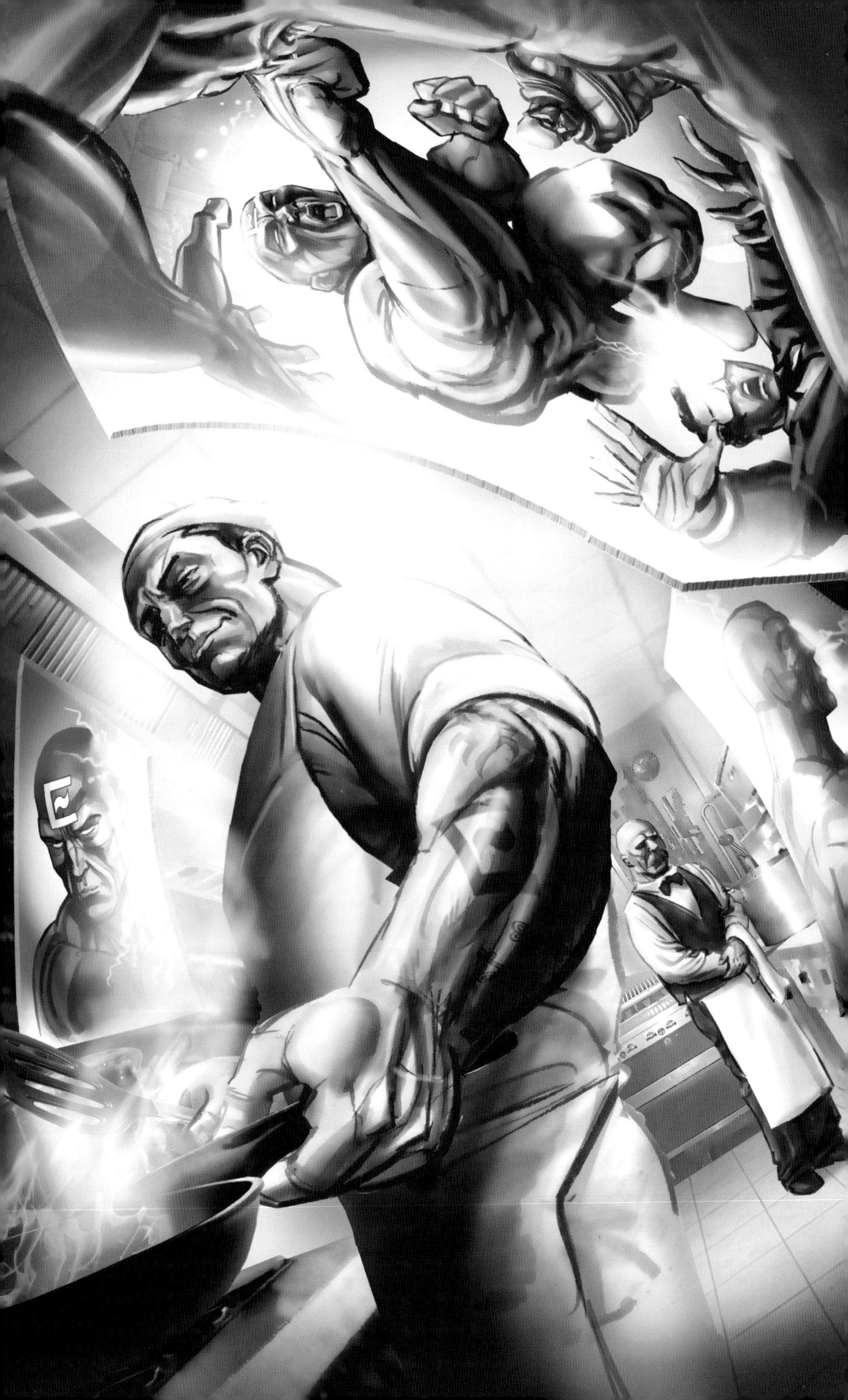

You don't expect to find a superhero working in a restaurant kitchen, especially one that he owns. But that's exactly where I find myself, watching fifty-five year-old, Egress, busy cooking for a house full of diners.

The Fourth Dimension is a restaurant located in Montreal, Canada, just off Boulevard Crémazie Ouest. Egress bought the business ten years ago as an investment for his future retirement but he's now spending more time devoted to the business and less time being a Super-S.

JS: You don't appear to employ many kitchen staff. How do you cope when the restaurant is busy?
E: I don't need more staff. Notice how the kitchen is covered in mirrors? That's not because I'm vain!

There's a flash of light and Egress disappears. A second later and he's reappeared on the other side of the kitchen. He turns some dials on the oven and rematerialises back next to me.

JS: I see! So, what's the nature of your power?
E: Well my main one is teleportation; I use the mirrors as a mode of transport. Their reflective surface acts like a dimensional door and once I'm inside, time outside just seems to stand still. I can then observe a multitude of events, as if I am looking thru windows at lots of scenes occurring outside. I choose an exit I want, open the door and in a second, I am there. To you it looks instantaneous, for me it's as if I am still operating in real-time.

JS: Which means you can pretty much run the entire kitchen on your own?
E: I never thought I'd be using my powers to keep the bellies of two hundred-plus guests full but, yeah, everything we create back here is down to me.

JS: Have you always enjoyed cooking?
E: Yes. When I was a full-time Super-S, it's something I used to do to help me unwind after a hard day 'on the beat'. Michelle, my wife, was the one who originally got me interested. I had an affinity for it, especially when I began incorporating my powers.

JS: What was it like when you were a full-time Super-S?
E: It became very hard to cope with the responsibility. Even with my power, I still couldn't be everywhere at once. I could cheat time, not control it. The failures began affecting me; I wasn't able to acknowledge all the people I saved, only the ones that I'd failed. Cooking became my outlet. The great leveller; I could create something that would make people happy, not sad.

JS: What was your greatest memory of being Egress?
E: That's an easy one! It was about twenty-five years ago – I'd teamed up with a 2nd Degree called The Revolution; a huge Russian guy who'd turned his back on his motherland's anti-western policies to work over here. A real nice guy, but his biceps were bigger than his brains, if you catch my drift. Anyway, the stupid ox got himself into some trouble and needed my help. He'd been captured by this supervillain called DownFall, a real nasty guy; he'd imprisoned Revolution in his lair, somewhere in Alaska. DownFall knew how my power worked, so he'd made sure there were no mirrors or reflective surfaces around. It turned out that he was in cahoots with some spineless government official who had supplied him with top-secret intel on both of us; seems there was some kind of issue between him and us, but I've never managed to find out what it was.

Well, fortunately, this government man wanted to gloat over the fruits of his deception, so he accompanied DownFall to see the incarcerated Revolution. That's where he made his mistake. I was in the mirror world, looking for clues to their whereabouts and, as government boy left the lair, he put his sunglasses on. Mirrored sunglasses. Need I say more? DownFall's face was a peach! I can still see him now, turning in horror, screaming at the guy to take them off. Too late. Way too late. Once I was in, I scattered polished ball bearings so there were lots of nice reflective surfaces all over

the place! They didn't stand a chance. Still makes me laugh. I've been dining out on that one for a while.

JS: Michelle tells me that you're thinking about concentrating on the restaurant full-time and retiring from the Super-S business altogether. Is that true?
E: Yes. I really enjoy it back here. Michelle is far happier now she sees more of me and she doesn't have to worry about whether I'll be coming home injured or if I'm coming home, period. There are plenty more Super-S and 2nd Degrees out there to fight the good fight. I hear there are even a few Super-M's creeping out of the woodwork now. Good for them.

JS: You're totally open about your past and your association with the restaurant. Aren't you worried that a supervillain or a Vader may turn up one day, hoping to settle an old grudge?
E: Well, most of them are locked up in high-security penitentiaries, so that shouldn't be a problem, but if one did turn up... well... even bad guys need to eat. One mouthful of my Foie Gras Poutine should be enough to settle any old score!

JS: What are your plans for the future?
E: More customers, of course! Seriously, I'd love to own a chain of restaurants; start with a few more here in Canada, then perhaps go global. I've really been thinking about that. I'd love to oversee each and every one, just to make sure each dish goes out with the Egress seal of approval. I'd need to invest in lots more shiny stainless-steel and mirrors!

JS: Wouldn't that become stressful? It's not an easy task being the head chef of one restaurant, let alone ten or twenty.
E: True, but it would be a different kind of stress. Presiding over delivery orders, managing staff and inventing new menus is a lot less worrying than preventing some madman from detonating a nuclear device in the center of Toronto's financial district.

JS: Those threats to our society still remain. Just because you've chosen a new career path, it doesn't mean the danger goes away.
E: True, true, and if fate decides that threat turns up at my door again, you can be sure I shall take the appropriate steps to deal with it. But I won't intentionally go looking for it. Trouble has always been there and it'll be there long after I've served my last entrée. We are all minor players in a very big game, Mr Stanley. There will always be substitutes waiting to take your place once you've hit your last puck.

JS: How will your fans feel – those that still see you as a Super-S and not a celebrity chef?
E: Give them a couple of months and they will have adjusted to the idea. At least, I hope so. After all, they are my primary audience to target when I release my own range of kitchenware!

A tall, barrel-chested man, dressed in a smart waiter's uniform, walks into the kitchen. He speaks with a thick Russian accent.

Waiter: Table two are asking where their lobster is and table three now want their steaks well-done.

E: Right. Be with you in a minute, Vlad.

Vlad nods and glares at me before returning to the dining area.

JS: Was that...?
E: The Revolution? Yes! After we split up the team, we remained good friends. When I opened this place I told Vlad that, if he needed one, there was always a job here for him. I guess he'd been thinking about moving on, too. It's great having him around. Put it this way, nobody skips on paying the check when Vlad's working! Hey, can you smell burning?

He looks over at the smoke billowing out of the oven.

Shiiiiit!

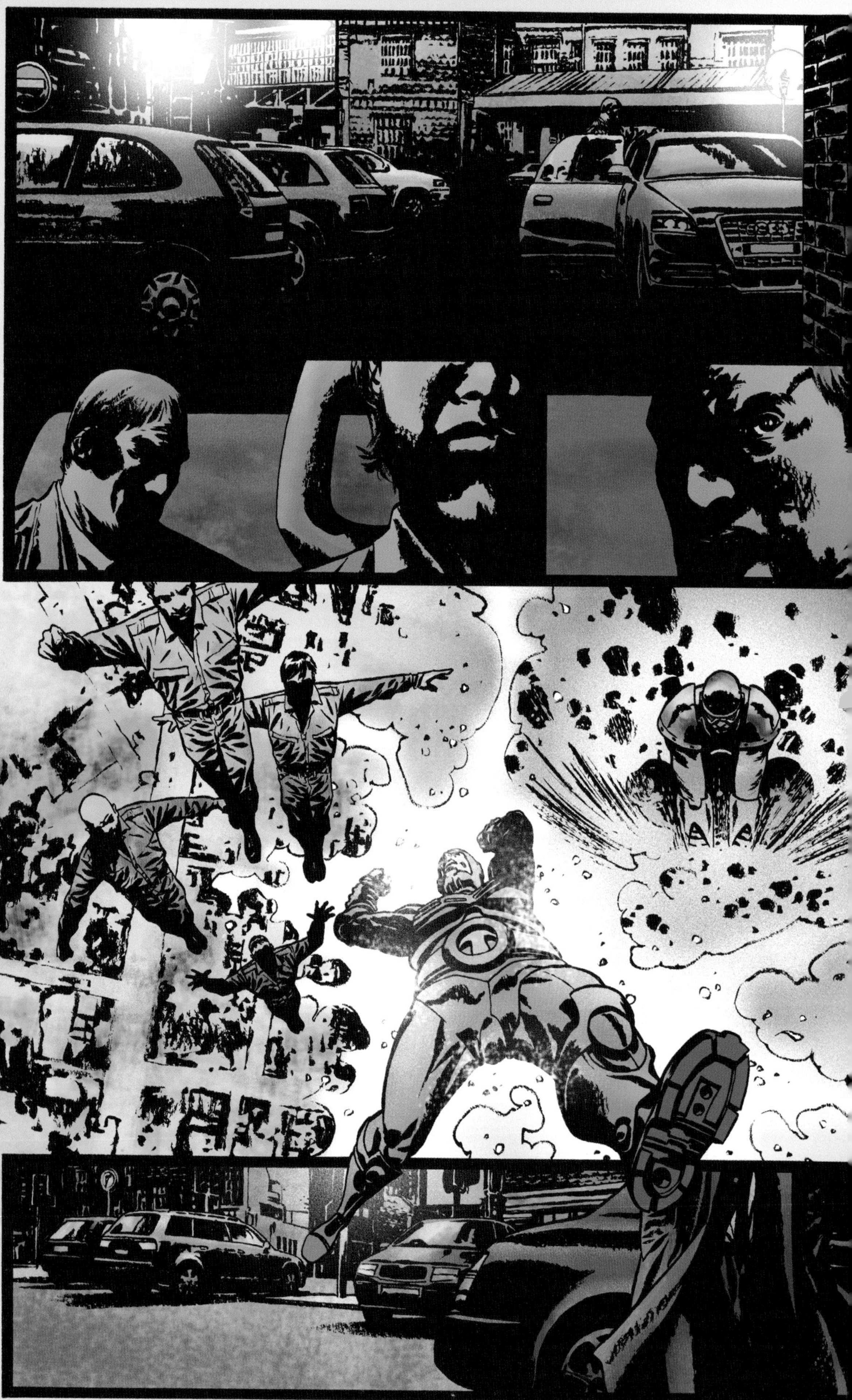

3am. It's late, or early, depending upon your point-of-view. I'm sitting in my car in a parking lot in Hamilton, Ontario, waiting for my interviewee to turn up; a high-ranking official with the infamous XoDOS.

I jump as the rear door of the car opens and someone gets in the back.

Mr. Doe: Please don't turn around.

JS: Mr... Doe?
D: Unoriginal as it is, it's a name that protects us both. Please don't turn around; the less you know about me, the better. Otherwise, I may as well take the gun I have in my pocket and blow both of our brains out right now. You know from our brief communication that XoDOS won't take too kindly to our meeting like this.

JS: I was sure I'd locked the doors.
D: You did. So let's get down to it. What do you think XoDOS is?

JS: Well, from what I can ascertain, it's a government organisation established to provide financial support and assistance to the public where they or their families have, or are diagnosed with, the Super-S gene.
D: Back in the beginning, that's what it used to be, but not anymore. That's what they still want you to believe. Now, it's an organization for the establishment of a new-world army, pure and simple.

JS: For what purpose?
D: We're on the brink of a war. A World War unlike anything the human race has seen in the entire history of military confrontation. We're talking Global participation. What do you think will be the most effective weapon in that kind of battle? The kind of weapon that would leave nothing standing?

JS: Nuclear strikes?
D: Wrong. Super-S. Or more precisely, the Super-S of tomorrow.

JS: The Super-S children?
D: The perfect subjects for psychological manipulation, unlike mature Super-S who are, by nature, flawed because they possess ideals. With the exception of a few, they are either impossible to convert or take too long to condition. 2nd Degrees are easier; they're already committed to the cause, are simple to influence and can be quickly integrated into active service. They need little coercion, but they can be unstable. And every country, regime or political power is frantically developing their own 2nd Degrees for the same purpose; the North Koreans, Iran, China, Russia.

Remember those purported WMDs in Iraq? You want to know why we never found them? There weren't any chemical weapons. They were, in fact, four 2nd Degrees. They escaped to Iran. I say escaped. I mean *flew*. Iraq had engineered 2nd Degrees with aerial powers.

JS: Where are these 2nd Degrees now?
D: We're not sure. We lost them over Iran. Wouldn't surprise me if they headed East. We know several 2nd Degrees have been indoctrinated into government programmes in various countries there, so it makes sense to think they would look for employment with the Chinese or the North Koreans.

JS: What of the educational facilities XoDOS have established? Are you saying they're primarily Super-S recruitment centres?
D: Why not? The President reasoned it was only a matter of time before our enemies came for us. We needed to be ready. Start them young and they're yours for life. We're not just talking ten, twenty kids here; we're talking hundreds, thousands; most either orphaned, abandoned, or born to parents that simply can't cope. Take them under the protective XoDOS wing, show them some love and attention and you've got yourself the perfect military candidates; dedicated, unwavering and committed. Think of it. Thousands of them.

JS: I've seen, with my own eyes, evidence of XoDOS turning up on delivery wards. Acting like an adoption agency. That's unethical.
D: Unethical or accessible? The way XoDOS see it, they're saving a lot of children from a meaningless existence, nurturing them to discover their true potential. You've done the research, spoken to enough of them, I'm sure. A Norman environment isn't the way to go. XoDOS believe the kids have a more productive future under their tutelage. And so will the rest of the American population.

Think of it this way, Mr. Stanley. Nuclear weapons are crude; they make no distinction between friend or foe, whereas a Super-S can make informed decisions *then* act with precision and ferocity. That's what makes them so dangerous, so destructive; the power of *choice*. If you could educate a weapon to differentiate between friend or foe, it would enable you to operate on a military level with more firepower and focus than this world has ever seen.

Initial tests in the Middle East and South East Asia have already proven to be successful, even though we made a few miscalculations. Remember the cyclone that hit Burma? That was us. It was actually meant for China. A 2nd Degree by the codename 'Turbina' went AWOL during the mission. It turned out he lost control of his power, somewhere off the Burmese coast. Over 22,000 dead; 41,000 missing. That mistake didn't stop XoDOS trying again. We sent another Super-S into China a few weeks later. That time we got it right; hit the mainland with several seismic earthquakes. Our weapon development was working.

Now, imagine if you could stockpile a WMD, right in plain sight and have the whole world completely oblivious to it. That's where our creation of the S-Zones comes into play; mass stockpiling of weapons at closely monitored and controlled locations, strategically placed across the country, ready for use, as and when required.

JS: So XoDOS are on one big recruitment drive to secure as many Super-S as possible? What part does The Lotus play in this?
D: I guess you would call her XoDOS's full-time careers officer. She's a highly-valued and extremely dangerous agent. She came to us through HomeLight, which was a rare coup for the agency. Her power is incomparable; she can bend your will to her own, making you believe anything and everything. She can work from a distance or in close-quarters, she's at the top of her game and is revered within the ranks. She recruits whomever she pleases and hunts down and annihilates anyone that is detrimental to the XoDOS cause. You need to be very careful, Mr. Stanley. We both do. If she knew I was talking to you we'd both be dead, understand? She'll have you believing you're a blind, paraplegic female, pregnant with the bastard child of Freddy Krueger before you can even blink. You do not want to make yourself a target for that woman. There have been many Super-S that have confronted her before and paid the price. Most with their lives.

JS: Why are you giving me this information?
D: I have my reasons and if I mentioned them to you it would be enough of a clue to put Lotus onto me. Certain members of the agency are pushing the government to be more pro-active in global politics. They're not interested in world peace but a One-World Order with themselves at the helm. They're stockpiling their weapons, ready for the day they can unleash them on the rest of the world. And that day is coming; there's something called the 'SkyLine Objective' which I've heard whispered in darkened rooms. Not even I'm party to that particular information. All I know is that it's close to being activated and I'm pretty certain it will spell disaster for the rest of the planet. For the good of everyone on this planet, Mr. Stanley, you have to let people know the truth about XoDOS and its super-crusade. Before it's too late to stop them...

The car door clicks open and the engine starts, even though I'm not touching the key in the ignition.

...otherwise, God help us all.

Artwork: Charlie Adlard - Mr Doe

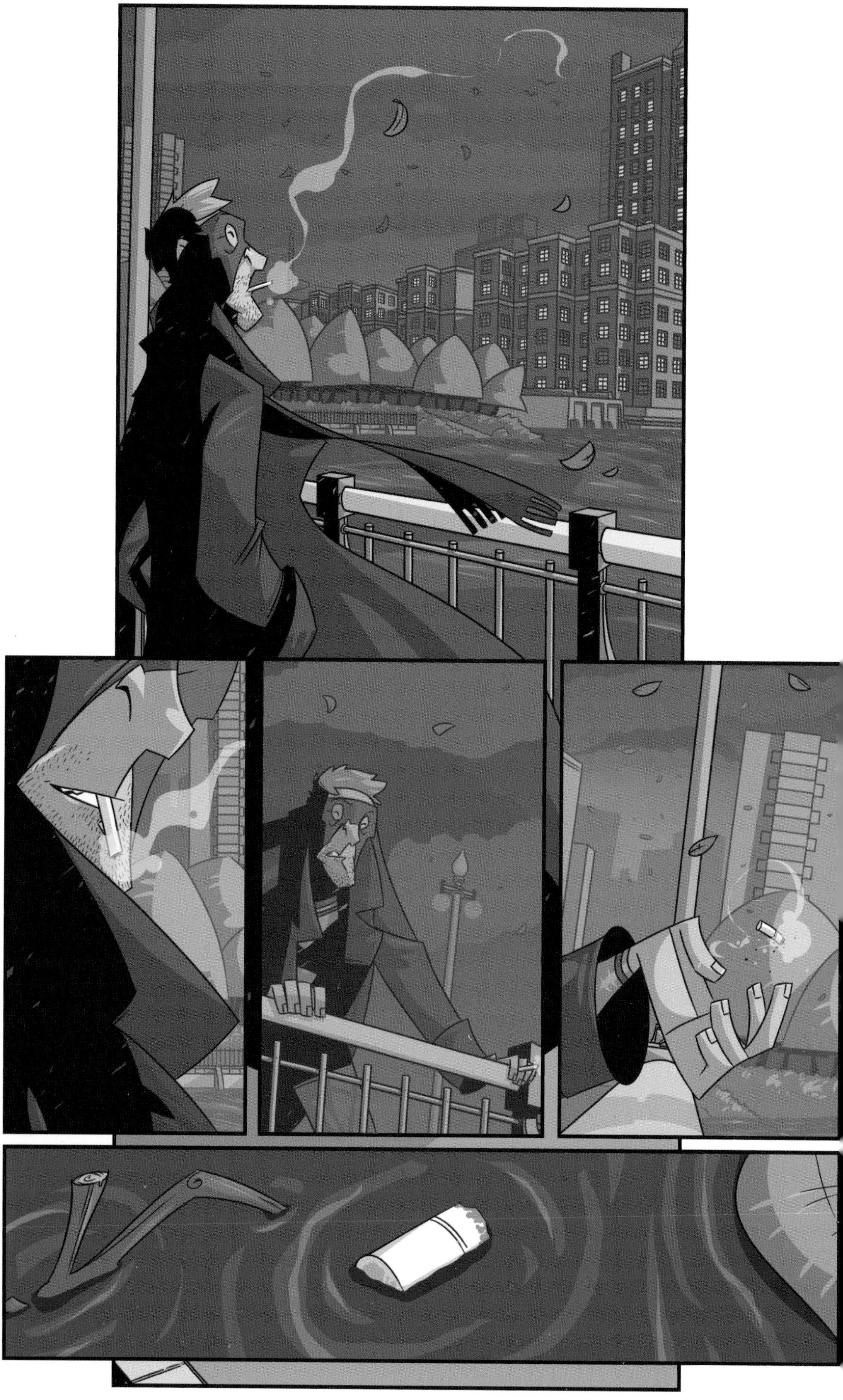

G-Core, aged fifty-seven, is a member of the Justice Crusade, a Detroit-based superhero team. He's recently agreed to step back from his full time role within the group.

We're on the MacArthur Bridge, looking out over the Detroit River. G-Core is dressed in a large overcoat, his ill-fitting costume just visible underneath. He's smoking a cigarette and gazing off into the distance.

JS: Are you okay?
GC: Apologies. I don't mean to ignore you standing there. Just... I'm a little preoccupied. It's been a weird few weeks for me.

JS: Is it something you want to talk about on record?
GC: Be a damn short interview if I didn't.

G-Core laughs.

GC: Sorry. Like I said, it's been a funny few weeks. You know, I used to come here as a kid and watch the boats going about their business. It helped me clear my mind. I was born a Norman (I'm a 2nd Degree) and I was a bit of a loner when I was a kid. Even the Norman kids that lived in my area didn't get me. I didn't mix well.

JS: What's brought you back to this place now?

G-Core hesitates a moment.

GC: I'm dying. No mistaking it, it's the big 'C'.

JS: I'm... sorry. Are you sure? When were you diagnosed?
GC: Sure as four separate, second-opinion doctors can be. Top boys, too. Guys the President himself uses. They gave me the news just under a month ago.

JS: Is it curable?
GC: It's highly unlikely. I'm already in an advanced state and it's extremely aggressive. If it wasn't for my body's ability to absorb and neutralize energy, I think it would have beaten me already. I guess I should've expected it at some point; my body's assimilated a lot of weird stuff over the years, consumed huge amounts of rads. I even helped you Brits out in the aftermath of the Strathclyde disaster a few years back. Jeez, that was serious; if we hadn't nullified the fallout, it would have taken centuries for the radiation levels to return to normal. You lost a good man that day.

JS: The Flying Scotsman?
GC: That's the one. Wonder what became of his partner, Bearach...?

JS: I met him recently. I don't think he ever really recovered from the ordeal.
GC: Pity, he was a good guy. It's hard being a superhero; challenging destiny, accepting fate. Something I must do.

JS: Is there anything they can do to slow the progress down? Make you more comfortable? Chemotherapy? Drugs?
GC: They're trying, believe me, but everything they pump me with doesn't do any good. Chemo and drugs don't work – I'm resistant to everything they've got. Who'd have thought my own power would rob me of a chance of a cure? I do find myself laughing sometimes, at the irony of it all.

JS: Who else have you told?
GC: Heh. With the exception of my immediate family and the 'Crusaders, you're the first. The team have been great, letting me become part-time, offering support when they can, but I know they're stunned. I'm the first of the crew to be in this position. I think it's really rocked them to the core – I hope they can put this behind them once I'm gone. I'd hate to think of it as the catalyst to the break up of the Justice Crusade. My wife knew at the beginning. She noticed the change in my skin tone and weight. I was also fatigued but put it down to several large skirmishes I'd been involved in. Thought it was the workload catching up with me. I'd never felt like that before. But she knew...

JS: You won't be able to keep this from the media forever.
GC: I know. I'm planning to call a private press conference with all the heads of the networks and publications. I'll sit them down, with the rest of the Justice Crusade by my side, and break the bad news. Heh, they'll be speechless, which will make a nice change. I'll ask them to respect my privacy, both for my family and for the people of Detroit. I do wonder how they'll react when I tell them. Part of me hopes that they'd come up and shake my hand, thanking me for my service to the city. They owe me that much at least; I must have saved each and every one of them on at least one occasion.

JS: What about your fans?
GC: They'll be utterly devastated. Most of them have been supporters since the very beginning of my Super-S career. I don't want an endless supply of flowers and sympathy cards sent to Crusader HQ, a grim reminder to the team and myself, but it's going to happen whether I like it or not. It'll compound the fact I'm a dead man walking. I don't deserve that. There'll be plenty of time to grieve when I'm gone.

JS: I guess the big question is, how long do you have?
GC: The best they can come up with is six months. It's hard for the doctors to determine these things in Normans, let alone a 2nd Degree like me. My ability doesn't help; one minute I'll stabilize, the next the cancer is progressing again. One thing's for sure; even if I'm not up to joining the team every day, I'm going to keep working as long as I can.

JS: Why don't you just retire completely from the Justice Crusade and make the most of your time with your family?
GC: If I retired I'd waste away a hell of a lot quicker than still being one of the team. Anything's better than sitting at home, waiting for the finger of death to tap me on the shoulder, right? I'm not out on the frontlines so much – that would just be reckless, both to myself and the guys around me – but I can support them in other ways, like advising back at command post, monitoring global situations as they develop, training up some of the newbies. I can still make a difference. I may not be putting my life on the line for the public every day of the week, but a fight's still a fight, even if it's one I'm dealing with on the inside. I'm up against the greatest foe I've ever faced and even though I'm crapping myself, I can't back down. I need to keep busy, take my mind off the disease. The moment I relax, drop my guard, is the moment it takes me. I'm not going down without a fight. My family understands. They'd rather have me live longer as G-Core than waste away in front of them in some private hospital ward. That ain't the way I want them to remember me.

G-Core sighs, exhaling the last of the cigarette smoke, and throws the butt in the water. For a moment, I see the fragility in his eyes, hiding behind the bright, red mask. He looks gaunt, tired; nothing like the proud, confident man I'd seen in the photos I'd researched.

You know, when you're a superhero you're always expected to adopt an air of invulnerability, always make it look like you're in control. Sure, you live life on the edge, but you never really consider the prospect of dying. Not really. All those things I was capable of yet here I am, helpless and riddled with a disease us Super-S believe can only occur in Normans. Well, I guess there's a part of me that's more human than I think I am. Do you know I've started praying? Even before I became a 2nd Degree, I never sided with one particular faith, never *got* Religion. Yet, every night this week, I've been kneeling by my bed, my darling wife sleeping next to me, praying that when I'm taken, I'm taken quickly. I don't want to fade away in a protracted haze of hallucinations, pain and agony. After all the good I've done in my life, I deserve better than that.

JS: What will happen if you don't get your wish? If your powers won't allow the cancer to act that efficiently?
GC: I've never backed down from a fight and I won't start now, but if I get to the point where I'm a burden, either to my team-members or my family, then you never know – a few months' time and that water might become a real tempting way of making things easier.

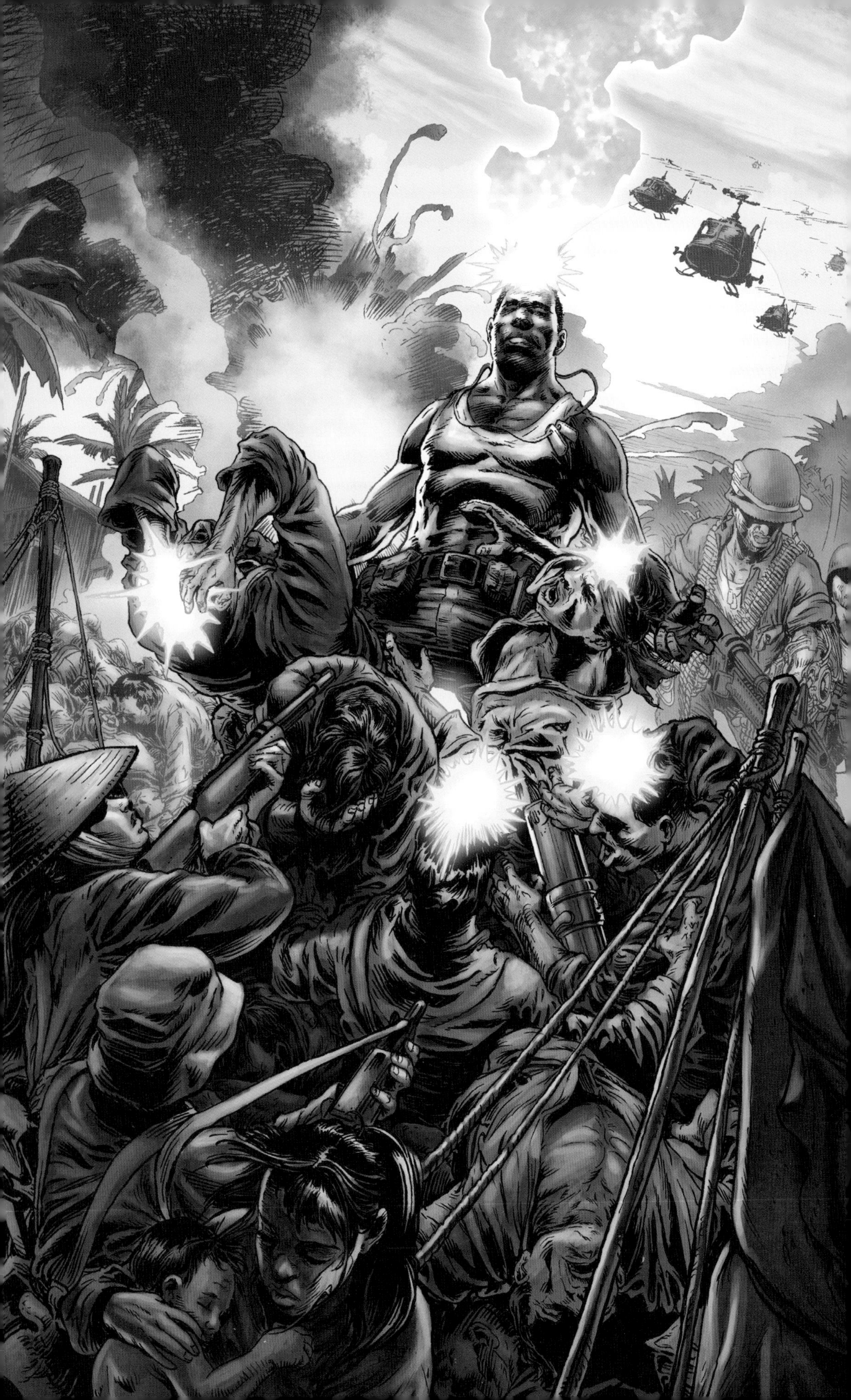

In all his adult life, fifty-nine years-old Flaky-J has never taken a vacation from his Super-S duties, so it's unusual to be sitting next to him, on a beach, taking in the ocean view on St. Lucia.

Locals and holidaymakers walk by, oblivious to the fact that there's an extremely powerful Super-S vacationing in their midst, and he's currently savouring a cold beer.

JS: For a man who declared he would never take a holiday from fighting crime, how is it that I find you in a Caribbean resort?
FJ: Heh. What can I say? Guess I came to my senses. All work, no play, and however the rest goes. I just needed a break; from my life, from everything. You fight for truth, justice and yakkity yak for most of your life, and for what? Back in the Sixties and Seventies, things were interesting and relevant; lending support for the BPP, leading the offensive against the gooks in 'Nam. I was there when the Tet Offensive broke out, assisting the frontline troops pushing Charlie back into the Mekong Delta. I was the face of the Stars & Stripes, a rally-cry for the corps. Those were good times. Made a lot of friends back then... lost a hell of a lot of them, too.

JS: How did you feel when you realised the war was lost as well?
FJ: Don't believe everything history teaches you. We made the choice to withdraw. There's a difference. Let's just say... our work there was done.

JS: But Vietnam embraced Communism?
FJ: That's right. But who said we were there at the end to fight a war? If it was a war, don't you think we would have won? No, man, we were sent in on a shopping trip; we went in to get something, or to be more specific, some*one*. And if we couldn't get it, we were to make damn sure Charlie couldn't get their hands on them. You get my drift?

Flaky-J raises an eyebrow at me and takes a swig of his beer.

JS: So, Super-S were involved? It was an extraction mission?
FJ: Now, I never said that. But you could see why we'd want to throw as much military firepower in there as we could spare, if that were the case, couldn't you?

JS: So, you discovered Super-S in Vietnam? Taking into consideration the United States initiative to quell the expansion of communist activity back then, I can see why their retrieval would become a prime objective of the war.
FJ: Yup. First of their kind over there. Only a handful mind, scattered across the country. It was Johnson's directive to get those subjects onto U.S. soil before Charlie found them and used them against us.

JS: What about those that you couldn't convince to come?
FJ: Booked on a one-way ticket to boot hill, as my great-grandpa would say. Let's just say, we had every eventuality covered.

JS: You're a 2nd Degree. How did you gain your superpowers?
FJ: I signed up for the standard corps. Turned out, I was prime material for a special division that was being put together, so I volunteered for that, too. The gene trials were a success and I came out of the incubation period ticking all the boxes. Funny thing was, based on my trials, the docs had predicted I would acquire enhanced physical attributes, but I ended up with psychological dynamics instead. Who knew?

JS: What role did you play in Vietnam?
FJ: Well, I can talk about this now because it's public knowledge; I was part of an elite, select unit sent in as frontline offensive. Once we'd made enemy contact, I'd unleash a cerebral attack on their entire company – or battalion – it didn't matter the size of the opposition; the more, the merrier. I'd work Charlie up into a mass frenzy, they'd be capping each other, pulling pins out of their own grenades, dicing each other up; saving our boys' the effort and the ammunition. The few that survived the assault would be finished off by a mop-up crew. Worked like a charm, every time. Fear was another trick I'd use. I'd create a blanket projection into an advancing battalion and have them imagining their worst nightmares. They'd be running in seconds, soiling their pants as they fled. They nicknamed me 'Agent Brown' after that. Heh.

JS: Even though you're still very active as a Super-S, you rarely make the headlines anymore. Is that intentional?
FJ: Unless it's a major event I'm involved in, I barely make a column, let alone a headline! It's certainly not intentional – I guess I'm just more of a behind-the-scenes kind of guy. Nowadays there's a lot of glamour and media pressure that comes with the job; there are way younger and more exciting heroes out there for the public to gush over, so who wants to read about a Super-S that's the same age as your pop? Still, if it means I can get on with my job without interference, then all the better. And it's kind of like being covert again, like the old days. I dig that. I haven't got a problem with anonymity.

JS: What about relationships?
FJ: Can't say it's something I'm successful at or interested in. What with the pressures of the job, I never have time to find the right girl and commit. I admire the guys and girls that do maintain relationships, even bring up kids. That takes a lot of effort when you do what we do. There was one girl I was involved with, back in 'Nam. I guess you could say she was the only girl I ever, truly loved. Lost her when a 'Cong hit-squad attacked her village while I was on a support mission in Da Nang. Bastards took the whole place apart; men, women, kids. It was a massacre. When I found them, I picked up enough residual psychic energy to be able to reconstruct the experiences the victims went through. Let me tell you, you don't wanna know what those devils did to them; it was the stuff of nightmares. But that wasn't the shocking part. I discovered my girl was two-months pregnant, with my kid.

I went AWOL after that. It took me two weeks, but I found every one of them sons-of-bitches. Tortured them for days before taking them apart with my bare hands. The Government pulled me out shortly after that; said my personal objectives were hindering the main purpose for me being there. I returned to America, spent a great deal of time in rehab then chose, in honor of her memory, to make it my life's ambition to make my homeland a better place. Been doing so ever since.

JS: I understand why you are so committed to your cause now. So this is your first vacation in over thirty years? How does that feel?
FJ: It's not a decision I've made lightly. When you know people are relying on you, it's hard to step away for a time-out, especially when you've been disciplined in the way I have. But the older I'm getting, the more I'm thinking I have to start putting myself first. Yeah, I've caught myself a couple of times on this trip checking the news channels and trawling thru websites but common sense has usually taken over and I've forced myself to go for a long walk with a cold beer. Besides, I keep telling myself, there are plenty of us out there now, they won't miss an old timer like me if I choose to take a couple of weeks of R & R, will they?

JS: Of course not. It's well deserved. Will you be making this more of a regular occurrence?
FJ: I think so. It's quite strange for me, forcing myself to not read people's thoughts or influence their actions, but it's been a healthy experience; given me a chance to be a little selfish, to just think about myself, think about my future, not think about how I can mould it for others. These bones have seen a lot of action, they take longer and longer to recover everytime I see active service. I'm taking that into consideration more.

There's a bunch of us Vets from my old unit reaching the same point in our lives, and we've been talking about a reunion. I think I'd be up for something like that, especially as I'm on my own and I don't have many friends. It'll be interesting to catch up, find out what they've been up to, exchange some numbers, stay in touch more regularly. I guess I'm re-evaluating my life having taken this break. I feel a lot more social. Like I need to take it easy, experience life some more. Hey, the way this one's working out, I might even think about retirement! Never say never. It's crossed my mind a couple of times since being here.

Artwork: Sean O'Connor - Flaky-J

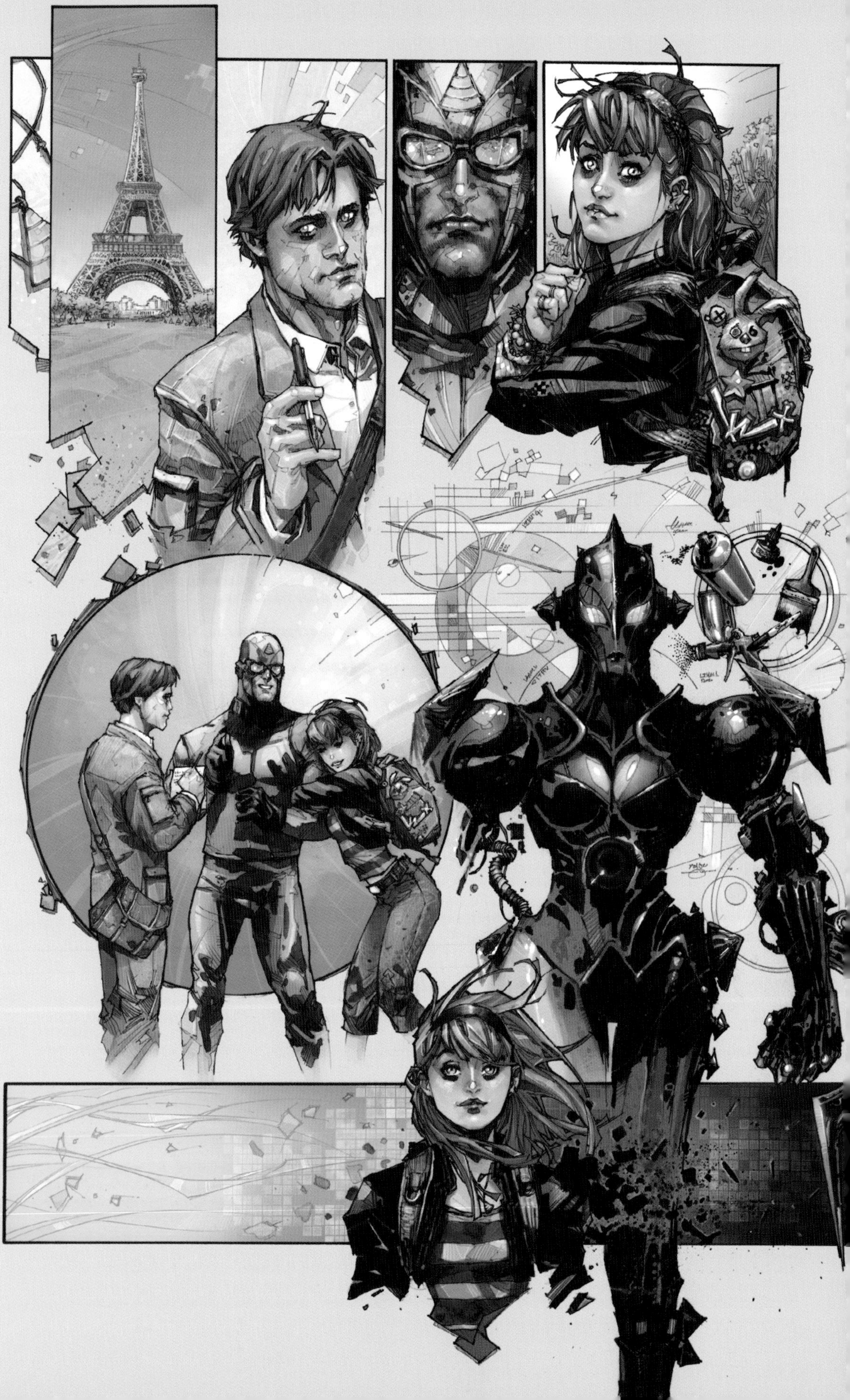

I've been granted a follow-up interview with the legendary superhero, UltraSonic, who is sixty years-old. He is the father of Hannah Hawkins, whom we last met at St. Pancras Station, London, leaving for Paris in search of her father.

I'm in a meeting room located deep in the heart of the French Defence offices, just a stone's throw from the Eiffel Tower. Opposite me stands UltraSonic. He cuts an impressive figure in his green costume and headgear. Next to him is the familiar face of Hannah, his daughter. She's wearing a huge smile on her face as she plays excitedly with the pendant around her neck.

JS: Congratulations, Hannah. When we originally met, you said you would do whatever it took to find your father. I see you stuck to your word.
HH: Ha, yeah! I remember saying I'd throw myself off the Eiffel Tower if I had to, but I'm glad it didn't come to that. I took a more obvious route; I knew Dad would have contacts high up in Interpol, so I made some enquiries and, fortunately, they were very helpful. They assigned an intermediary and, once Dad had agreed to a conciliation, it all steam-rollered from there. It was awesome!

US: Hannah certainly is resourceful. It's nice to see she shares some of my traits.

JS: It's been, what? A few weeks since you met? How are you finding life with the famous UltraSonic?
HH: It's... totally... mind-blowing! My head's still spinning trying to make sense of it all. I keep pinching myself to make sure it's real. He's nothing like mum said he was. He's just a lot more, I dunno, it sounds a bit stupid saying it out loud, but just... great! Just like his photos, but better. There's certainly a connection there, something tangible, you know what I mean?

JS: Yes. What about you, UltraSonic? How do you feel about being a father now?
US: I wouldn't say I'm a father. Not yet. I need to earn the right to have that title. I've always followed Hannah's progress but I promised her mother that I would never make contact. It was the hardest decision I ever made, one that tore me up inside every day I was away from her. I wanted to be a part of her life but I had no choice, my calling came before my family. Being an active Super-S was something Hannah's mother could never accept. It was hard leaving them both but I thought it was the best thing at the time, Now, I'm not so sure. I've missed a lot.

It's fantastic being reunited after all this time. In my heart, I'd hoped that, one day, she would want to find out who her father was and come looking for me, but I couldn't guarantee that would ever happen. Hannah was always a jpeg in a folder, a screen-grab from a security camera, to me; out of reach, unobtainable. Ironic when you think that it's usually the likes of us that are unobtainable to Normans. Hannah's resourcefulness and ambition is wonderful; I'm not going to let this opportunity slip away. Credit where credit is due, I have her mother to thank for that.

JS: Have you spent much time together?
HH: Yes, but not crime-fighting, thankfully! I think I'll leave that kind of stuff to my dad. We've been talking a lot; about my life, about his. As you can probably imagine, we both had a whole bunch of questions that needed answering, gaps in our lives that needed filling.

US: We've also been doing a lot of cultural things. Paris is beautiful this time of year and I've had great fun showing Hannah the city. I've never really spent any time doing tourist stuff since I've been here – I've always been too busy working – but it's wonderful being able to take time off and spend it with my daughter.

HH: Yeah! He's been great, too. Three weeks and I'm not even bored of his company-

US: Hey, cheeky! Your old man's not that boring... you know.

They both laugh. UltraSonic gives Hannah a hug.

JS: Obviously, UltraSonic, you'll have to go back to work soon. How will you stay in touch and how frequently will you see each other? Is it going to be difficult living so far apart?
US: Well, I've asked Hannah to come and live with me for a while, as long as she has her mum's consent. We'll be staying together in my apartment, with me in my alter-ego status, so I have to make sure Interpol organise the appropriate documents for us. I can see it now; messy rooms, boyfriends, mood swings, late nights...

HH: You wind-up merchant! You'll be the one I'll have to worry about with your late nights and missions!

US: Actually. I have a little surprise for you. I wasn't going to mention this until your eighteenth birthday but, what the hell, seeing as James is here...

HH: What surprise? Don't keep me in suspense, now that you've mentioned it!

US: Let's just say, being a well-connected superhero has its perks. What would you say about working with your old man? On behalf of the French Ministry of Defence? You'd be an Exo-S. You'd get the best martial-arts and ballistics training, along with an integration period with your suit. In fact, they're already developing a prototype for you, we just need to get you down to Bordeaux for a fitting. So, what do you say?

HH: No way?! You mean... I'm going to be like, RollCage?! Are you winding me up? Of course! That's amazing!

Hannah embraces UltraSonic.

US: Only if you're sure. I mean, it's a big responsibility.

HH: As long as it comes in black and chrome, and it's sleek and sexy, I'm totally in!

US: Well, the black, I know I can do...

JS: That's a big decision to make, Hannah. Shouldn't you take some time to think about it?
HH: Are you kidding? Oh my god, this is something I've been dreaming of ever since I found out about who my Dad was. Now I have the chance to learn from him, to be like him. We could be like a super-duo!

JS: What about your mother's opinion? Won't she be against your decision? It's going to be dangerous, you'll face scenarios that will push you beyond your limits.
US: You're right, of course this decision can't be made without talking to Hannah's mum first. I'm aware of that and respect her position in this.

HH: She'll probably be completely against the idea, but I'm almost eighteen and she has to understand that I really want this. It's about my happiness. I've always thought about a career that involves helping people and this would be an awesome way of doing that. How cool to be able to fly over to war-torn communities and deliver medical or food supplies, or use my powers to help build hospitals and schools. Dad, this is so cool! It definitely comes in black, right? Oh my god, I need to choose my name. Something classy, like The Iron Maiden, or The Noir, what do you think?

US: Hey, you need to learn by my mistakes and not choose a name you're going to regret later on, okay? Trust me, it happens! But let's just take things one step at a time, shall we? We need to talk to your mum first.

HH: Sure thing, dad. You're the best! Mum is so gonna have a fit.

US: She sure is, princess. Don't worry, she'll forgive you, in time. Me, on the other hand...

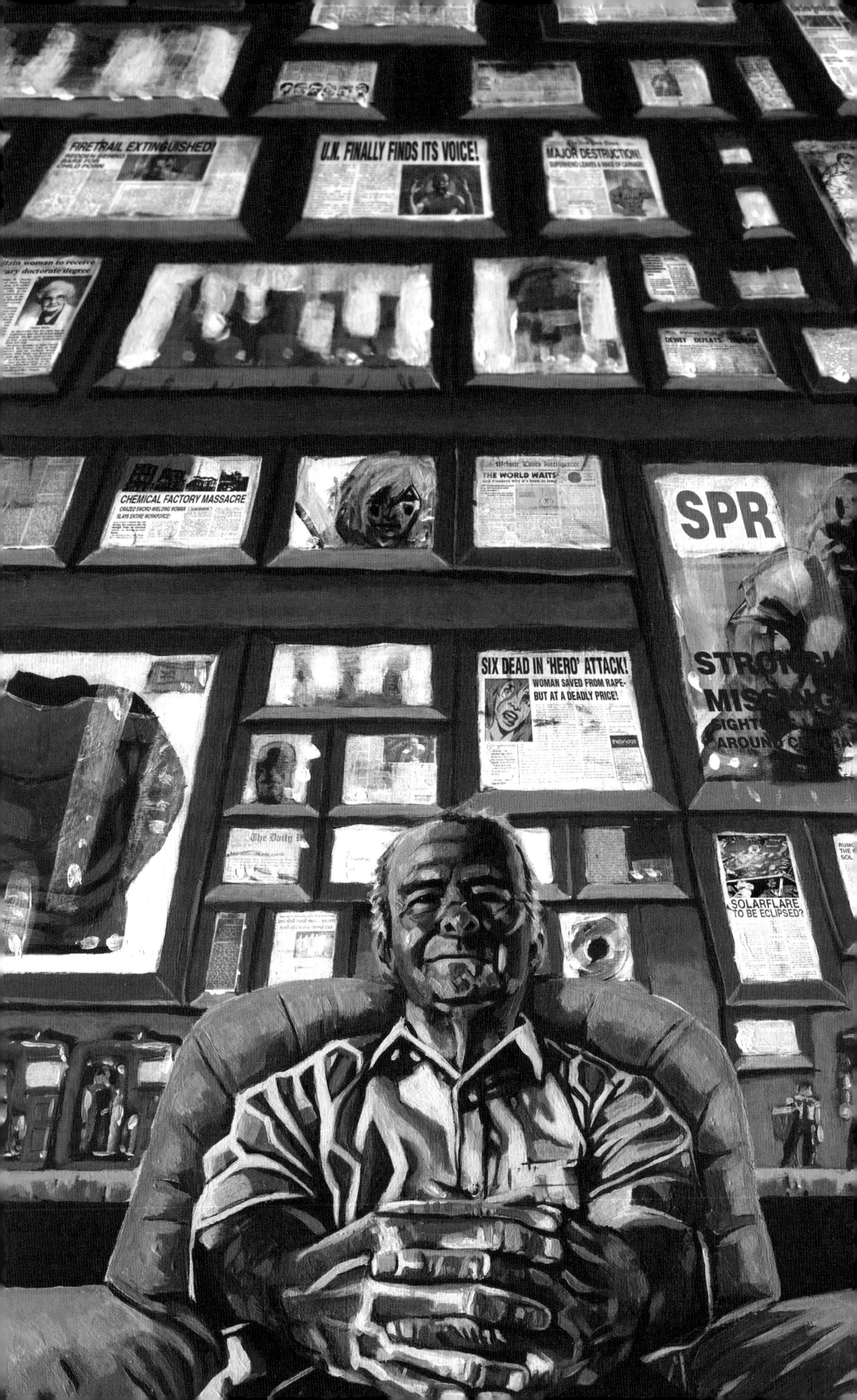

FIRETRAIL EXTINGUISHED!
U.N. FINALLY FINDS ITS VOICE!
MAJOR DESTRUCTION!
CHEMICAL FACTORY MASSACRE
CRAZED SWORD-WIELDING WOMAN SLAYS ENTIRE WORKFORCE!
THE WORLD WAITS
SPR
SIX DEAD IN 'HERO' ATTACK!
WOMAN SAVED FROM RAPE- BUT AT A DEADLY PRICE!
SOLARFLARE TO BE ECLIPSED?

At sixty-two years-old, Joe Maloney is the self-proclaimed "World's Greatest Super-S Fan". He's been collecting Super-S-related news articles, mementos and collector's items for over fifty years. He lives in Springfield, Illinois.

I'm standing in an immaculately-kept room. Every inch of wall space is dedicated to Super-S, from the past, right up to present day. It's an impressive display. There are many familiar faces I've already met; RollCage, G-Core, DarkMatter, to name but a few.

JS: You have an amazing collection, I don't think I've ever seen so much memorabilia in one place.
JM: Why, thank you. I'm pleased you know your stuff. It's been extremely time-consuming, but I've managed to keep the enthusiasm going, even through several marriages, kids and grandkids! It's certainly been a labor of love.

JS: So, what prompted you to become a collector?
JM: Why, uh... heh... me, actually.

JS: Really?
JM: Well, let me explain. You see, I haven't always been a Norman. Once, I was like them.

Joe motions to the news clippings.

A knight of the sky.

JS: You were a Super-S?
JM: 2nd Degree, actually. I was a kid. Electrical accident. I was playing with my buddies, near a power generator, ignoring the warning signs when, *zap*, I got slammed with ten-thousand volts! Woke up from a coma two-weeks later, charred and a little worse for wear with a hunk of fancy abilities for my efforts.

JS: What powers did you acquire?
JM: Really odd stuff, and not the sort of things you would immediately associate with electricity. The main power I attained was one where I could convert my body mass into thick, black, inert gas, yet still think and move as if I was still in human form. Sounds weird, but it was an incredible sensation. So, there I was, a ten year-old kid with the prospect of becoming a Super-S. Can you imagine the excitement?

JS: So at what age did you become a Super-S?
JM: Sadly, I didn't get the chance to be officially recognized as one. They kept me in the hospital, under observation, and ten days after I'd awoken from the coma, the powers just stopped working. Disappeared. No matter how much I tried to summon them, nothing happened. One day they were there, the next they weren't. For a few days though, I thought I was destined for greater things. I guess you could say, if you excuse the pun, that my dreams disappeared in a puff of smoke.

JS: How did you cope with the sudden loss of your powers?
JM: Even though I hadn't had them for long and hadn't gained full control over them, I was very upset. I became quite depressed and once I'd returned home from the hospital, I spent a lot of time in my room. I didn't even play in my own yard, let alone meet up with my pals. I felt I had been cheated out of my future, I was so angry.

JS: Did you turn to collecting as a means of getting through the darker days?
JM: You could say that's where my obsession started. Once I'd had a taste of the power, of what it must be like to be special, the collecting gave me a kind of connection to the whole fraternity, to those that had embraced their calling. It became my therapy, researching different heroes, following their adventures, cataloging their outcome. I even kept tabs on the Vaders. They're all here; those that turned and those that were born that way. I keep them as a reminder of the potential price of failure.

JS: What's your favourite piece?
JM: That's an easy one. This one, over here.

Joe stands up and walks across the room to a small, framed press clipping that sits above the fireplace. I look around. StateSide features heavily in Joe's collection; there are complete sets of action figures, boxed and sealed within glass cabinets; tins full of buttons and signed posters; VHS films; autographs; comic and graphic novel collections. There are even superhero-licenced clocks and lunchboxes and Super-S-branded candy from decades ago... all unopened and in pristine condition. Joe hands me the picture frame.

Heh. This is my favorite.

It's a very old black & white photograph of a young boy, sitting up in a hospital bed, with tubes attached to his arms and head. He is smiling, shaking hands with President Eisenhower. His parents are standing next to his bed, along with a number of important-looking gentlemen in suits. I read the faded words printed on the yellowed paper. "A FIRST FOR ILLINOIS!" proclaims the headline. "Proud parents, Mr and Mrs Maloney, look on as President Eisenhower congratulates their son, Joe, on his newly-acquired super-abilities." states the sub-heading.

Not too shabby, eh?

JS: That's very impressive.
JM: Of course, he lost interest once my powers disappeared. After a couple of months, they all did. Every now and then a suit would turn up at the family home and introduce himself. My folks would invite them in and they'd spend half an hour talking to me, finding out what I'd been up to and maybe run a few health-checks. They said they were from the hospital, but I think they were more important than that.

They dressed extremely well and had great cars. Even let me sit in them before they left. Their visits became less and less frequent until, by my sixteenth birthday, they just stopped calling altogether. I guess I had nothing to offer them once they realized my powers weren't coming back. Still, it was nice while it lasted. The first in Illinois, eh? Guess I got my fifteen minutes of fame.

JS: I can understand why it's your most prized piece.
JM: Yeah. The grand-kids always ask to see it when they come visit. I love showing them this room. They know not to touch anything, though!

Joe smiles.

JS: You do have an amazing accumulation of ephemera here. It appears to be a very well-researched, important database of Super-S activity from the past fifty years or so. Do you have any arrangements for it?
JM: Well, I'm not planning on going anywhere just yet, heh, but I do wonder what the family would make of it if I left the entire collection to them. With the exception of my most treasured piece, I don't think it holds the same, special meaning to them as it does for me. It would probably end up on some shopping channel, or on one of those internet sites people use nowadays.

I've been thinking about this for a while now and I've decided I'm going to open a museum, right here, in my hometown of Springfield. Nothing fancy, just a small place where I can put everything on permanent display to the general public. Got a lot of people interested in financially supporting me; from the local mayor and fans like myself, to investors that wish to remain anonymous. I'm going to donate the whole room. The world needs to realize how important Super-S have become and how committed to us Normans they are. It'll be good to give them a little something back.

I point to the framed newspiece of Joe.

JS: What about this one? Are you going to donate that, too?
JM: Heh. Well, everything except that one. That one I'll be keeping for myself. As my wife keeps telling me, heh, I'll probably end being buried with it and taking it to the afterlife with me. No, even though I was Illinois' first Super-S and I'm a bit of a celebrity, I'm sure they'll forgive me for keeping that one.

Artwork: Seb Antoniou - Joe Maloney

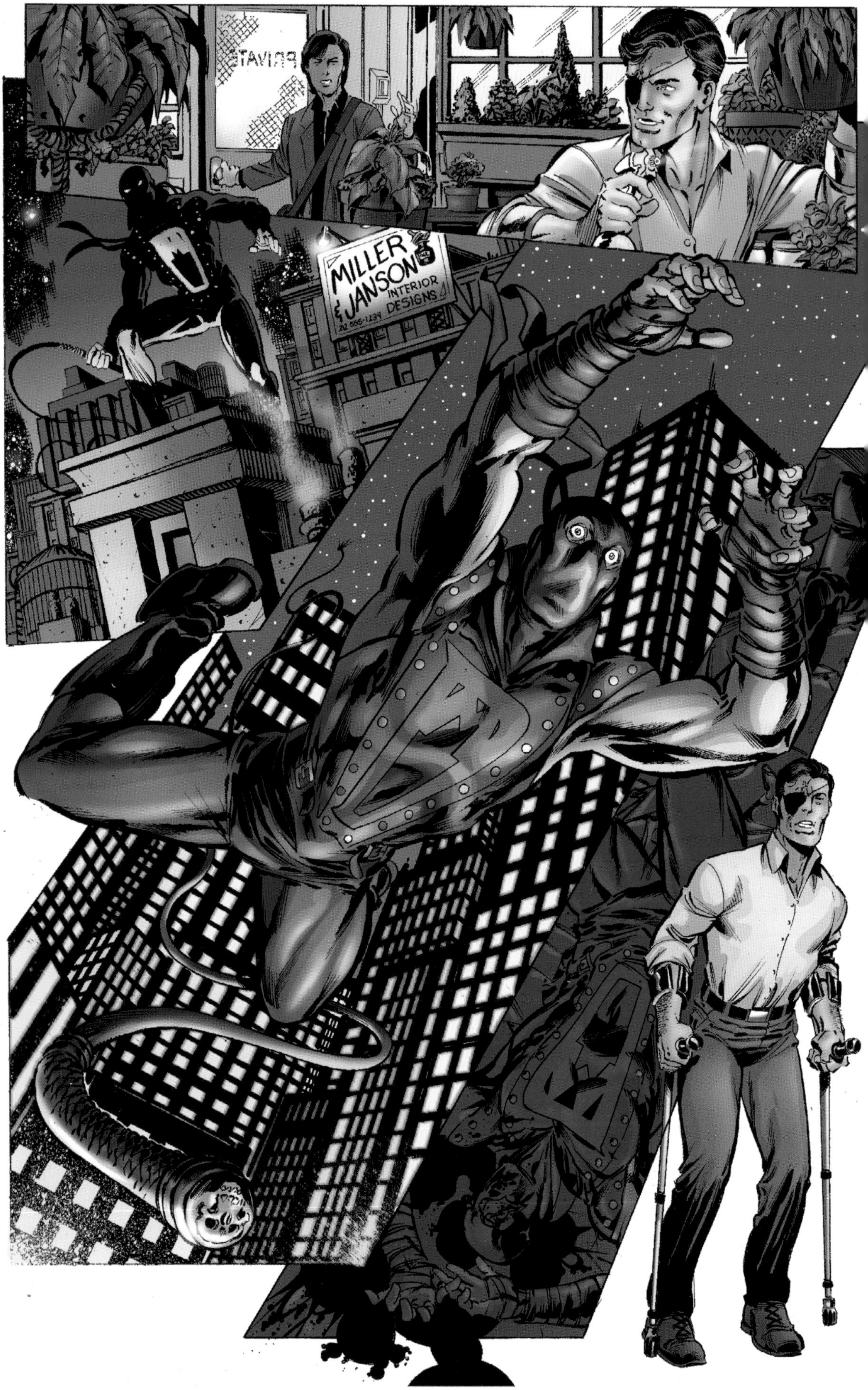
PRIVATE
MILLER
& JANSON
INTERIOR
DESIGNS

I'm standing in the garden of retired, sixty-eight year-old Max Osbourne*, formerly known as Max-Dex. Max was famous for his incredible acrobatic skills and daring, base-jumping antics. New York City was his playground, and upstate New York is now his home.

Max is tending to his plants in the atrium at his house. He greets me and invites me inside.

JS: You've been retired for, what, ten years now? Do you miss the Super-S business?
MD: Oh, most certainly. But I don't regret retiring at the age I did. Considering my skills were primarily dependent upon my endurance and dexterity, I do feel it was the right thing to do. That's not to say that it was an easy decision to make; I still felt I was youthful, adventurous but, at fifty-eight years-old, I think the only person I was kidding was myself.

Even into my late-forties, I felt on top of my game. I was very proud that I kept my fitness levels optimized and I thrived on the fact that I could still whip most of the young kids' asses when it came to straightforward battles of strength and agility. I still had that naivety you have when you're a young start-out where you have no awareness of your own mortality. I was out there, in my middle age, trying to prove I was the best, disproving the critics and the cynics. I always said that, when you're a Super-S at the top of your profession and you're reliant upon your physical attributes, there's really only one direction you can go: down. It took me a while before I listened to my own advice.

JS: Do you regret announcing your retirement in the way you did? By responding to that article in *The New York Times* that questioned your aptitude for the profession?
MD: I was never big on the whole fame thing, I was never interested in staying abreast of the media coverage, so I didn't see the piece until it was shown to me. I had been considering my options at that point anyway, so once I'd read it and they'd put forward some valid arguments, it kind of made my mind up for me. I didn't realize the public would react with such sadness and affection; you see, I'd always been a covert operator, working the streets at night and keeping myself to myself, so I didn't really think it would be a big deal, or something that would create so much attention.

I'd always seen my abilities as being more enhanced physical prowess that I had to work hard to maintain, rather than proper superpowers; far less special than, say, the gift of flight or super-strength. I never believed myself to be particularly special; just a normal guy able to do some cool things. I really didn't think it would make much difference when I chose to retire, so when I did say my farewells, I thought I'd do it quickly, without too much fuss. I guess the public didn't want to see it that way.

JS: Did you doubt your abilities as a Super-S?
MD: There's always doubt, no matter how confident you feel in your abilities, always that quiet, unnerving sense it could be your last night on earth, but stubbornness and self-confidence always prevail! I didn't fit the typical Super-S mould in the way I approached my work; I guess you could say I operated more on a vigilante level than a high-profile, government-approved one. I certainly erred on the side of caution when dealing with situations. That boiled down to acknowledging that I was fallible; I didn't have invulnerability or toughened skin to protect me if I came out worse in a scrap, all I had to rely on were my agility and wits.

That's what kept me alive and sane, no room for mistakes, and that's why I have a near-perfect track-record for saving Normans – unlike some Super-S I could mention. Oh, I've heard of heroes waking up in the middle of the night, screaming the names of the people they didn't save, haunted by their failures. Some of them have even sought professional help to recover from major incidents they've been involved in. I never looked at it like that. Once you identify your failings, it helps you cope with people's opinions of you and helps you deal with your responsibilities to society.

JS: It sounds like the world needs more heroes like you to look up to. Do you think you could be tempted back for one last swan-song? What if the Mayor requested your help?
MD: I really doubt that would happen, there are already too many heroes laying sole claim to the title Protector of the City, I don't think there's room for any more! If he did ask, I would have to politely decline; I'm happy growing old gracefully. Besides, it's been a long time since I donned the costume; the only excitement I have in life now is an infestation of aphids on my roses! No, I'm not up to the job anymore. I don't think I'd be much use to the City. My abilities are virtually non-existent now.

JS: So your powers have declined over the years?
MD: Yes, very much so. I still keep in shape and exercise regularly, but the older I've become, the more my skills have deteriorated. I'm ashamed to say, towards the end of my career, I didn't listen to my body, I listened to my ego. I found I was taking longer to recover from injuries, making silly errors when exerting myself; miscalculating jumps and landings, that sort of thing. But my stubbornness pushed me on.

JS: Nothing too serious, I hope?
MD: Well, it's not been documented, but the key factor in reassessing my career occurred when I was out on a routine patrol of the City one evening. I tried to make what should have been a very simple maneuver to jump the gap between two alleys; I miscalculated and fell, ten storeys. Thanks to my training, I managed to tuck and roll, to break my fall, but I still ended up nursing a damaged retina, a broken leg, and my right knee popped out. I was in agony. I managed to crawl behind a dumpster and change back into my civvies before calling emergency services for an ambulance. The embarrassing part was, I had to tell the medics I'd been hit by a truck to explain away my injuries. I was in recovery for months. At least it gave me time to reflect upon my situation. I was lucky to have escaped with my life. That's when I made the decision to retire from the profession gracefully, instead of ending up a mangled mess somewhere down a dark alley again or headlining the obituary section of a national newspaper because some younger, stronger supervillain had gained the upper hand on me.

JS: Speaking of bad guys, are there any out there that may still hold a grudge against you?
MD: I would have thought most of them have retired, like me, but I've heard that Hydromek is still active; he was my nemesis for twenty years or so. Boy, he must be in his late-seventies by now! You don't hear much about him, but the old guy's probably out there, somewhere, plotting my downfall. I'm glad he never discovered my alter ego or my secret hideout.

JS: What would you do if he showed up looking for you?
MD: Well, at our age, I'd hope we could resolve his issues amicably over a hearty brunch or a cup of coffee. I'd be happy to buy, of course! He should come to terms with the fact that New York won't be suffering by his hand any time soon and will still be standing, strong and proud, long after we're both worm-fodder. I'd like to think his antics are more mischievous than nefarious nowadays; like giving false directions to tourists, or skipping the fare on the subway. I hope he's at least contemplating hanging up his costume and spending quality time with any family he may have instead of concocting villainous traps, or devising elaborate bomb-plots. It wouldn't be right for him to end up in some nursing home, dribbling over his cape. Not right at all. He should be enjoying his later years, like I am. Even villains should bow out with some dignity, don't you think?

I shake Max's hand.

JS: Well, I wish you all the best. I know it was never acknowledged publicly, but privately I'd like to say thank you for everything you've done and for all those people you saved.
MD: Thank you, son, that's real nice of you to say so. It makes all those years of joint-ache, muscle pain and effort all worthwhile!

Artwork: Anthony Castrillo / Colours: Thomas Smith - Max-Dex

*Interviewee name has been changed

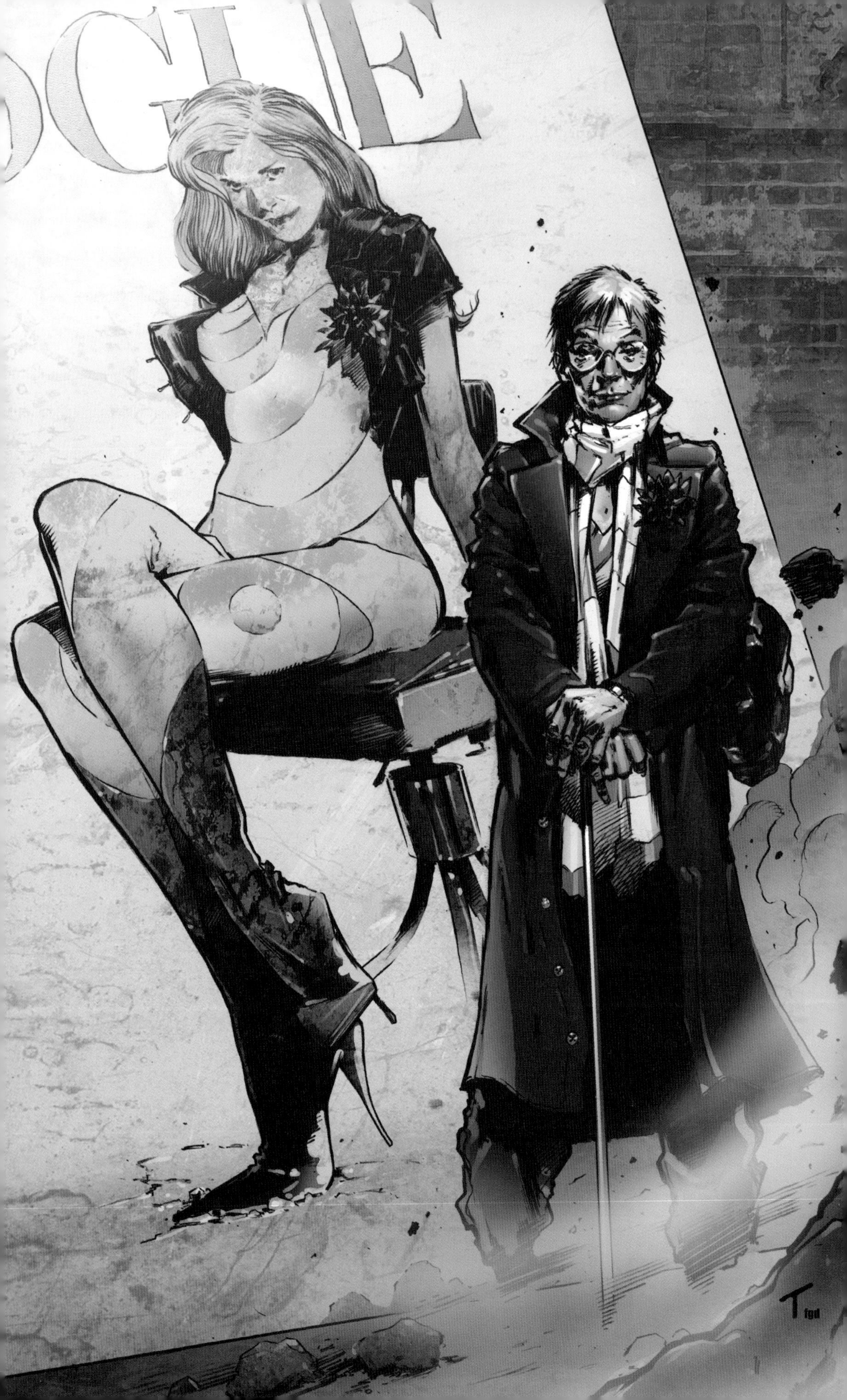

At the venerable age of seventy-four years-old, Dorothy Smithfield, aka Aftershock Girl, is one of the oldest Super-S still in active service. She's from the small village of Westcott in Surrey, England.

I'm sitting in Dorothy's living room, partaking in afternoon tea. It's hard to believe that the elderly lady sitting opposite me is the formidable Aftershock Girl. To reinforce the point, Dorothy hands me an album full of black and white photos of herself when she was younger.

JS: Wow! These photos are great. You look stunning.
AG: Oh, thank you, dear! Though, we've been through many winters since then! I loved the way I looked in those days; I always kept my hair long and could wear pretty much anything I fancied. I used to be on the cover of magazines, you know? They said I was, "The Face That Shook The World." I thought that was such a lovely thing to say.

JS: I love your costume; very old-school and refined, but extremely flattering. It certainly captures you in all the right places. Did you have trouble trying to find someone to make something like this back then?
AG: Not at all, I made all my own costumes. My mother helped – she was very good with a needle and thread. That one took almost three months to make; advancements in textiles were very hard to come by back in those days. Mother had the material shipped from Oregon. She always wanted to make sure the costumes were just right. She'd never let me go out in public in just any old thing, you know.

Dorothy smiles as I hand back the photo-album.

JS: So you're one of the oldest Super-S still on active duty. Where do you find the energy to keep going?
AG: You know what they say; you're as young as you feel! I might not look like I did in those photos but, in my mind, I still feel that age. How old are you, darling?

JS: Thirty-six.
AG: Ah, yes, when I was your age, the world was calming down a bit. It gave us Super-S a chance to relax and take a well-earned break. Although, I never got that whole hippy-thing a lot of the youngsters were into; I always liked to keep my appearance more refined and glamorous, unlike that loose, flowing, polyester stuff they used to wear. Oh, don't get me wrong, I liked the colours and the patterns, but I wouldn't have been seen dead in goat-skin! And when it was wet – oh, the smell...

Of course, then all those nasty skinheads and punk rockers started popping up everywhere and everything became anarchistic and anti-establishment. Awful hairdos. That's when things became much busier for us again. Sorry, dear, you'll have to excuse me, I'm rambling. Where were we? Ah, yes... Energy! Well, you have to keep active when you're my age, otherwise everything starts seizing up. There are also some wonderful supplements on the market for retired Super-S that I would recommend, but they are quite expensive. You can apply for government benefits to help with costs, but the tests and paperwork are horrendous. Back in my day it wasn't all about the celebrity lifestyle that these young'uns enjoy today; you certainly didn't enter the profession for the financial rewards, let me tell you.

I like to keep the old grey matter ticking over as well, keep my brain active. I read quite a lot and my grand-daughter bought me a computer, so I like to surf the internet. Lots of crosswords and sudokus help, too. The last thing you want when you have abilities like mine is dementia! Can you imagine it? It's hard enough remembering to put your underwear on, let alone how to implement your superpowers!

JS: Considering your age, how effective are your powers? Are you still battling Vaders across the rolling hilltops of Surrey?
AG: Cheeky! You know I'm too old for all that frantic stuff besides, I don't think my hip could take it. But, yes, I still have my powers,

albeit in a much reduced capacity. And when I do use them, I become quite tired and have to rest afterwards. That's why I only stay locally now, helping out in the village; neighbourhood watch, the odd, rowdy mountain-bike party, that sort of thing. Though saying that, I've recently returned from a holiday in China with the ladies from the Women's Club. We had a wonderful time.

JS: China? That's a big trip to take.
AG: Yes, I know. So many of my friends have lost their husbands, so we organise these trips to keep each other company. China was one of those places I never got to experience as a youngster, so it was lovely to be able to visit the Great Wall and the Forbidden City. Such beauty. Shame about those terrible earthquakes; so much damage and mayhem. The intensity of those shocks put even my powers to shame.

JS: Were you caught in the quakes at all?
AG: Fortunately, we ladies were staying at a hotel quite some distance from the whole affair, so it didn't affect us. I did offer my services to the authorities though, but they politely declined. I suppose the last thing they wanted was a Super-S whose powers emulated the actual disaster events becoming involved. Looking back, I would probably have been stretching myself too far if I'd helped but, even when you're my age, you can't ignore the cries for help if they're out there. That's not the way I was educated.

Take this village, for example; we had a spate of vandalism a few months ago and the town councillors asked if I could help, so I stayed up one evening to catch the buggers. It was way past my bedtime; I caught a gang of boys, no older than fifteen or sixteen, smashing car windows as they made their way down Milton Lane. I confronted them in my Aftershock Girl outfit. Well, they laughed when they first saw me; especially as my suit isn't as flattering as it used to be, although I've integrated a trenchcoat now to hide all my lumpy bits.

Let me tell you though, they weren't laughing for long. The hooligans tried to attack me – talk about no respect for the elderly – so I gave them a taste of my walking stick. Luckily, it was designed for me when I had my hip replaced, so it was extremely light and very durable. Unlucky for them, I've had fifty years of melee weapons training and the stick had become an extension of my own limbs. Oh, it was funny. I didn't even have to use my terra-disrupting abilities on them.

Their faces were an absolute picture; especially as I'd organised for a newspaper photographer to be in attendance. He captured every, single, uncompromising position! The next edition of the local paper headlined with, "Elderly Lady Teaches Yobs A Lesson". They didn't do it again. You need to stand up to these types. I can't abide rude, disrespectful people. Mind you, I'd be lying if I said I didn't enjoy that evening. It took me back a few years!

JS: How often are you called upon to help in situations now?
AG: Oh, not very often at all, now. Cats up trees have become a speciality of mine; a few shakes, they fall out and they're as good as gold. I can't say the same thing about one of the local tom cats though – the little devil keeps popping into my garden and doing his business in my perennials!

Dorothy looks through the window, out into the garden.

Ooh. "Speak of the Devil and He shall appear." I'm sorry, we'll have to end the interview here. I need to go teach a cat a few toilet manners. Then, I'm afraid, I have friends coming 'round for our weekly Bridge meeting. I hope you don't mind letting yourself out.

Dorothy picks up her walking stick and shuffles into the garden. Seconds later, a small tremor rumbles through the floor of the house. The tea in my cup ripples and a framed photograph sitting on the sideboard falls over. I walk across the room and pick it up. It's a picture of Aftershock Girl, X, and a young, attractive woman; all looking very close, almost like a family unit. I feel slightly unnerved knowing there's a lot more to this lady than she's letting on...

Artwork: Trevor Hairsine / Colours: Frank D'Armata - Aftershock Girl

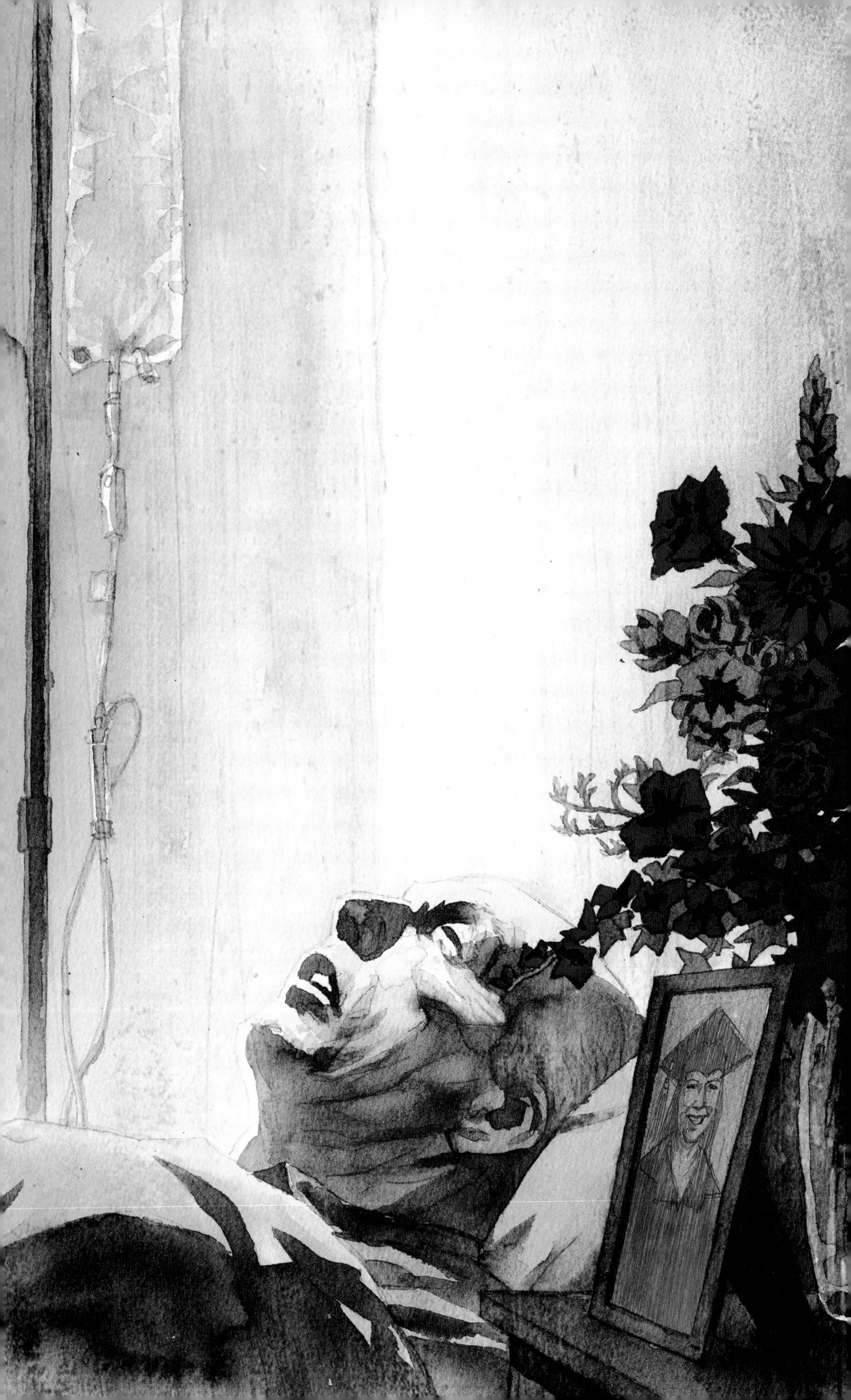

Eighty-seven year-old StateSide lies in a hospice, somewhere in the leafy outskirts of Washington D.C. The epitome of an iconic superhero; StateSide served his country with honour and distinction, a true defender of the people. Now, wired to heart monitors and attached to intravenous drips full of pain relief, his body is failing.

I'm in a private room in the hospice watching StateSide sleep, his chest rising and falling with each laboured breath. Hundreds of cards from well-wishers across the country adorn the private room. He stirs and blinks, trying to focus on me.

JS: Hello, sir. I'm James Stanley. I spoke with your grand-daughter about the possibility of a short interview with you? If it's too much trouble, I can come back another time?
SS: Hello, son. Yes... I remember... No, no, it's fine. Could you pass me some water please?

I pour a glass and help him raise it to his lips. He takes a sip and lays back on his pillow.

SS: Thank you... What would you like to know? I hope you want to talk about the past, because the future's not looking too peachy...

StateSide manages a feeble laugh through his coughing and spluttering.

JS: Are you in much pain?
SS: It's a different kind of pain to the one you're thinking about, my boy. Unfortunately, the morphine doesn't numb that kind of hurting. I should know, they've pumped enough drugs into me to down an elephant these past few hours and it isn't going away. No. Failure. That's what hurts most. When you try your best and it just isn't good enough... Civilians... Family... You try and create a balance between both but you always end up letting one of them down.

JS: I don't think anybody would say you let them down. You were an icon; always maintaining an air of dignity in everything you did and the way you handled your affairs. Your support towards the end of the Second World War was absolutely essential in boosting the morale of the Allied troops. You've been an incredible influence on modern society.
SS: Heh... There's no special secret to my success; just good, old-fashioned honor and bravery. The public admired me because I kept a low profile and did my job. I didn't do it for the smiles and the gratitude, I did it because I believed I was making a difference. If, in all my years, I've been a positive influence on just one person, I'll die a happy man.

JS: XoDOS tried to recruit you on a number of occasions, but you turned them down. Why was that?
SS: By the time XoDOS was officially established, I was well into middle-age. They had plenty of enthusiastic, younger Super-S waiting to join their ranks, what would they want with an old-timer like me? Anyway, I didn't totally approve of their attitude – just had this gut feeling about them. And like any good Super-S, I always went with my gut.

JS: I've heard they didn't take too kindly to your rejection.
SS: Maybe not, but there was nothing they could do about it. I'd said "no" and that was my final word on the matter. They didn't dare retaliate; I had an entire nation of supporters behind me. Offend me and they would have had the tax-paying public to answer to. No, they didn't want to get involved in anything like that, not when they were drumming up support and funding for the organization through the various political channels. Hats off to them though – devious bastards that they were – they used my media coverage to promote their own heroes and the pro-Super-S programs they were initiating.

StateSide coughs violently.

JS: Going back to your career, you never knowingly took a single life in all your active service. That's exceptional in your line of work and something to be very proud of. Is there anything you wished you'd done? Anything you haven't achieved?
SS: Not that I can think of, no. It's all about the Oath, you see? About how much of a contribution you want to make to society and the morals and aspirations that come with that decision. I'm not just talking about Super-S here, young man, I'm talking about the significant benefits *every* human being can make to this world, if only they put their hearts and minds to it. I've been fortunate in that I've been blessed with a gift and a public platform from which to voice my opinions, but it's within every person's grasp; every living soul has the capacity to improve the environment in which they live. Even the bad guys.

StateSide begins to cough more frequently. The heart monitor next to his bed drops to 54 BPM.

Boy, you just can't imagine how fulfilling a public role like mine can be. Take these cards here; this is just a selection that the nurses have put on display from the thousands I've received since I've been hospitalized. Who do you think they're from?

JS: Your fans and well-wishers?
SS: Heh... Some of them. But about eighty percent are from people I've saved. *Saved.* How great is that? Each one, a note of thanks, a show of support and a prayer of hope... for me. The feeling I have when I look at all these; you can't buy that kind of sensation. I just... just wish... wish that Sarah, my daughter, could understand. Then she'd know why I did it, why I had to spend so much time away from the family. She... hasn't visited yet. I was hoping... in some way, my situation would prompt a reconciliation. My grand-daughter, bless her, keeps on at her Mom to visit. She hasn't yet, but I'm still hoping...

StateSide coughs again. His heart rate drops to 41 BPM.

I... *was* a good man, wasn't I? I didn't let you down? I tried my best, you know... always tried my best. Do you think I was a good Dad? I tried my best... I'm sorry if I let you down...

JS: You have nothing to be sorry for. So many people owe you so much for what you've done over the years. The last thing you should be feeling is regret.
SS: Regret...? I do feel regret, you know. I regret that I don't have more time. I just wish I had a little more time. I could have... I could have saved more...

StateSide's heart-rate drops to 30 BPM and he closes his eyes. His breath becomes laboured and raspy. I press the alarm button and a male nurse enters the room. He takes a blood sample from StateSide's arm and checks his pulse.

Nurse: He's slipped into a coma. He doesn't have long now. I've made him as comfortable as possible. Please, keep talking to him; even though he's unresponsive, he can still hear you. It helps comfort them when they've come this far.

I hold StateSide's hand. He replies by subtlely squeezing mine. Despite his age and condition, I can still sense an incredible power within him. His breathing slows even further.

JS: Sir, I've only just met you, yet I've known of you my entire life. Trust me when I say, you've been an inspiration to so many people, including myself. I want to take this opportunity to thank you from the bottom of my heart, on behalf of an entire population, for everything you've done. You are chivalry incarnate. No one could possibly ask anymore of you than what you've already given. If there is a God in the heavens, he is keeping a special place for you by his side. Know that you're not alone in your next journey. You will never be alone. Trust me when I say, America is with you, the World is with you. And that means Sarah is with you.

With those final words, StateSide loosens his grip and breathes one final, long breath. The nurse returns and smiles, sympathetically. I know he's fought his last battle. As a nation mourns a true hero I hope, somewhere in the midst of their numbers, a daughter is mourning her father.

Artwork: Dom Reardon – StateSide

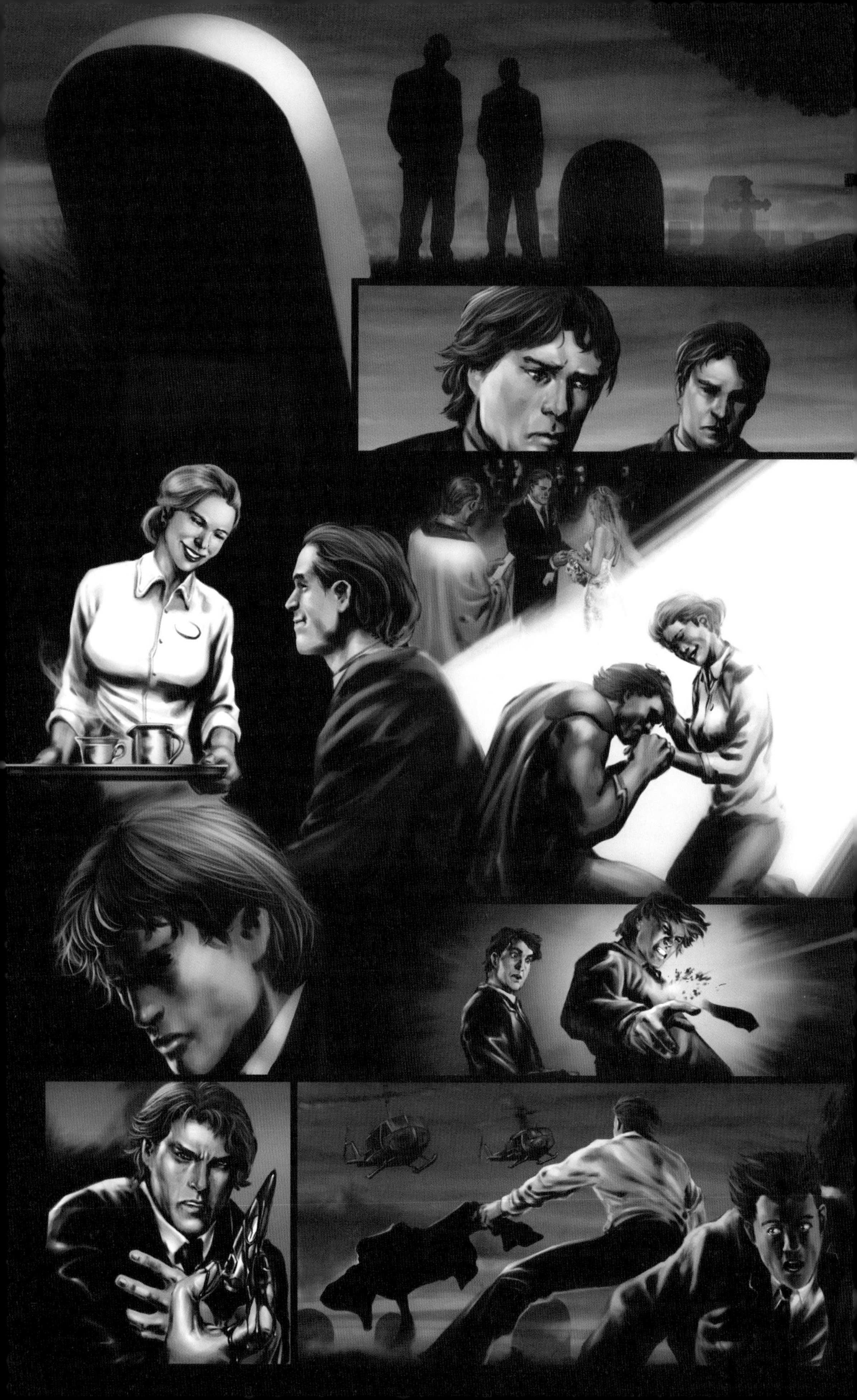

Saint Francis Cemetery, Kansas. The headstone reads:

Gillian Laidlaw*
Beloved Wife. 1985-2009
She found her path was growing steep,
so God came down and said to her "sleep"

SkyLine and myself stand in silence, staring at the grave in front of us. He's here to pay his last respects to the woman he's loved for the past three years.

SL: I've never been able to get used to outliving the people closest to me.

SkyLine was born, not only with the power of super-strength and flight, but with the gift of immortality – a bitter-sweet attribute, he tells me. As we stand here, mourning the passing of his wife, I'm suddenly very aware of my own mortality.

JS: I'm sorry for your loss...
SL: Thank you. I knew this day would come, but I still feared going through the grieving process again and starting over. Do you know what's so ironic about this situation? I loved Gillian so much I would have died for her. How is that possible? How can you love someone that much yet know that, even if you were put in the situation, there's no way physically you could make the ultimate sacrifice? My immortality – the greatest gift I could ever have been given; never falling ill, never growing old, invulnerable to harm and yet, for my physical imperviousness, I suffer emotionally like no other human being ever could.

JS: How old are you?
SL: In years, I'd put my current age at one hundred and fifty-six, although I don't know for certain exactly how old I am as I have been plagued with amnesia since I awoke from a coma in 1878, in a hospital bed in Boston City Hospital. The doctors estimated I was about twenty-five when I came to and I haven't aged a day since. That's how I arrived at that calculation. Prior to that I have no recollection of who I was or where I came from. I've been trying to uncover my past ever since.

JS: How did you discover your abilities?
SL: I was very weak when I awoke but, over the subsequent days, my powers of strength and flight appeared relatively quickly. But, I did not realize I was immortal for a long time after; I fell in love with Margaret May*, the nurse who tended to me when I first turned up at the hospital. We married two years to the day after I was admitted. She was twenty-one. It wasn't until many years later that we realized something wasn't quite right. We had always joked that the years had been kind to me, but when you're a forty year-old that still looks as young as he did the day he woke up on the ward, you've got to have an inkling that something isn't quite right.

Initially, Maggie maintained she was the luckiest girl in the world, what with having an ageless, strapping man for a husband, but as the years drew on, I saw the envy in her eyes when the younger women would stare at us in the street and make comments. She chose to distance herself from me and eventually, we parted ways. Maybe it was for the better – I did not feel the need to grieve as much as I have done over these last few weeks. For all the enemies I have encountered throughout the centuries, loneliness is my nemesis; it haunts me, eating away at my sanity.

JS: Is it such a bad thing to find someone to share your life with?
SL: Not from a Norman's perspective, no, but when you've been in this situation on numerous occasions before, as I have, the disadvantages become apparent. The ache I feel in my heart is the only concept I have of what physical pain must feel like. Immortality is a cruel twist of fate; my powers border on omnipotence, yet I am allowed to experience the love of another person, almost as a reminder that, even if it is through the pain of losing someone, some little part of me is still Norman. It would be better if I could fight the urge, to deny myself the joy and passion of loving someone, but I've long given up trying. It seems to be my destiny.

JS: I can't imagine what it must be like to love someone, knowing that you'll eventually lose them, no matter what you do to try and prevent it happening. Something that is just so... inevitable.
SL: And when they're gone it's even worse. I met Gillian when she was twenty-two. We fell in love the moment our eyes met across the restaurant; she was working as a waitress and I was a customer, dressed as a Norman, of course. We began talking and we clicked straight away. I asked her on a date. We were married within six months. It was sublime; a textbook romance. Little did I know it would also be a textbook tragedy.

JS: Did you reveal you were a Super-S?
SL: On her twenty-fourth birthday. But it wasn't planned as some kind of special, unique surprise; I did it because she'd been diagnosed with cancer. And it was terminal. To hear those words from one so young, was... numbing, to say the least. I was so used to watching my partners age gracefully over the years, giving me time to prepare for that fateful moment, and here I was with the woman I loved, who had but months to live. Destiny was even denying me a relationship that should go the natural term. So unfair. I owed it to her to tell her, so that we could share those precious few months we had left together in trust and love.

JS: How did she take the sudden revelation?
SL: She was extremely receptive. She had known of my secret for some time, yet had never let on that she did. She reasoned that the day I did confide in her was the day she knew I truly loved her. She attested that, of all the gifts I could bestow upon her, of all the experiences we'd shared together; to have spent but a fraction of my life with her was the greatest honor anyone could ever make. She knew how important and valuable the gift of time was. To all of us. It sounds ironic, but she was unlike any woman I'd ever met. She was quite... wonderful.

SkyLine crouches down and places his hand on the recently-dug soil.

SL: Goodbye, my love. I'll never forget you... Now, if you'll excuse me, Mr Stanley, I have a few more respects to pay whilst I'm here.

JS: A few more?
SL: Yes. All my wives are buried here.

I watch SkyLine walk away. He suddenly looks up, shielding his eyes from the setting sun. A heavy, chopping sound interrupts the silence as three Hueys appear over the tree tops. A red dot appears on SkyLine's jacket and a bullet hisses by, ploughing into his chest. He staggers backwards and stares down at the dark, wet, crimson pattern forming on his pocket.

JS: What the...?! I thought you were indestructible!
SL: So... did I. Looks like... someone's R&D department has... been working... overtime.

JS: Who would do this? An old enemy?
SL: XoDOS. They've never stopped... they want me... want my immortality. You have to... get out of here... now!

JS: But... that bullet?

A red spot appears on my lapel. Another on my arm. And another.

SL: I said NOW!

SkyLine pulls me towards the cover of the trees. A hail of bullets rip into the earth around me.

SL: How DARE you defile the sanctity of my family!

In an instant, he leaves the ground, hurtling through the air towards the helicopters. He punches through the fuselage of one, sending it spiralling to the ground, just beyond the gates of the cemetery. I hear a brief, solitary scream from SkyLine as he lands in the open doorway of the second unit until everything audible is drowned out by a massive explosion. I run, turning briefly to see a plume of black smoke rising from behind the trees. I continue running and don't look back again.

Artwork: Carlo Pagulayan - SkyLine

*Interviewee names have been changed

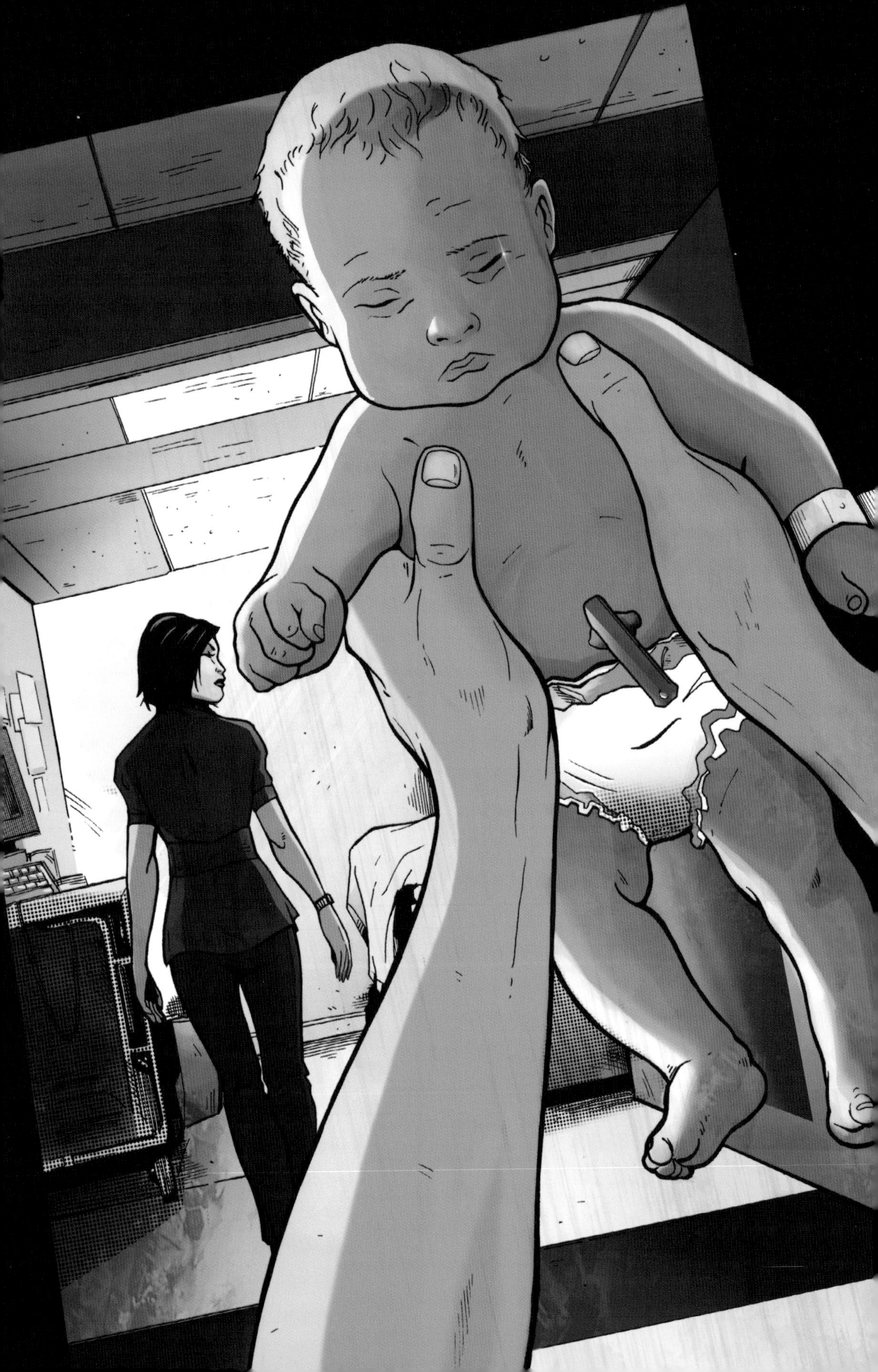

I've forgotten how long I've been sitting here now, waiting for news on my wife and child. The delivery room had been relatively calm. That is, until we heard that ominous word; complications. My wife had started bleeding. Badly. They call it a placentural abruption. It meant both my wife and my baby – our baby – were in trouble. The doctor wanted my consent to perform a C-section. The situation was too serious for a local anaesthetic, so they insisted it must be general. They assured us it would be quicker and easier that way. I looked at my wife in panic. I could tell as she looked back at me that she wanted the baby out, wanted to hold it in the safety of her arms. I gave my consent. In an instant, there was a flurry of activity as the medical team whisked her away to the operating theatre. I looked at her for a fleeting moment as they wheeled her through the doorway and mouthed the words, "I love you", although it never means enough in moments like that. She looked at me and then, she was gone. As quickly as the room had filled with people, so it was empty again, my only reminder of her ever being there was a pool of her blood on the delivery room floor. Flashbacks of my experience with Zip and Kate plagued my mind. I tried to banish the thought; it wasn't needed here, I needed to stay positive.

After what could be hours or days (time really has no relevance to me at this point) my immersion in my thoughts is broken by the midwife entering the room. My fears are allayed as she hands me a small, white bundle of blankets and congratulates me on the birth of my son. A boy! She asks if we have chosen a name for him yet and I tell her, Zack. A lovely name, she enthuses. I think so, too; at this moment in time, nothing about him is less than wonderful! After reassuring me that Mum is also doing well and promising to return soon, the midwife leaves me with my son.

I stare in awe as I cradle his tiny features, peaking out of the swaddling; like the most precious gem, protected from damage by the folds of a velvet cushion. I feel somewhat helpless as he yawns and attempts to feed off his blanket. How important a mother's presence is at this time in a baby's birth. We both miss my wife. Yet, I smile, comforted by the bundle of joy I hold; so small, so fragile, so perfect. Whether my son is a Super-S or not, at this moment in time, in my eyes, he's the most incredible, exceptional human-being that has ever existed.

Super-S? With that thought, realisation dawns upon me and I'm quickly grounded in reality. Fear replaces euphoria. Recalling the surprise on Michael and Felicity Brown's face when they gave birth to their son, The Legend, I find myself holding Zack very tightly, wondering if he'll suddenly levitate. Ridiculous as that sounds, I chuckle to myself, yet as I try to make light of the situation, I realise I have no idea what, if any, power lurks hidden within his fragile frame. I unfold his blanket. There are no obvious external marks, no outward clue to his future potential. I breathe a small sigh of relief yet at the same time, I am consumed by despair.

I had been searching all this time for answers to the question, "What if my child was born with superpowers?" and suddenly here we are alone, just the two of us. Even after the recent events surrounding my incredible interview with SkyLine and his subsequent disappearance, I find myself more afraid than I have ever been. If Zack is a Super-S, it's inevitable that They will come for him. She will come for him. From what I've been told and from what I've surreptitiously uncovered, They won't accept 'no' for an answer, especially from me. Naively, I have put my family and my son's future at risk. I don't want my son to be a Super-S if I could potentially lose him to an organisation like XoDOS, or to the pressures and demands of a critically-demanding public. From my interviews it's clear; for every positive contribution a Super-S can make to society, they will be faced with an equally opposite negative.

I don't want my family rounded-up and housed in an S-Zone, forced to integrate into a community until XoDOS decide to reveal their master plan; waiting for the day they can use my son as a weapon for their twisted, misguided, machiavellian beliefs. So many risks. So much unhappiness. But then, I recall the honour of meeting heroes like StateSide, who have dedicated their entire lives to serving the human race; right until the end. If it weren't for their tenacity and spirit the world would be a far darker place. Even us Normans can learn from the way they address themselves and the pride and commitment they project. Suddenly, I feel humbled and ashamed; I expect so much from my child, yet there is so much room for improvement in my own life and the way I conduct myself. As a father, it is my duty to lead by example, to give Zack

someone to look up to, someone who should be his primary role model. I stare at his innocent, emotionless face. He's my responsibility until he's old enough to decide otherwise. It's my obligation to be the father he deserves and needs. You don't need special powers for that.

If he's a Norman, he'll be free of the XoDOS grasp, their inevitable influence; he can grow up in a world where he can look to the skies with fascination, not down from it in pity. Yet I wonder, what future would he face if XoDOS does carry out it's threat of world domination? I could still lose my son, as a casualty of war instead of as a piece on the chessboard. I'm afraid for his future, whether he be Super-S or not.

I have to act, do something. Mr Doe said it was up to me to let the world know. I know it means becoming a target, a thorn in their side, but it's not about me, not even about my son; it's for all the sons, for all the daughters, and their children. For humanity's sake I need to do something. Me, a Norman. With no exceptional ability other than a resolute determination not to fail. What I wouldn't give right now for super-strength. Or speed. But first, I need to make sure my family are safe, away from prying eyes, away from XoDOS. And that commitment starts now.

As I carefully lay Zack back down in his cot, there's a gentle knock at the door. A pretty nurse enters the room, carrying a folder.

Nurse: I just popped by to see if everything is okay. How's the little one?
JS: He's doing fine.

The nurse walks to the cot and gently pushes the swaddling back from around his face.

Nurse: Hello, gorgeous, what's your name then?
JS: He's called Zack.

Nurse: Hello, Zack. You're a special little fellow, aren't you? Who's going to grow up and make his daddy proud?

JS: How's my wife?
Nurse: She's fine. You should be able to see her soon as she's just being moved from the recovery room to the ward. How are you holding up? You must be tired?

JS: Shattered but at the same time, running on natural adrenaline! It kind of pales in comparison when you think about what my wife and son have just been through though.

Nurse: Well, try get some rest and look after the little one. He seems to be doing absolutely fine. I'll come back to check on you again soon.
JS: Will do. Thank you.

The nurse smiles and leaves. Seconds pass and our midwife re-enters the room.

Midwife: How are we doing, Mr Stanley?
JS: Good, thank you. The nurse said Zack's doing well.

She hesitates and looks at me, quizzically.

Midwife: What nurse?

JS: The pretty one; with long, dark hair. She just left.
Midwife: You must be mistaken. There are no nurses on the ward yet. I'm the only one on duty.

JS: No. She was here a minute ago, checking on Zack. I saw her.
Midwife: No-one's been in to see him yet. I was just coming in to do that myself. The other staff aren't due for another half an hour. What's wrong, Mr. Stanley...?

It can't be. She can't be here. Not unless... fearing the worst, I turn and rush over to Zack's cot. He's still there. Relief. I pick him up. As if to reassure me, he opens his eyes and stares straight at me. And our souls connect for the very first time.

The Vault

The following pages include additional art, interviews and concept sketches. Enjoy.

Interview with James Stanley that appeared in Forth Magazine (September 2009).

Interview that appeared in Varoom Magazine (November 2009). Varoom magazine published a PR piece themed as a James Stanley 'rejection' interview featuring a Super-S called 'Hawaiian Slammer', originally intended as transcript #12. Art by Gus Vazquez, colours by Tom Chu. Nov 2009.

Alternative page art for interview #5 by Bob Wiacek

Alternative page art for interview #5 by Alvin Leigh

Amy Turner concept sketch by Jock

Concept sketches by Dan Brereton, Randy Green, Sally Hurst, Rufus Dayglo

Simon Bakersfield concept sketches by Andie Tong

Katrin Dupuis study by Steve Sampson

Katrin Dupuis concept sketch by Steve Sampson

BlueSpear concept sketches by Calum Alexander Watt

Concept sketches by Neil Edwards, Kenneth Rocafort, Robert Atkins

Concept sketches by Fiona Staples, Bob Wiacek, Kit Wallis

Concept sketches by Anthony Castrillo, Eduardo Francisco, Frazer Irving

Concept sketches by Ross Dearsley, Boo Cook

Twister and DarkMatter concept sketches by Barry Spiers

The Annex concept sketches by Gary Erskine

Concept sketches by Admira Wijaya, Dave Ryan, Kevin Kobasic, John Higgins

Flaky-J concept sketch by Sean O'Connor

Hannah Hawkins and UltraSonic character studies by Andrew Wildman

Turncoat concept sketch by Ben Oliver

Concept sketches by Matt Timson, Carlo Pagulayan, Tim Vigil

Concept sketches by Seb Antoniou, Dan Boultwood, Rodin Esquejo, Simon Coleby

Aftershock Girl concept sketch by Trevor Hairsine

The Lotus character study by Calum Alexander Watt

BlueSpear character study by Calum Alexander Watt

I'm watching the world go by from my table in a quieter part of Soho, London. It's not often I find myself nervous before an interview; years of journalism prepares you for most things. But this time, I'm the one who's being interviewed.

I turn back to look at the young woman sitting at my table. Her name is Angela Dace; she smiles politely, tapping her pen on her writing pad. She takes a sip from her americano before writing my name on the top of the page followed by a number: James Stanley. 45.

JS: I'm not that old!
AD: Excuse me? Oh, yes! Funny. Thanks for agreeing to the interview today. To be honest, I wasn't sure you'd be up for it, it's strange for me to be interviewing a fellow-journalist.

She shifts uncomfortably on her chair, brushing the hair from her face. How old is she? Twenty-two? Twenty-three? I suddenly feel quite old.

AD: Okay, let's start at the beginning; can you tell me about yourself and the nature of this "45" project?
JS: I'm James Stanley, a freelance journalist, who isn't 45 yet. I've been a fan of superheroes for as long as I can remember. It's my interest in their world that has brought me to where I am today. "45" will be a series of forty-five interviews with those individuals that have been gifted with the Super-S gene or those that have developed a super-power later in life – what's called a 2nd Degree. I assume you've done your research and know already that my wife is expecting our first child?

AD: Yes, congratulations to you both. Was it her pregnancy that inspired the idea of the forty-five interviews?
JS: In part, yes. But it was really after we declined the "Super-S" test that the idea really began to take shape.

AD: The *Hale-Criterion*, you mean?
JS: Yes. The test designed to determine whether an unborn baby possesses the Super-S gene that activates at birth, enabling the child to evolve physically and/or mentally far beyond the range of a normal human's abilities. It's extremely rare, of course, but it had me wondering – what if my child was born with such faculties?

AD: What are you hoping the reader to garner from these interviews?
JS: I'm trying to interview Super-S from all walks of life and age-groups. I'm hoping my book affords the reader an insight into what it's like to not only live life as a Super-S, but also what it's like to live WITH one.

Before I conducted any interviews I'd have said a Super-S should aspire to be a legend in their own lifetime, adored and revered, successful and famous, feared by the wicked, loved by the good. I've discovered over the last few months that it's not as simple as that. My interviews are not just with those with the Super-S gene that have '*made it*', but they're also with those who haven't. So it's not really a series of interviews with "superheroes", per se. They're not necessarily all heroes - that's for the reader to decide.

AD: I see. So what sort of people have you met?
JS: Everyone, from proud parents at the birth of their newborn baby, through to teenagers with super-abilities struggling to define their own identities. I'm hoping to encompass the entire spectrum of age-groups, to truly understand the life-cycle of an individual with extraordinary powers. This isn't as straightforward as you may think.

AD: What do you mean?
JS: Well, for starters, say you've decided to become a superhero – what's your superhero name going to be?

AD: SuperGirl?
JS: Not possible! Taken already. Now, try thinking of one that isn't already taken by a comic publisher; one that a true superhero can own without infringing copyright.

Angela is stumped.

JS: Not easy, is it? Now throw in puberty, pushy parents, family breakdown or, for example, dating - how do you explain your double-life or ability? What about superheroes that want children of their own? How do they cope? It's not just about wearing a cape or mask and adopting a persona; it's about what's under the costume that's just as important.

AD: So why "45"? What's the significance with the number?

I can't resist a wry grin.

AD: Did I say something funny?
JS: Just a private joke I have with my editor. There is a reason why it's called "45" but to explain now would be unfair. You need to read the interviews yourself to work it out.

AD: You're approaching the way you document your interviews in transcript form, right?
JS: I wanted to approach the project from a unique angle; the people I'm talking to need to be heard. I wanted to give them the appropriate conduit; I think the readers will appreciate that. By leaving the interviews in transcript form, there's nowhere for the truth to hide. There's something you may not be aware of; I'm aiming to pair each interview with an illustration, drawn by one of the many talented comic book artists from around the globe. I think it'll be a memorable way of capturing the moment.

AD: It sounds very ambitious. What does your wife make of the project? Wouldn't your time be better spent preparing for the birth of your baby and supporting her through the various stages of her pregnancy?
JS: She's being very supportive. She agrees that this is something that shouldn't be ignored. The timing was never going to be great but it is both critical and relevant to the book. When I'm out of the country, we communicate daily. If there were any cause for concern, I'd be on the first flight or train back to be with her.

AD: How many interviews do you have left?
JS: I have a trip to New Zealand and Japan scheduled, then it's back to the States. I didn't realize there would be so much travelling involved. Oh, to be able to fly!

AD: Who is publishing the book? Have you approached one of the nationals?
JS: I doubt a national would be able to publish the amount I have to tell in one go. I have a publishing deal with an independent company called Com.x. They understand what I'm trying to achieve with "45" and are very excited by it.

AD: When is it scheduled for release and where will people be able to buy it?
JS: Pending delivery of the final few pages of art, we are scheduled for a December 2009 release. It will be available anywhere comic books are sold; comic stores, online stores, bookstores, etc.

The alarm on my phone rings.

JS: Sorry, you'll have to excuse me, I have another interview with a Super-S scheduled here in London which I have to attend.
AD: Well, James, thank you so much for your time. I hope our readers will be intrigued to see the finished book.

AD: One more final question before you go. Are you hoping for a Super-S or a normal baby?
JS: Right now, we'd just be happy with healthy... anything else we'll leave to fate.

As I stand to leave, I glance at her interview notes. She hasn't written anything beyond my name and the title "45" at the top of the page. She catches me staring.

AD: Don't worry, I have an *exceptional* ability for recalling these things...

She flashes a knowing grin.

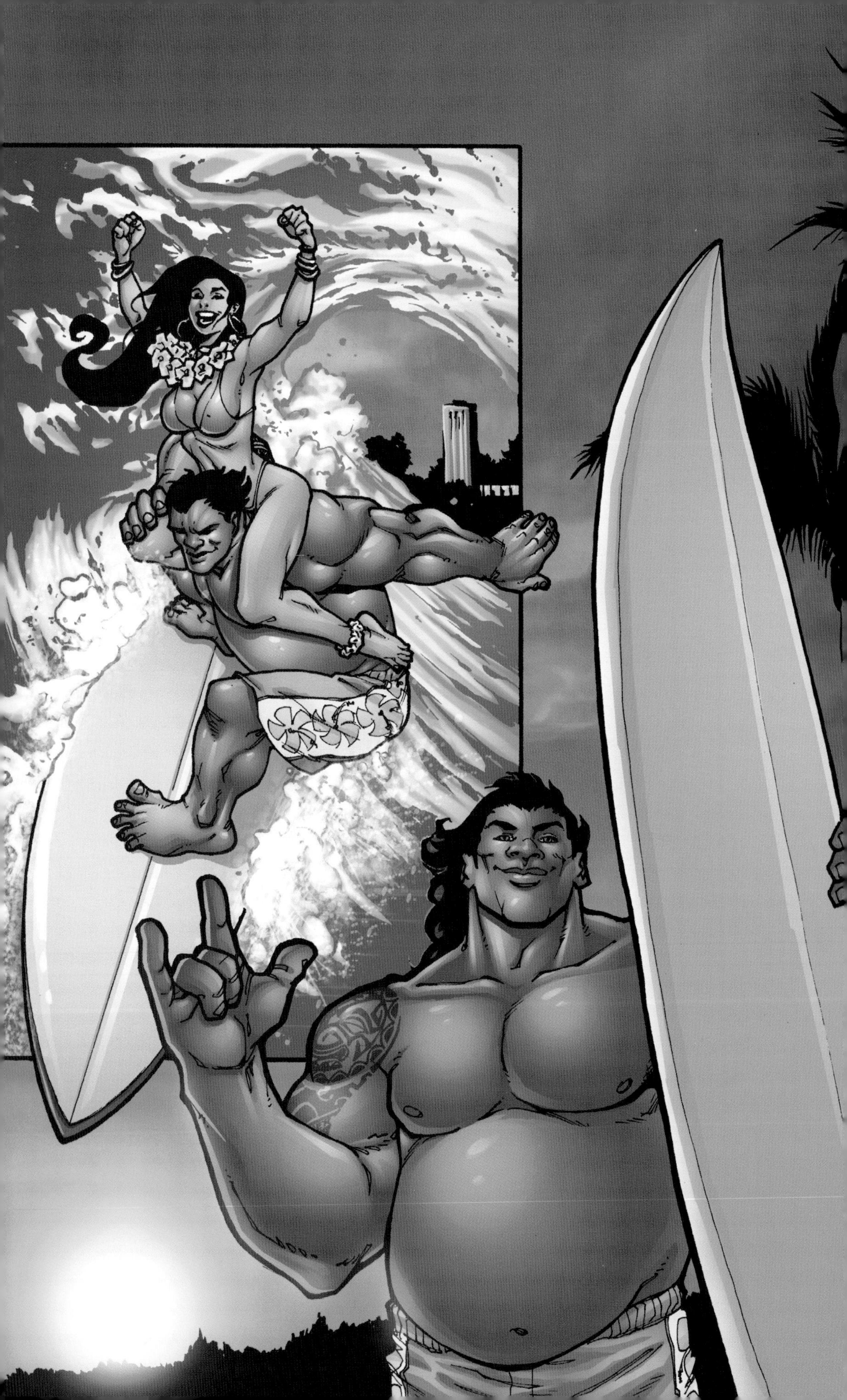

It's early evening and I am sitting on the steps to a bar, not far from Waikiki Beach, Oahu. Inside, the lounge is a hive of activity, as workers are in mid-clean up, busy repairing broken tables and chairs and plastering over holes in the walls. From the extent of the damage, it looks like a large vehicle crashed into the building.

The general level of clatter and hammering inside the bar isn't helping alleviate the discomfort of my jet-lag any. Out, beyond the shore, I can see a large, dominating figure carving a swathe through the turbulent waves on his surfboard. The surfer is Hawaiian Slammer, a twenty year-old local superhero whom I've been waiting to interview for over two hours.

Barman: You're going to be waiting a lot longer if you're here for the The Slammer.

James Stanley: Excuse me?
B: You're not local, that much I can see. And this isn't exactly the height of tourist season. That leaves two options; beer and the Hawaiian Slammer, and as most of the beer is being mopped off my floor right now, I'd say it's the latter.

The barman motions towards the Hawaiian Slammer who is swimming back out to face the gigantic waves.

JS: What happened to your bar?
B: The Slammer happened, that's what. That kid sure knows how to party – I just wish he didn't have to party so hard on my bar. It started off peaceful enough, but then it always does. Before the night was over, he'd got a little too familiar with another guy's girl and, as usual, the results were four trips to E.R., including two staff members, and twelve troopers called in to bring him under control.

A car pulls up outside and a thin man steps out and gestures to the barman.

Thin Man: Hi Ethan.

E: Hey Josh, come by to help out?

J: Yeah, I heard from Mia that he kicked-off again. Jesus, he really wrecked the place, huh?

JS: So this a regular thing for The Hawaiian Slammer?
J: Once a month, like clockwork, he comes in here, lets his hair down and enjoys himself. Trouble is, he has no concept of the word 'moderation'.

JS: Have you tried barring him?
E: You try barring a guy with an oversized arm that can punch through plate steel! The Governor of the island puts the entire police force on alert when he's in town! Trouble is, I'd rather have him drinking here than at the competition; he has quite a fan-base, I can tell you – although probably one less just for today.

J: If you ask me, he's more trouble than he's worth.

E: You don't mean that, Josh. You know he's got a good heart, he just likes to take it to the extreme sometimes.

J: The guy is going to get someone killed someday.

JS: Have you tried discussing his behaviour with him? Maybe some form of meeting on how to avoid such incidents in future?
E: Sure, we've talked about the idea of some sort of mediation between The Slammer and the locals, but we never seem to agree on what sort of restrictions to impose, or if he'll even pay attention to them.

J: The police don't know what to do with him – if they do manage to subdue him, they just throw him in the cells to sleep it off for the night and he's back on his way in the morning. I think it's all part of the fun for him; they know he could simply bust his way out if he really wanted to. I get the feeling he's having one big laugh at ours and the rest of the taxpayers' expense.

JS: Can you get him legally removed? I'm sure there are organisations that can deal with rogue superheroes?
E: Don't get us wrong, we love the kid, really we do. Despite his downsides, he's done a lot of good for this community. It's just a phase he's going through that we need to ride out.

J: Better hope he doesn't wipe you out before then. Look at this place, how much damage this time?

E: It's cool, really. His mother will cover the costs. She's a very powerful woman, works for a large government agency. Not sure what she does exactly but I think it's pretty important. His father died quite a few years back, when he was about eight years-old.

J: Killed, you mean.

JS: Killed?
J: Seems like more than just a rumor to me. The Slammer's father worked at the same agency as his wife, in the research department. That's where the accident 'happened'.

E: Don't listen to this fool. He loves spreading a good rumor.

J: Well "rumor" has it The Slammer's pop was working on a project that had something to do with those HALE-CRITERION tests that are available. The story goes that one day, he leaves the house as normal but doesn't return at the end of the day. Hours go by and his wife, sensing something is wrong, calls the agency to find out where he is. Security does a sweep of his office and can't find him, so they check the labs and find his personal effects in a pool of blood on the floor and a bloody 'X-shape' spattered on the wall, but no sign of a body. Forensics come back two days later and confirm both sets of blood belong to his pop. Worse still, they find traces of his DNA profile in the wall. He was *in* the fucking wall! Not behind it, or plastered into it, I mean *in it*. It was as if the wall and his body were fused into one. He never left the room! That is some weird-shit rumor.

E: It's still just a rumor, Josh. Whatever really happened, I guess we'll never know for sure. The official verdict was "unfortunate accident at work". His wife seemed happy with the verdict and still continued working for the agency until it closed down some years later, so best leave it be.

JS: The agency he worked for – it wasn't called 'XoDOS', was it?
E: No, but I didn't live on this side of the island back then. And I was only in high-school myself, so didn't pay much attention to the news. No-one mentions it when The Slammers' around and he and his mother never speak about it–

J: –Let's just say his mom ain't really the motherly type. She's mother in title only, that's why the kid's a law unto himself; no discipline.

E: Which is why we have to cut the kid some slack.

JS: It would certainly make sense, not having a father-figure to look up to and to learn from. Let's focus a little on the good – what does The Hawaiian Slammer do for the community?
J: You mean beyond starting and finishing bar fights?

E: Ignore him, he's just yanking your chain. We do alright by him, you know? He's stuck around when the flash-floods hit bad back in the storm season. He was a full-on hero that day, I can tell you. Can't begin to calculate how many people he saved. He was everywhere; rescuing people from drowning, pulling others free from trapped vehicles, damming up the floods with his bare hands. Yup, a real hero, no doubt. He became a real man that day. He was awarded the National Bravery Award by the Governor for his efforts. His father would have been proud.

J: And how does he thank us for that? How does he thank *you*, Ethan?

E: Go easy on him. He just needs a father-figure in his life, that's all. A bit of parental guidance to get keep him on the straight-and-narrow. Isn't that what mentors are supposed to do?

We watch as The Hawaiian Slammer continues to rip through the water, pulling the board in as he disappears into a tube. Seconds pass and he appears spectacularly from the other end. His huge right arm punches the air triumphantly before he turns back for the next wave.

E: Doesn't look like you'll be interviewing him any time soon. When he's on that board, it's like he's on his own little planet. There's no way that boy's coming in until he's ready.

JS: And when will that be?
E: Sorry, only *he* can tell you that.

Resigned to the fact that this interview will have to wait for another time, I pack up my things and I say goodbye to Ethan and Joshua. I have another plane to catch; this time, Auckland, New Zealand. I leave The Hawaiian Slammer to enjoy the solace of the sea.

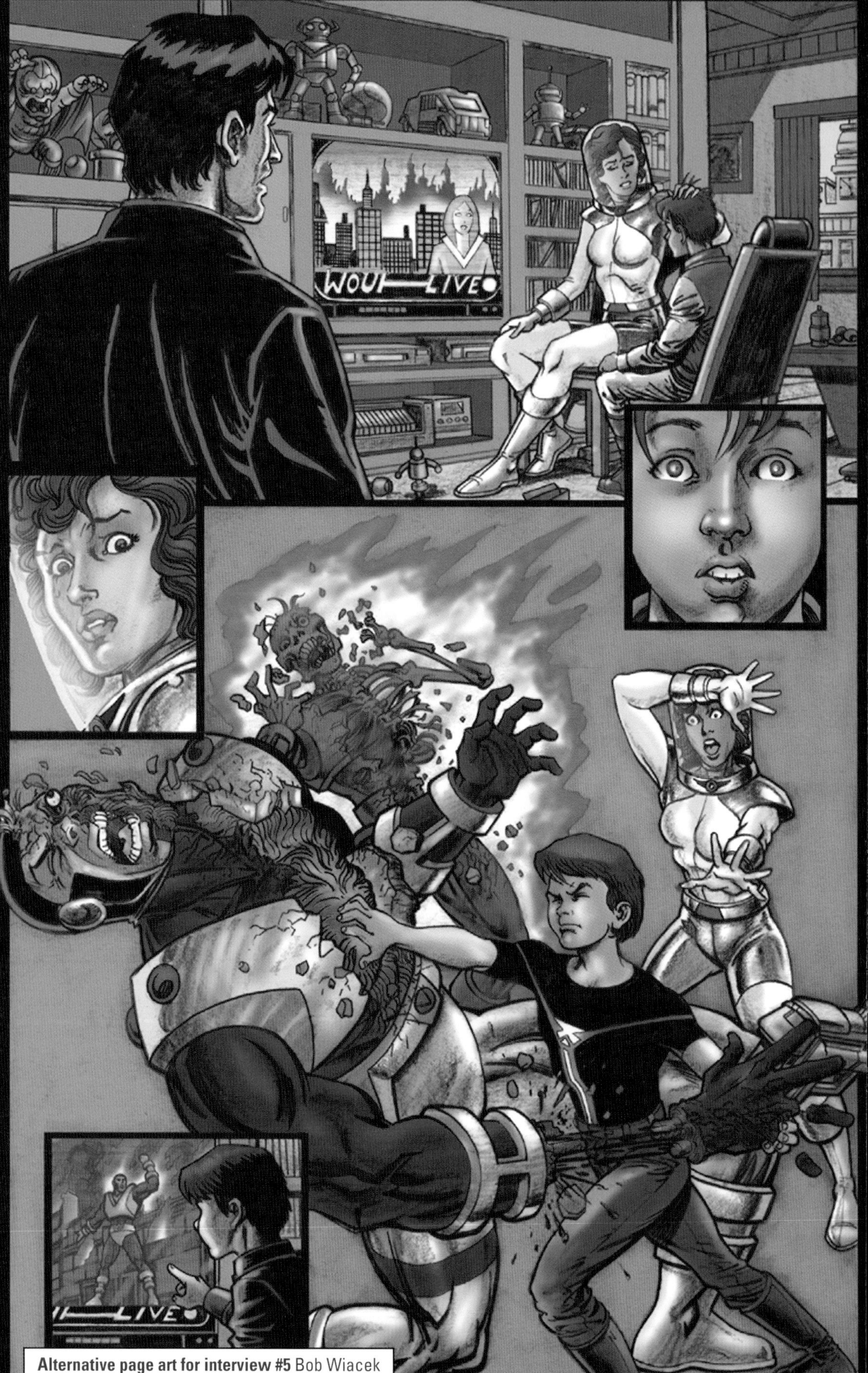
WOUI—LIVE
LIVE

Alternative page art for interview #5 Bob Wiacek

Alternative page art for interview #5 Alvin Leigh

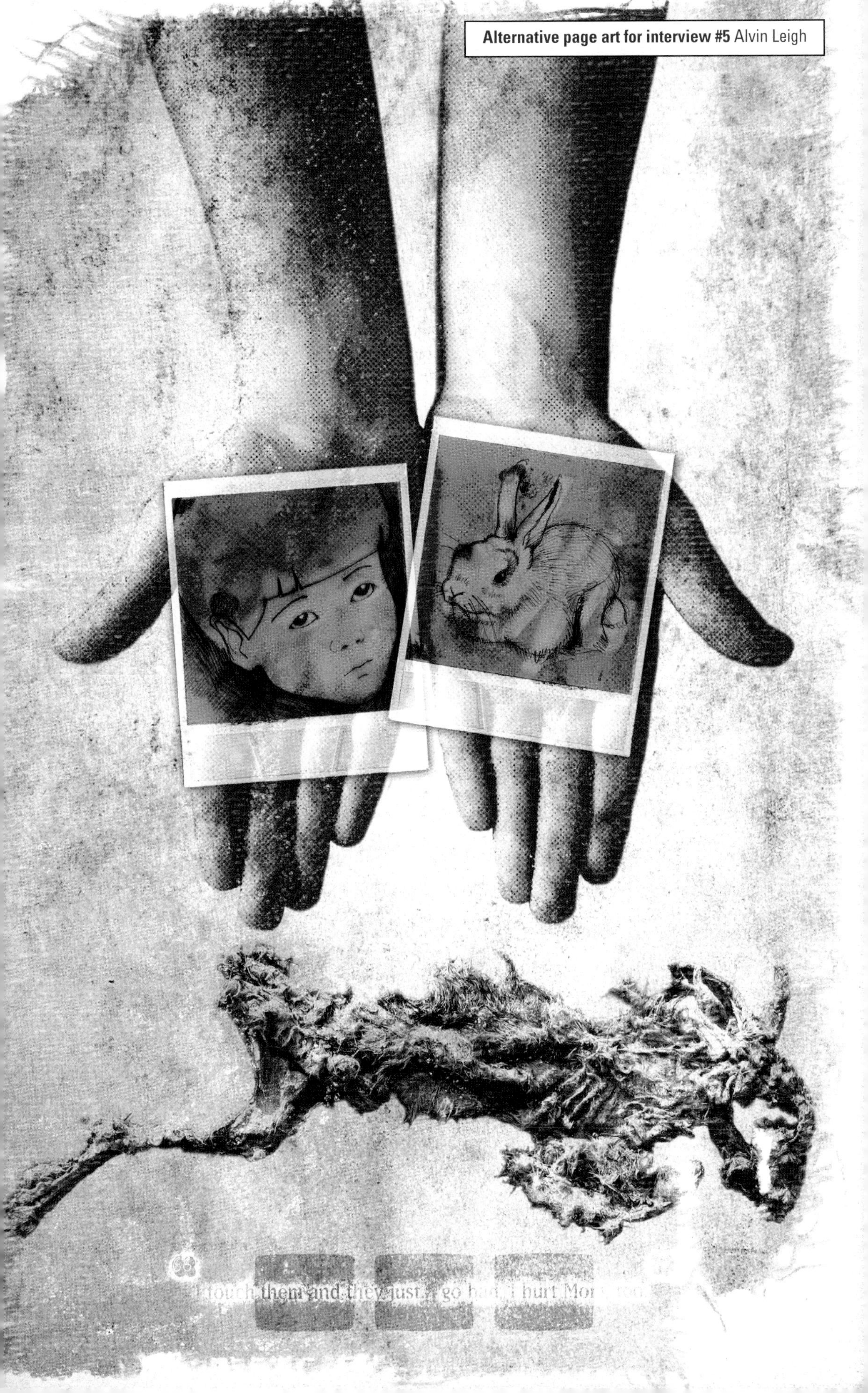
I touch them and they just... go bad. I hurt

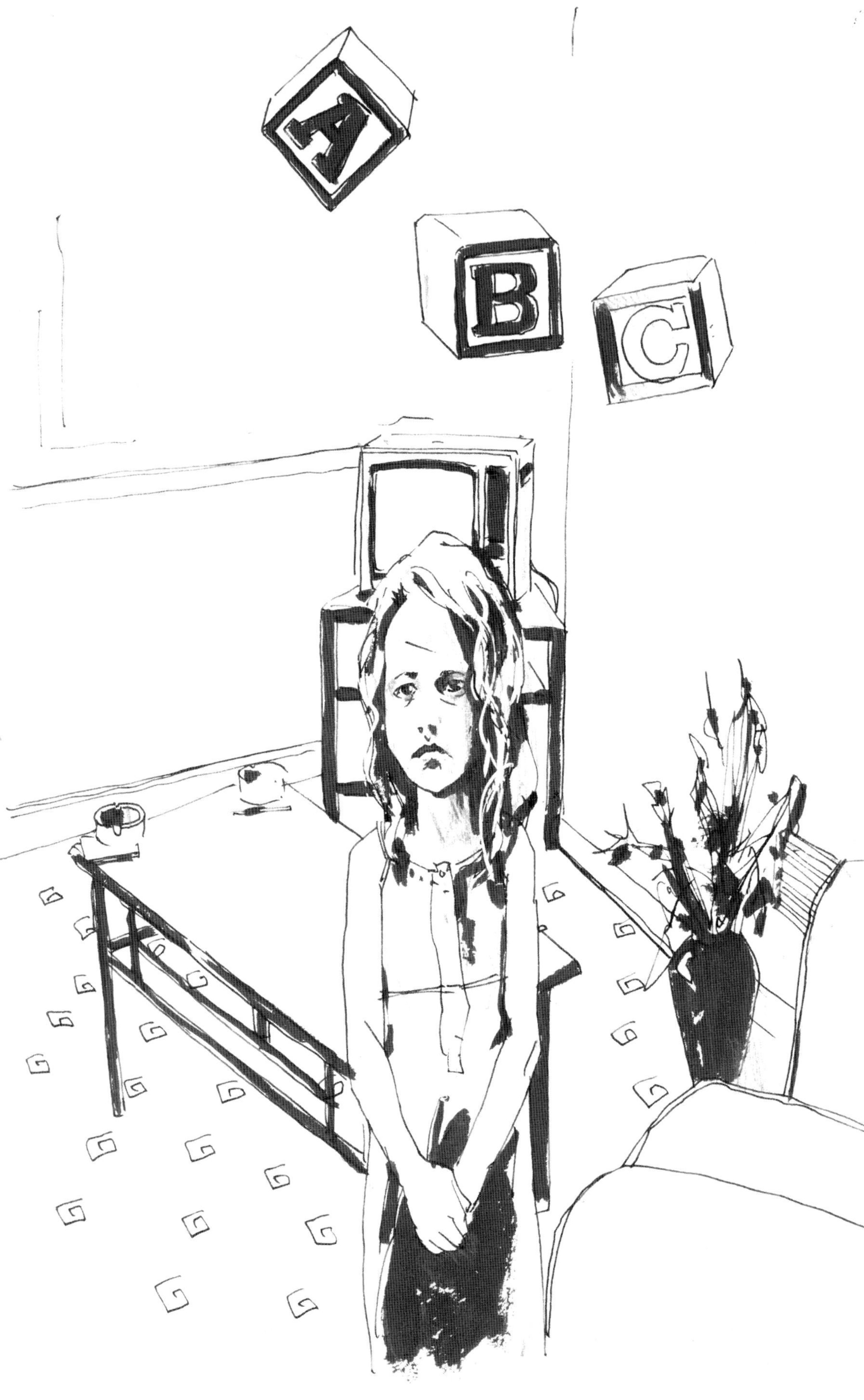
A
B
C

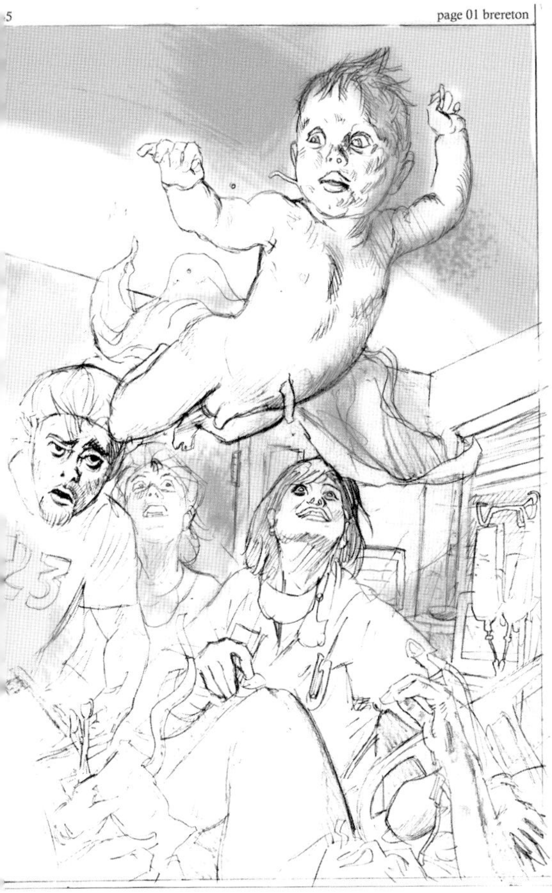
page 01 brereton

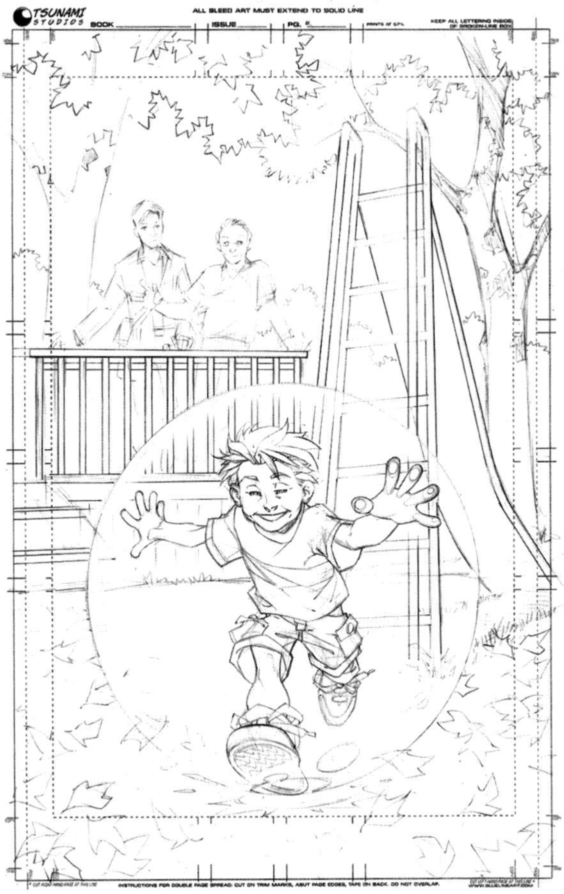
TSUNAMI STUDIOS
ALL BLEED ART MUST EXTEND TO SOLID LINE
BOOK
ISSUE
PG.
KEEP ALL LETTERING INSIDE OF BROKEN-LINE BOX
INSTRUCTIONS FOR DOUBLE PAGE SPREAD: CUT ON TRIM MARKS, ABUT PAGE EDGES, TAPE ON BACK. DO NOT OVERLAP.

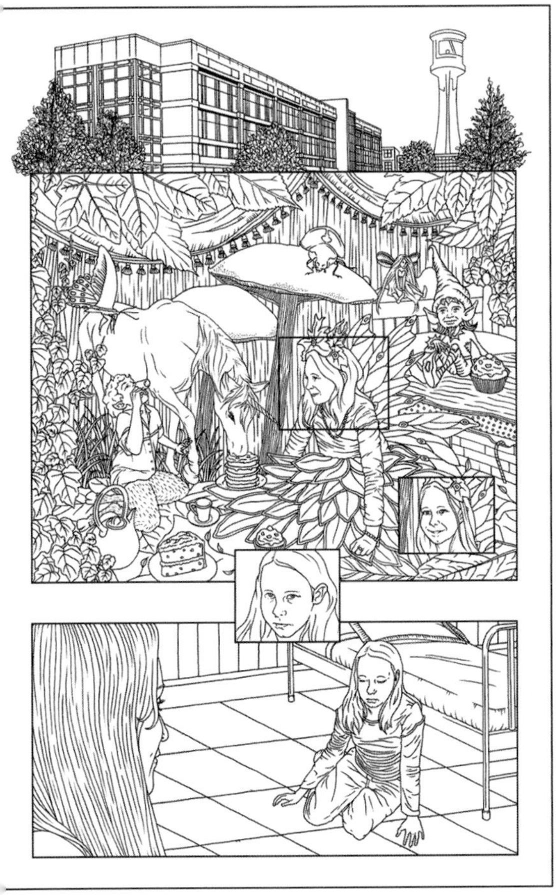

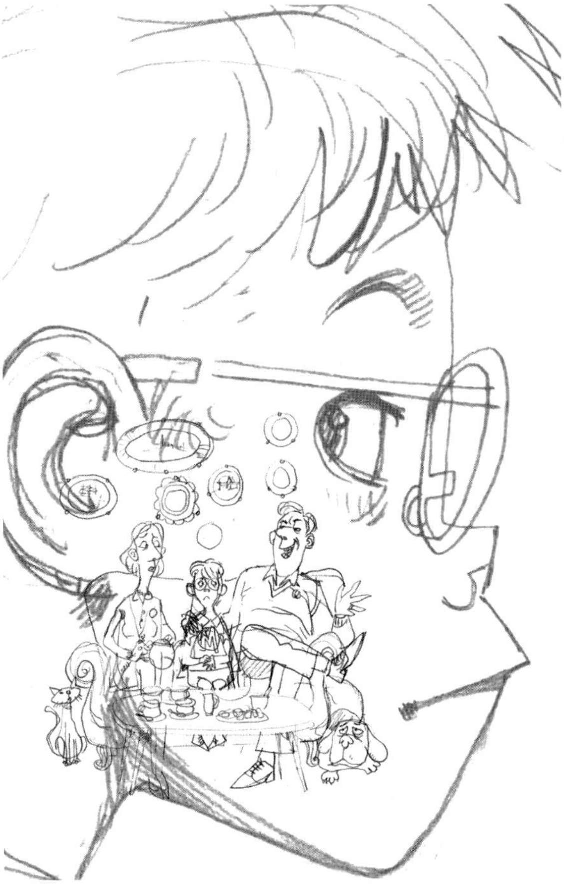

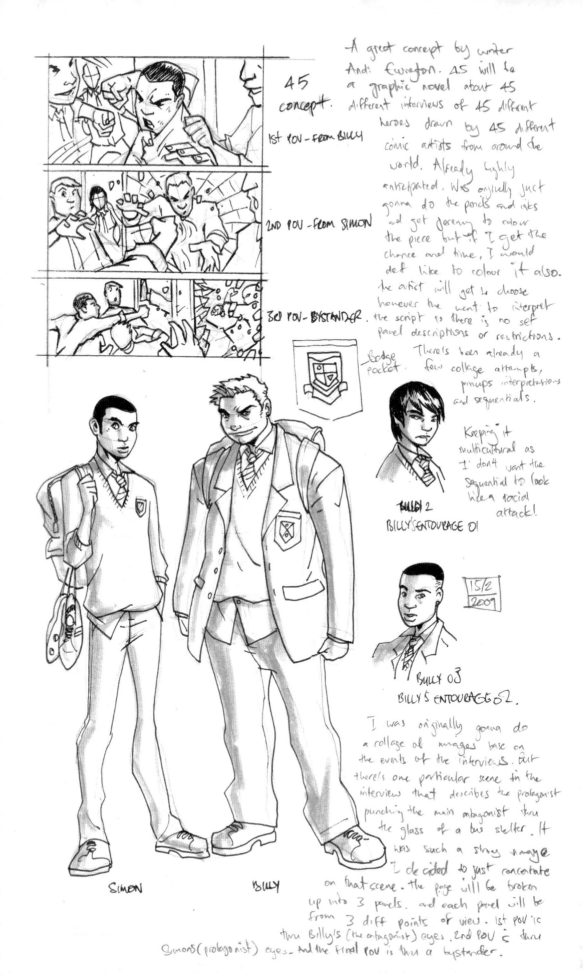

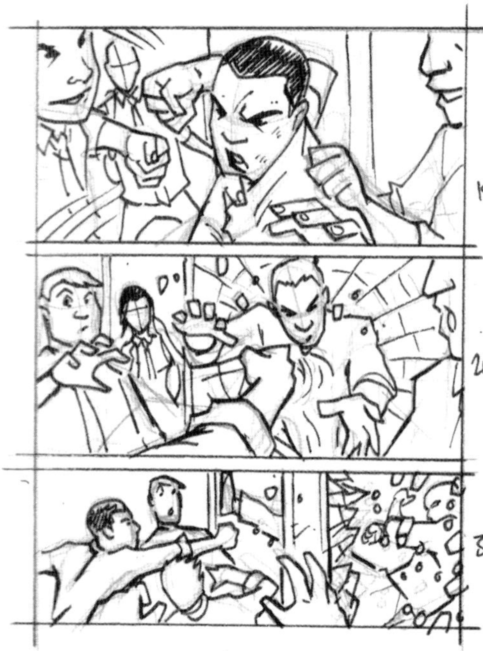
45
concept.
1st POV - FROM BILLY
2ND POV - FROM SIMON
3RD POV - BYSTANDER.

A great concept by writer Andi Ewington. 45 will be a graphic novel about 45 different interviews of 45 different heroes drawn by 45 different comic artists from around the world. Already highly anticipated. Was orignally just gonna do the pencils and inks and get Jeremy to colour the piece but if I get the chance and time, I would def like to colour it also. The artist will get to choose however the want to interpret the script so there is no set panel descriptions or restrictions. There's been already a few collage attempts, pinups interpretations and sequentials.

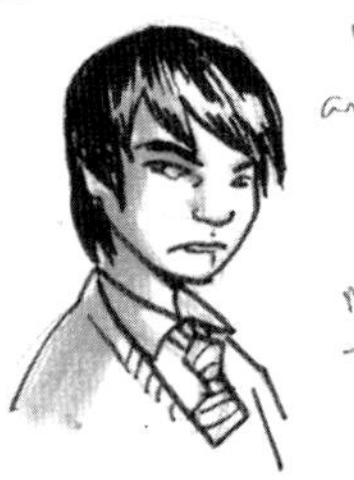
BILLY 2
BILLY'S ENTOURAGE 01

Keeping it multicultural as I don't want the sequential to look like a racial attack!

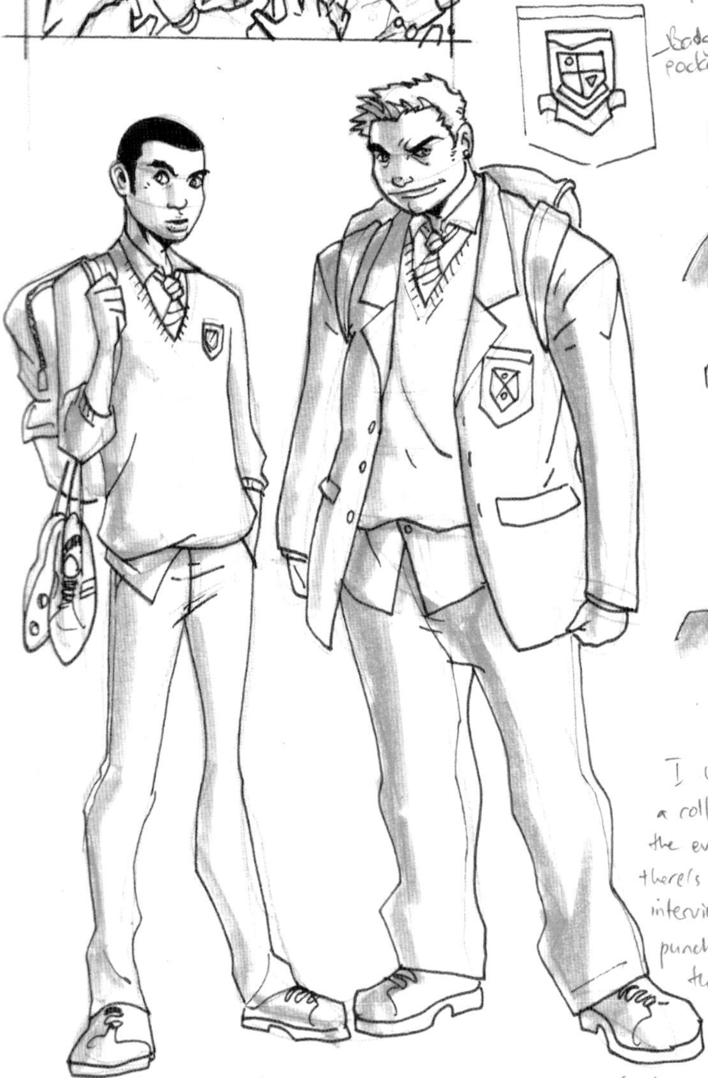
Badge pocket.
SIMON
BILLY

15/2
2009

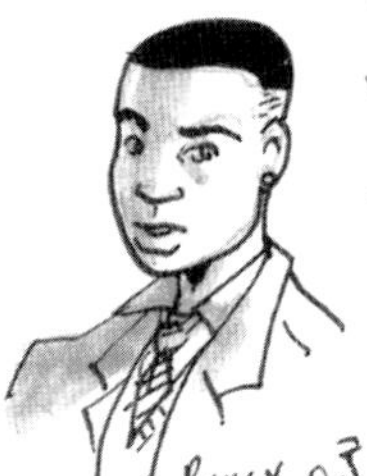
BILLY 03
BILLY'S ENTOURAGE 02.

I was originally gonna do a collage of images base on the events of the interviews. But there's one particular scene in the interview that describes the protagonist punching the main antagonist thru the glass of a bus shelter. It was such a strong image I decided to just concentrate on that scene. The page will be broken up into 3 panels. and each panel will be from 3 diff points of view. 1st POV is thru Billy's (the antagonist) eyes. 2nd POV is thru Simon's (protagonist) eyes. And the final POV is thru a bystander.

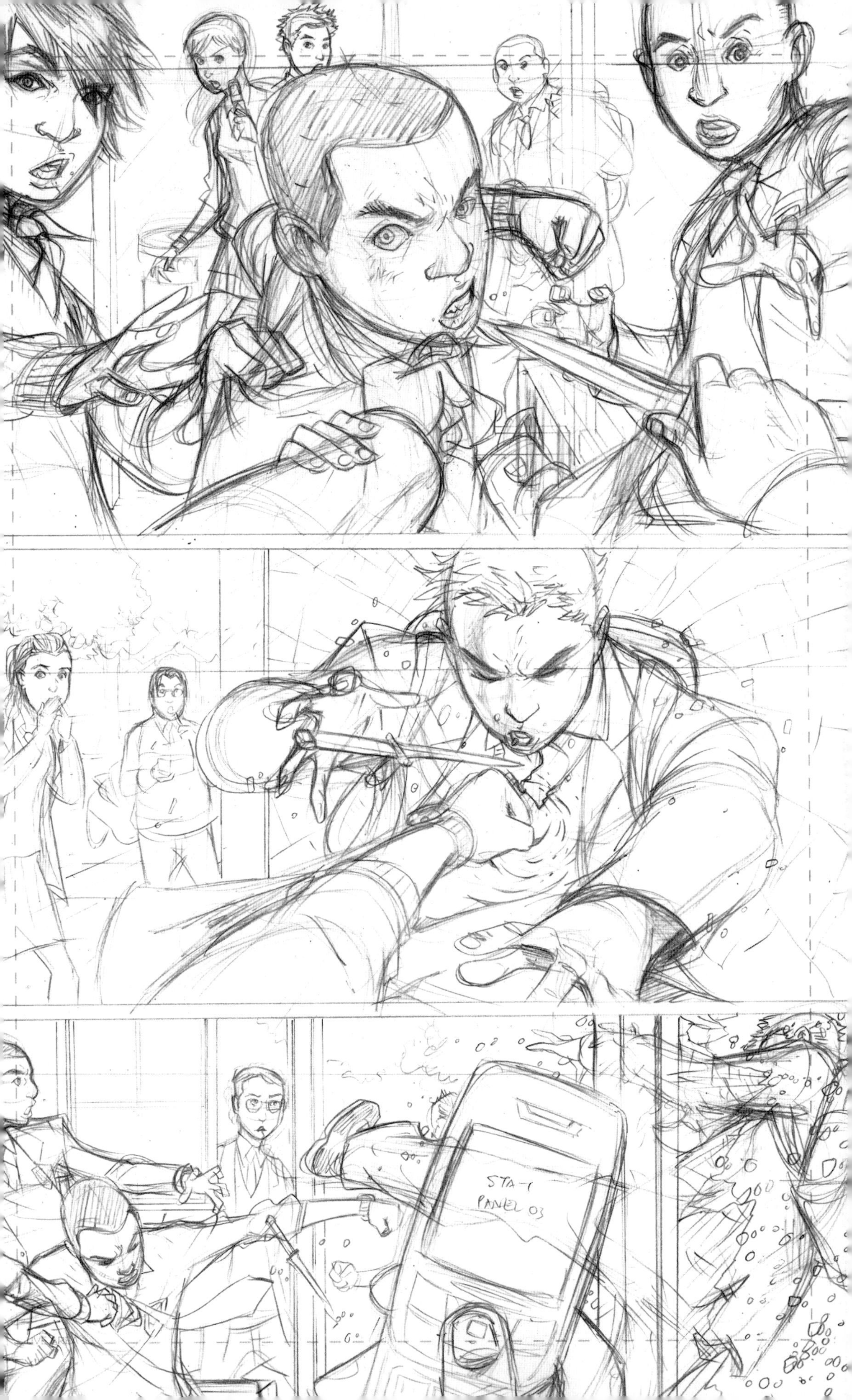
STAT
PANEL 03

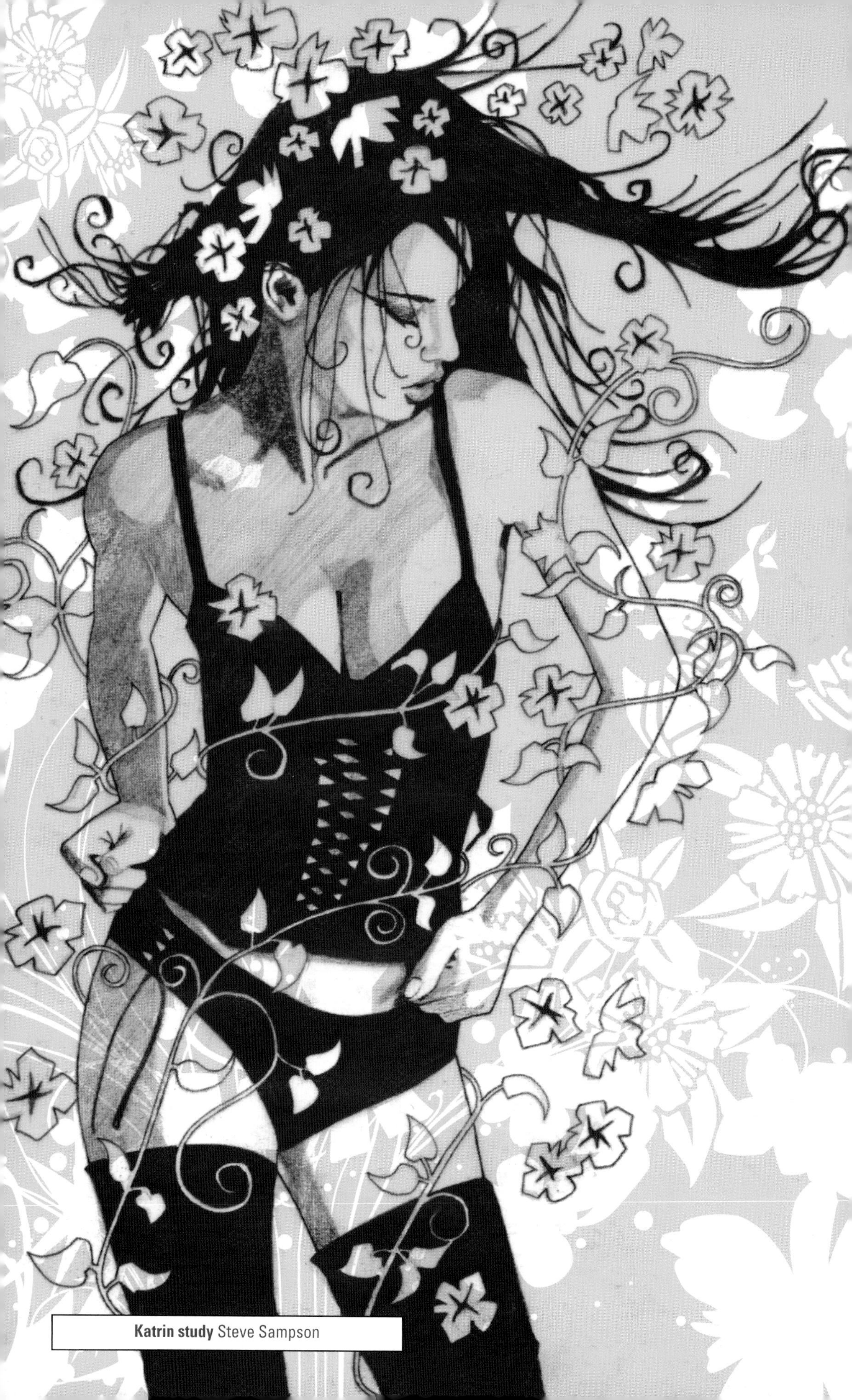

Katrin study Steve Sampson

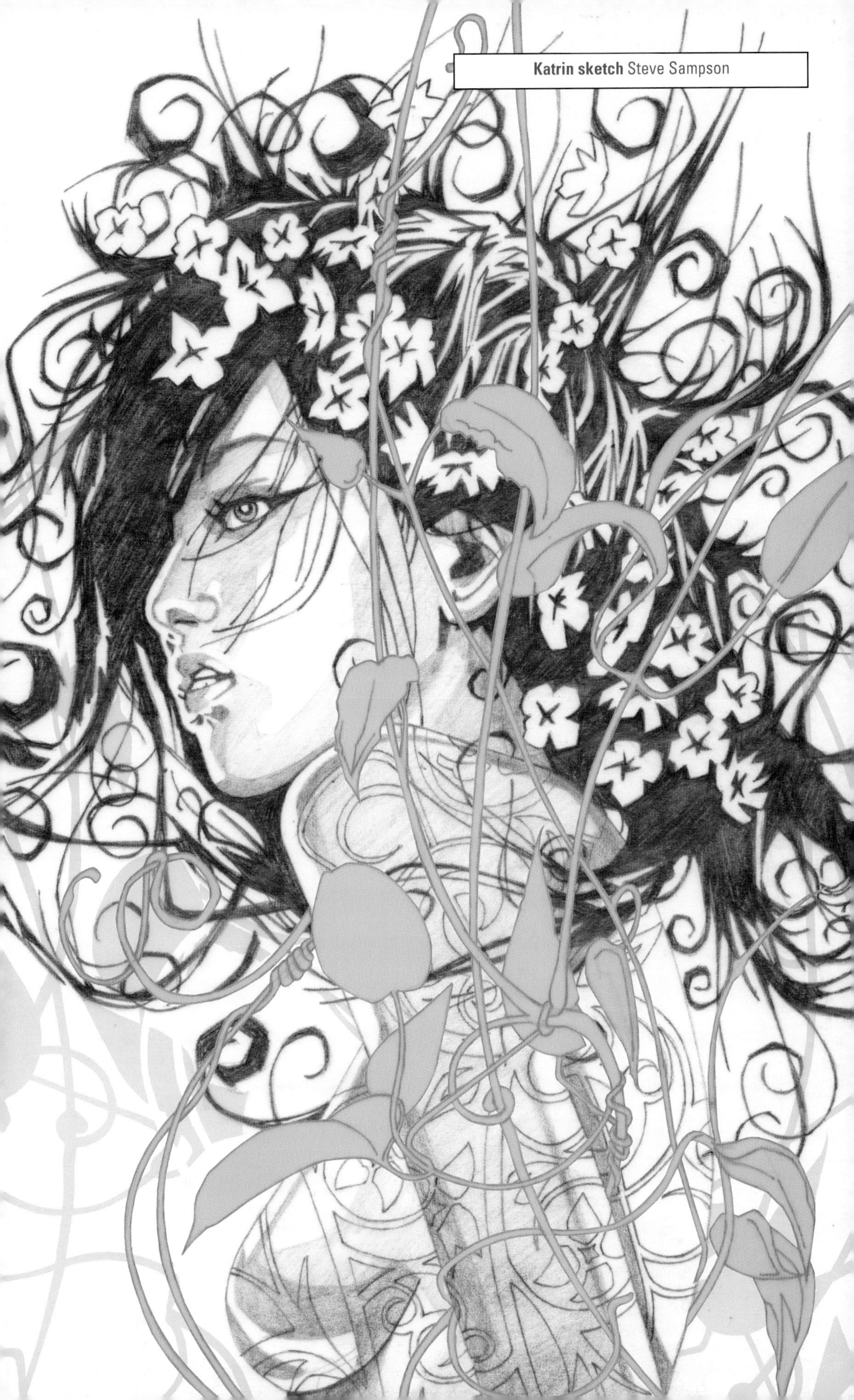

Katrin sketch Steve Sampson

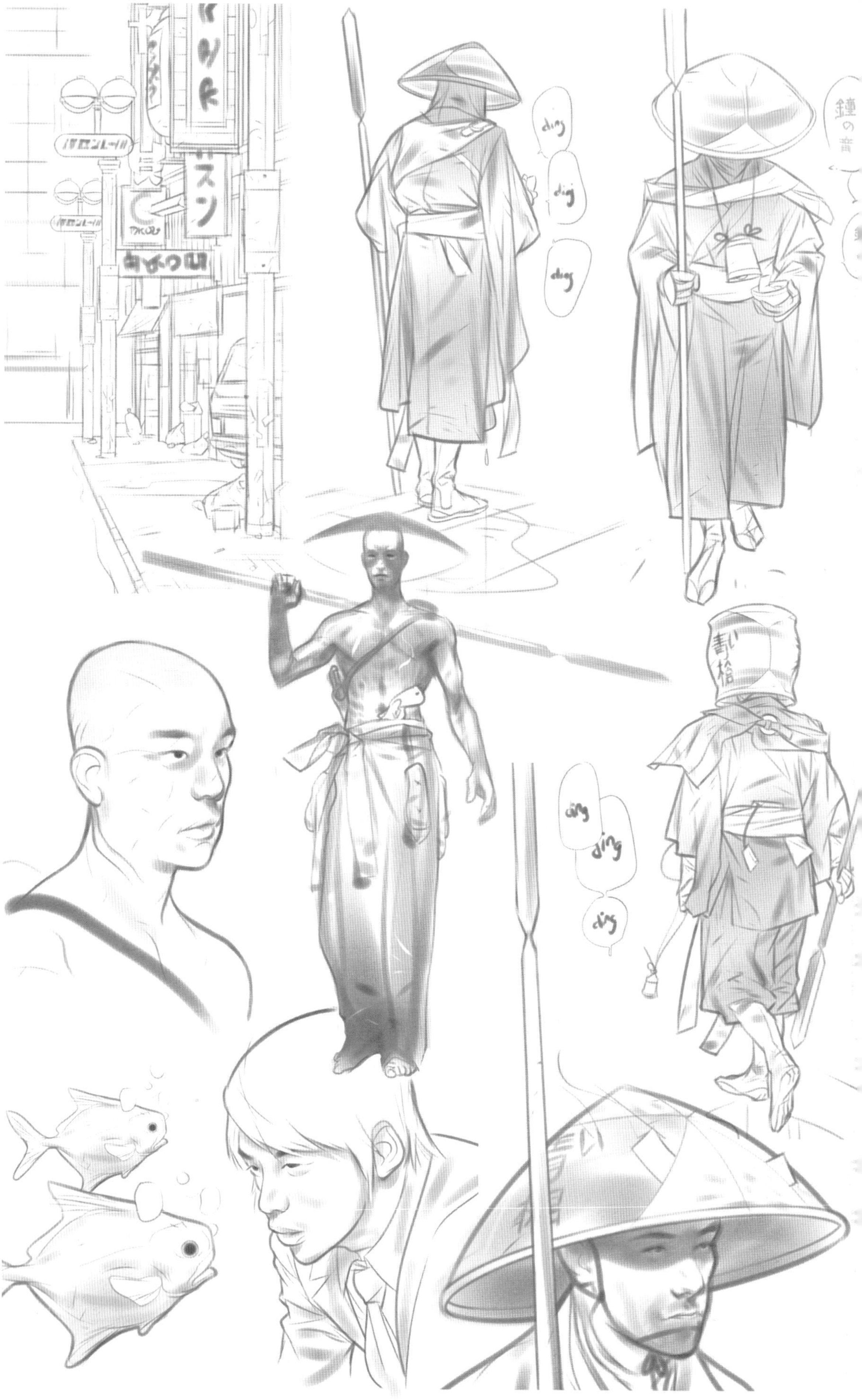
ding
ding
ding
鐘の音
ding
ding
ding

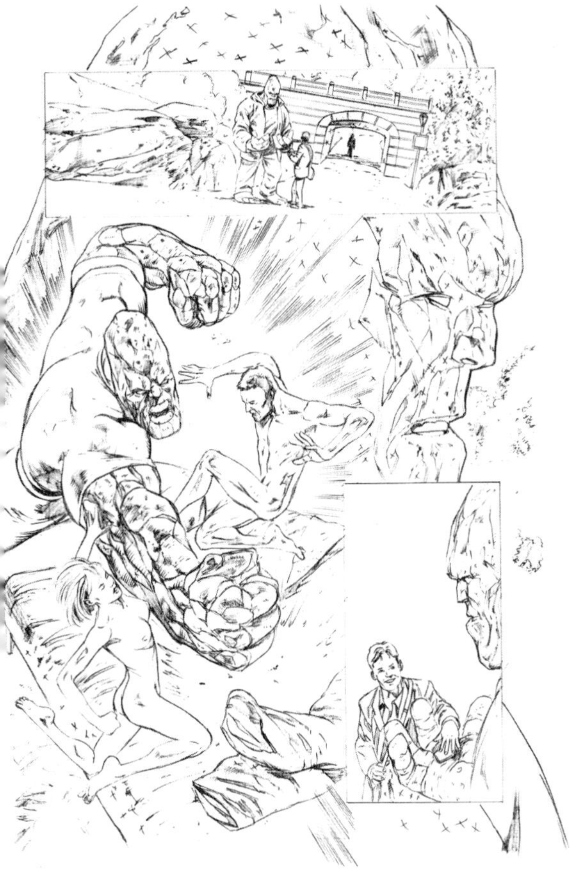

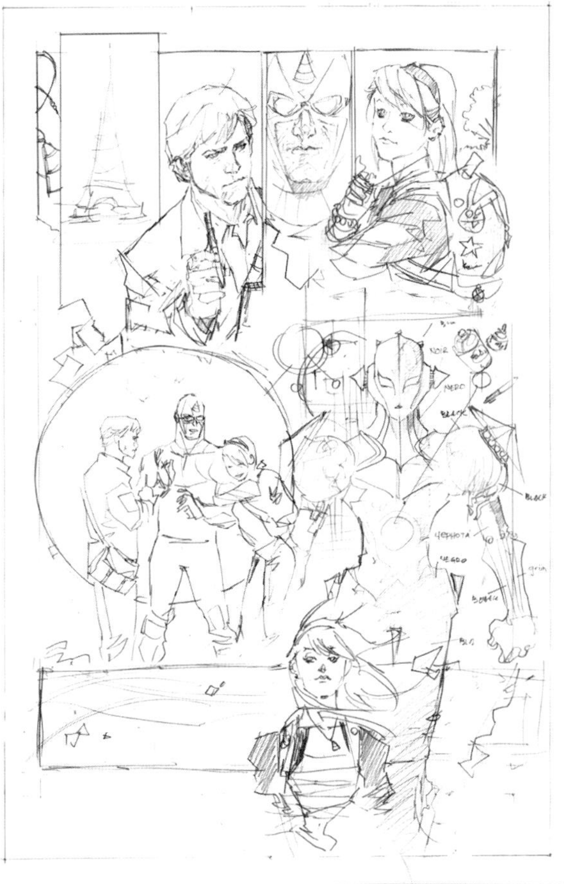

ROBERT ATKINS

45: FULLY ARMED

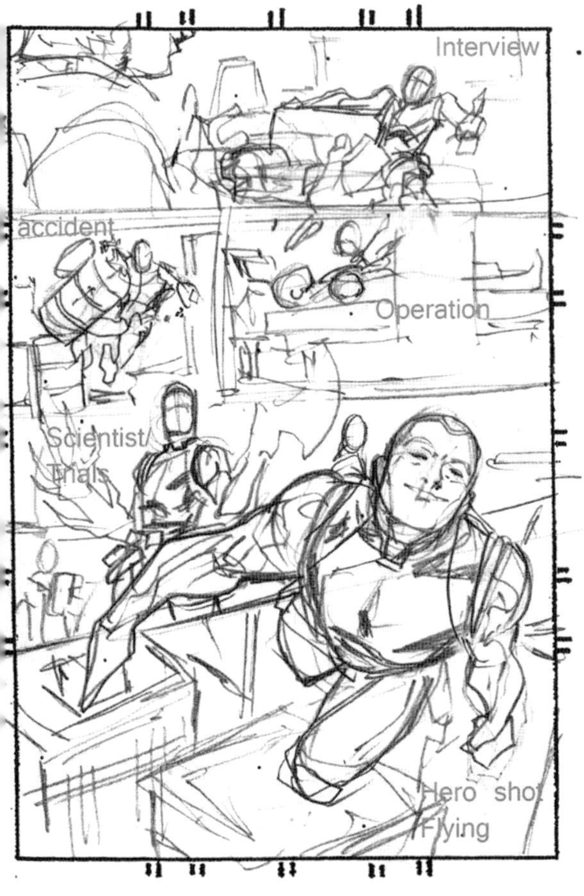
Interview
accident
Operation
Scientist/
Trials
Hero shot
Flying

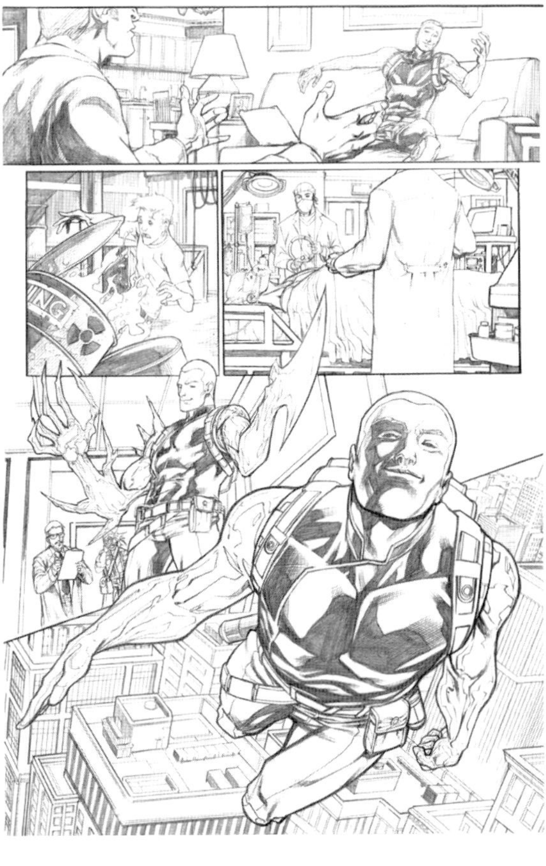

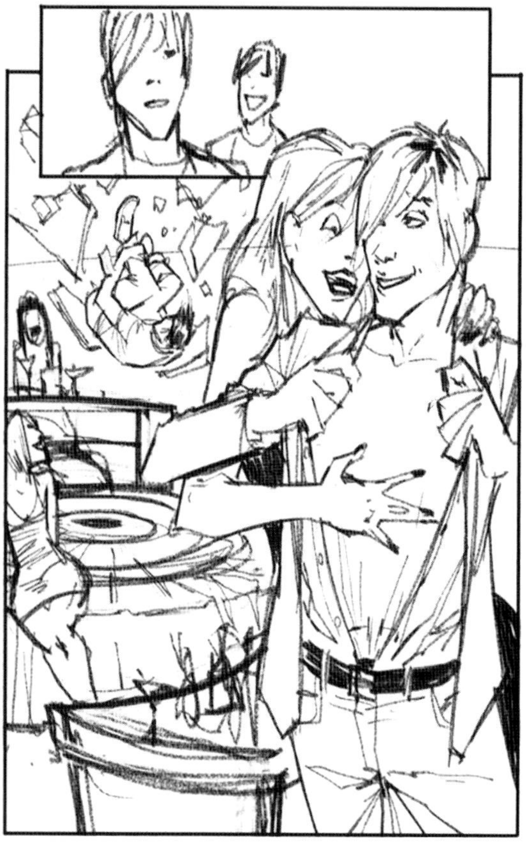

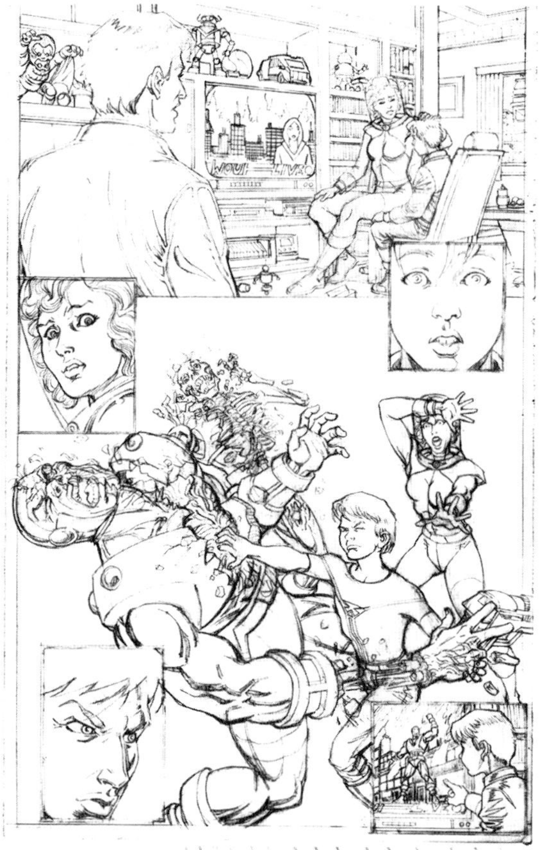

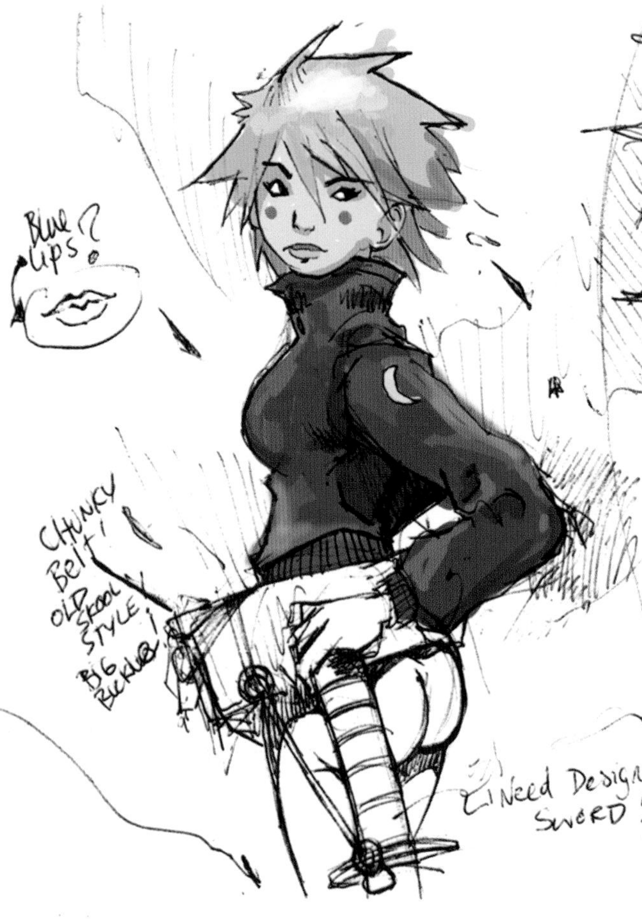
Blue lips?
Chunky Belt! Old Skool Style! Big Buckle!
Need Design for Sword!

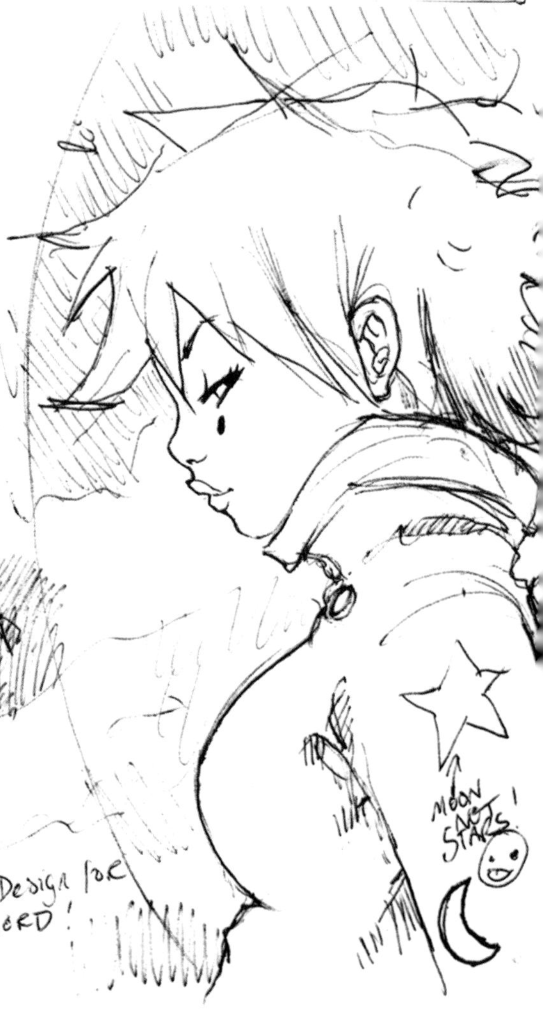
Moon and Stars!

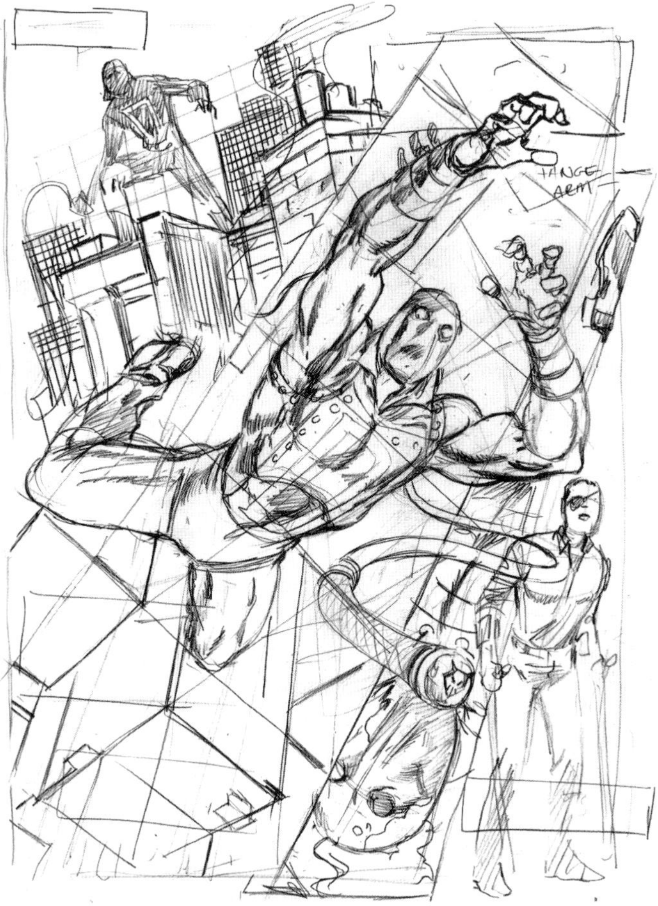

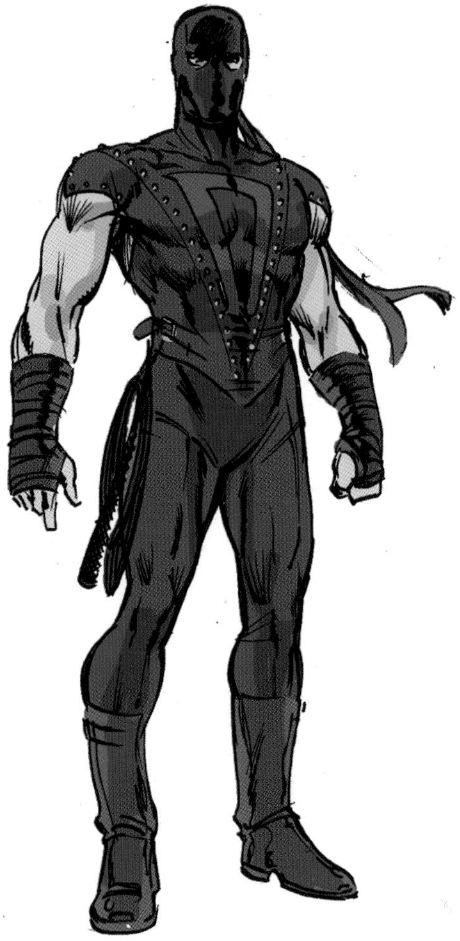

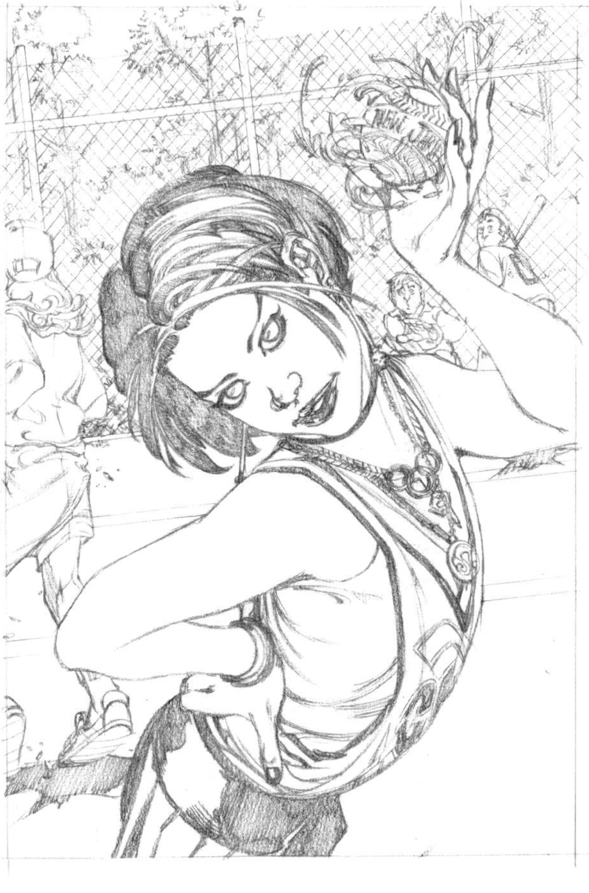

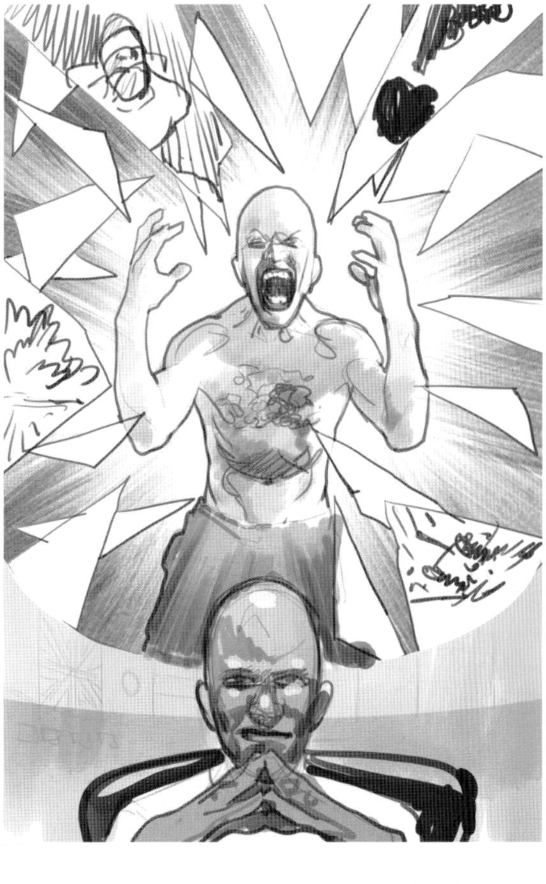

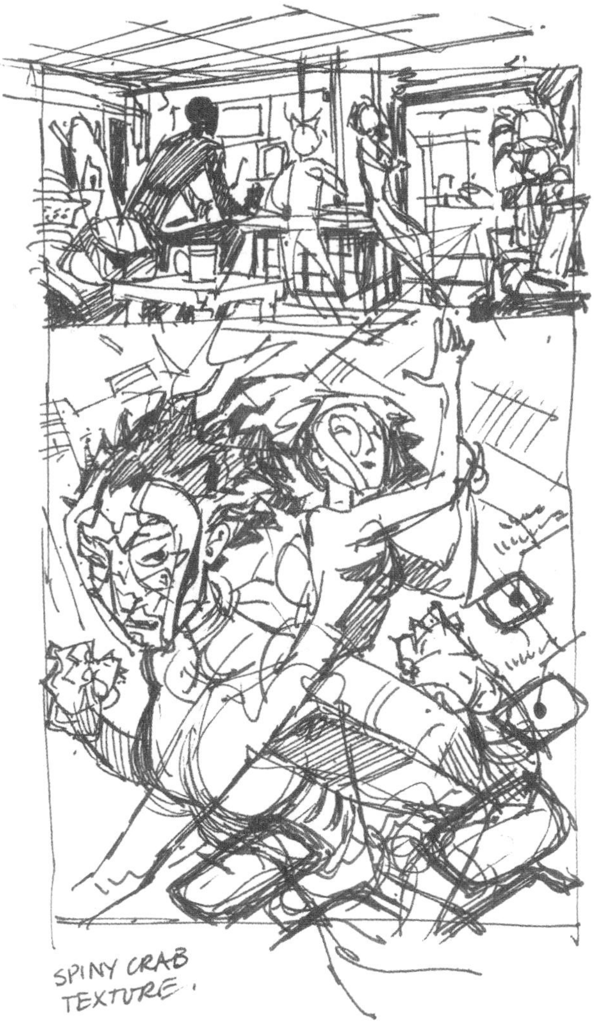
SPINY CRAB TEXTURE.

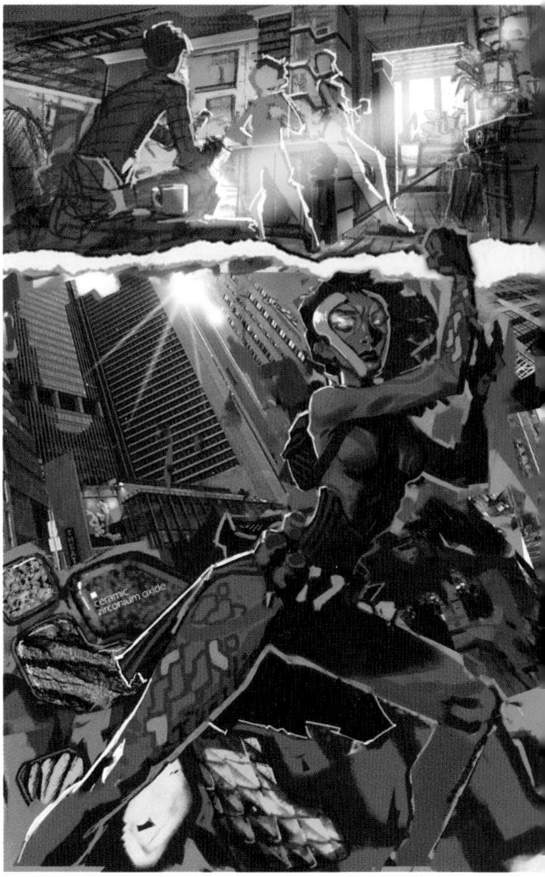
ceramic zirconium oxide

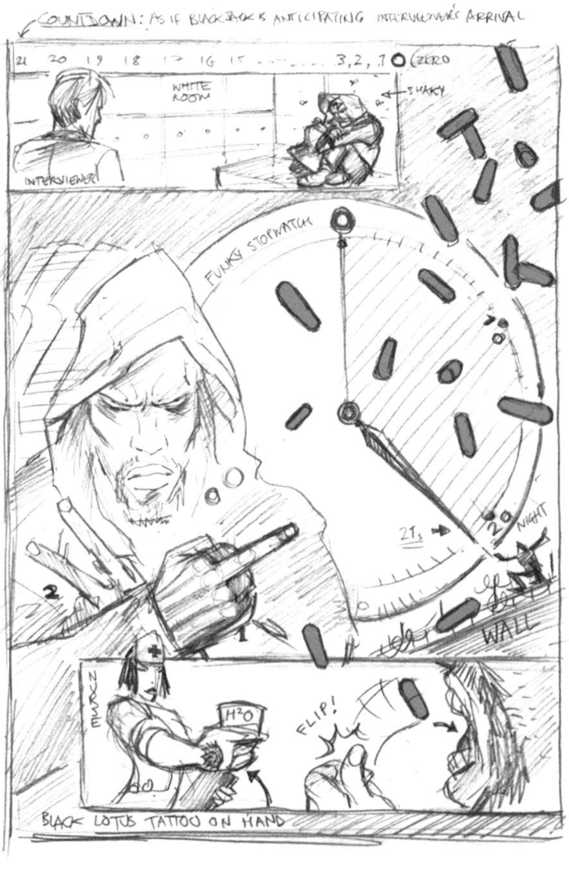
COUNTDOWN: AS IF BLACKJACK'S ANTICIPATING INTERVIEWER'S ARRIVAL
21 20 19 18 17 16 15 3, 2, 1 0 ZERO
WHITE ROOM
SHAKY
INTERVIEWER
FUNKY STOPWATCH
21s
NIGHT
WALL
NURSE
H2O
FLIP!
BLACK LOTUS TATTOO ON HAND

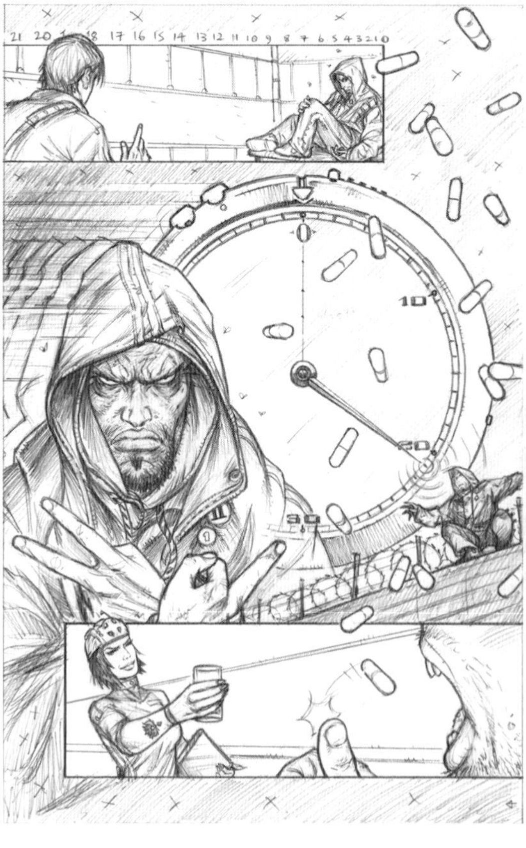
21 20 18 17 16 15 14 13 12 11 10 9 8 7 6 5 4 3 2 1 0
10
20
30

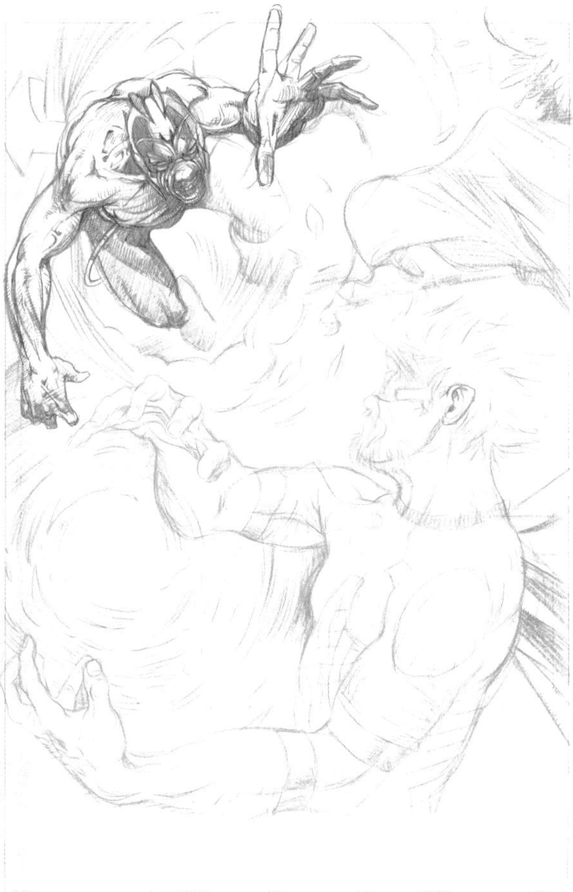

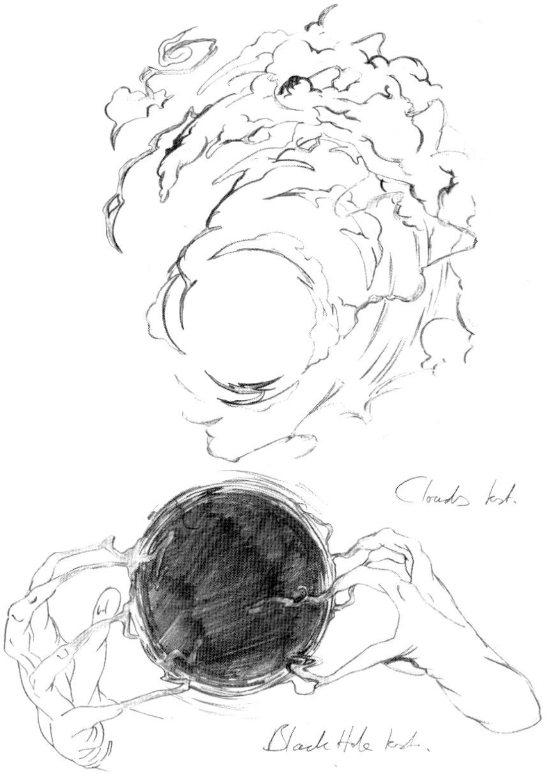
Clouds test.
Black Hole test.

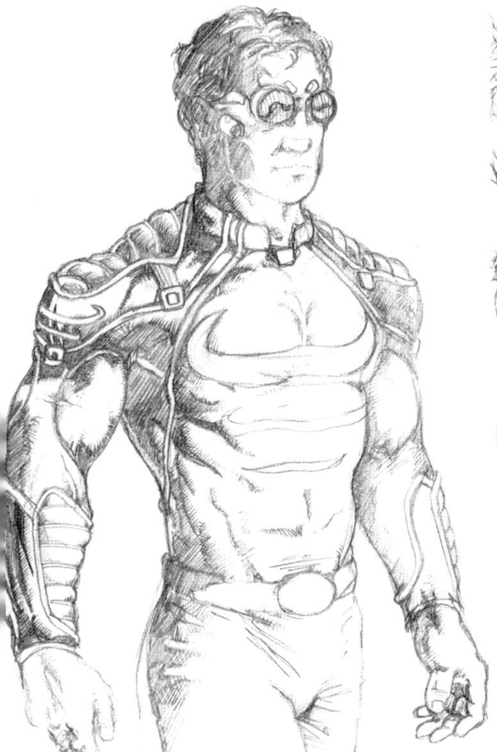

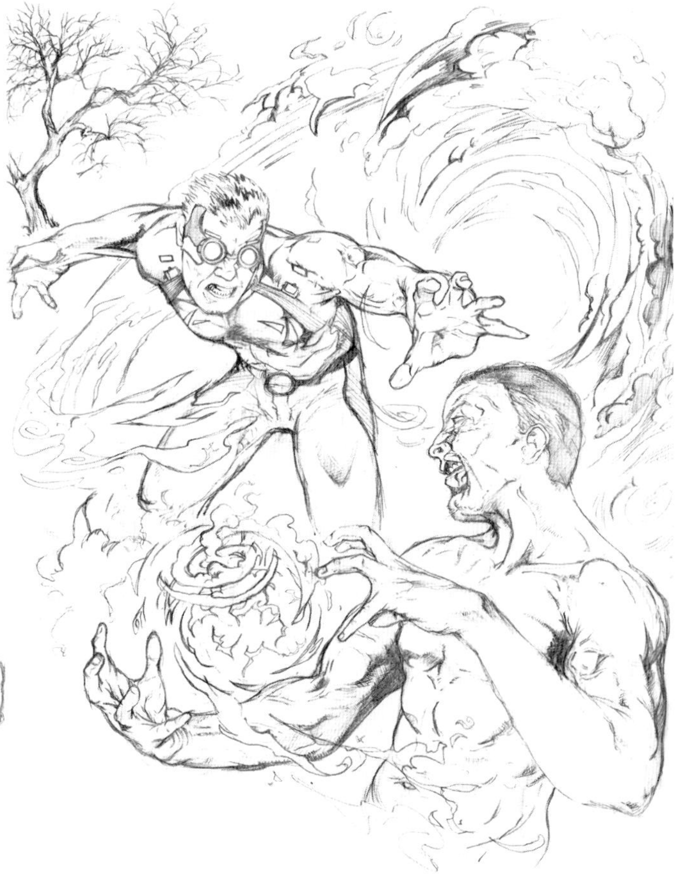

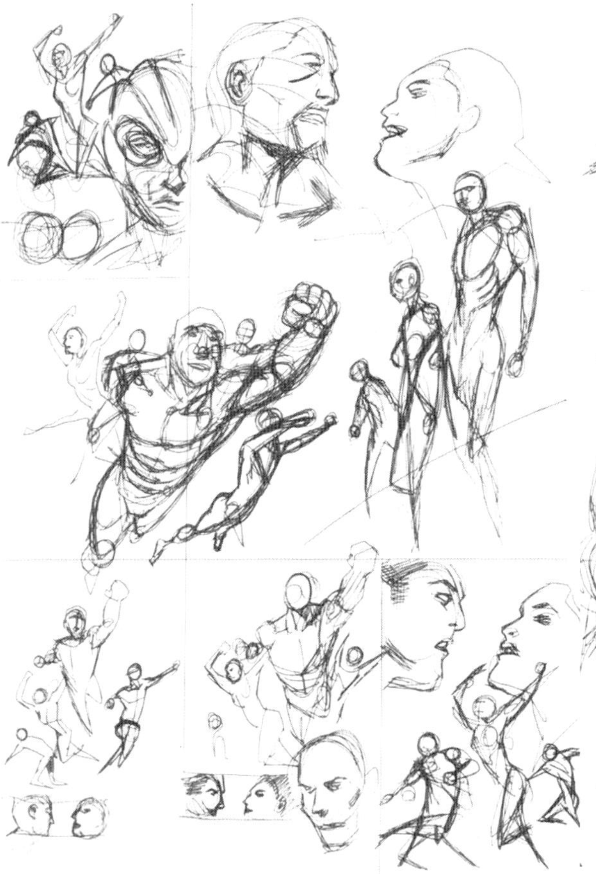

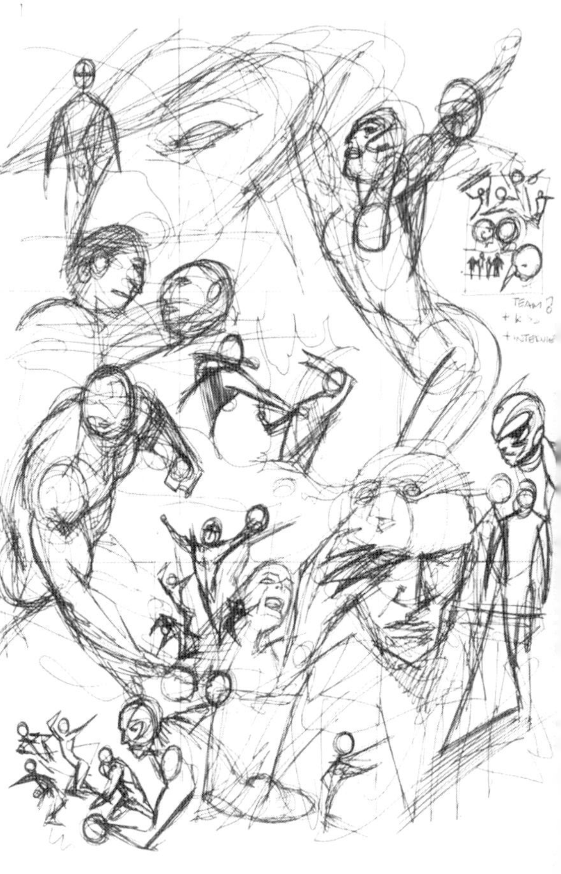
TEAM

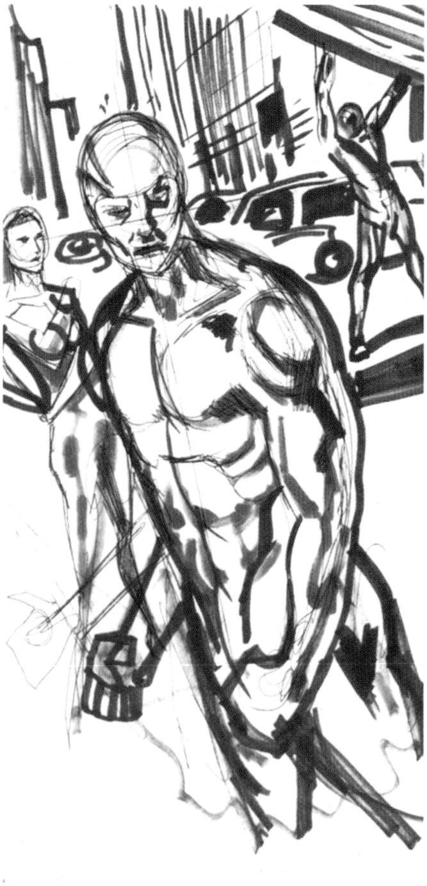

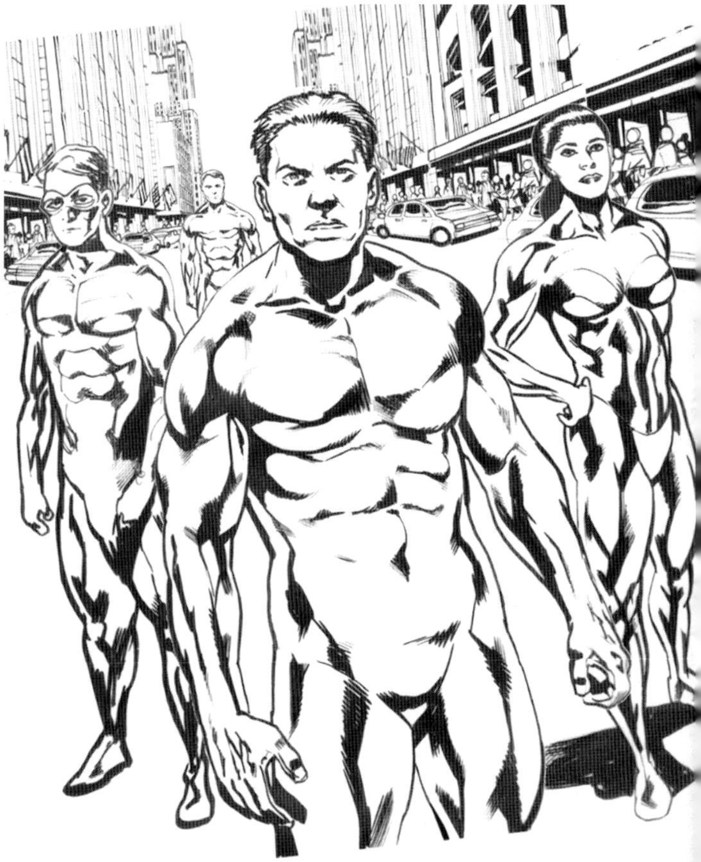

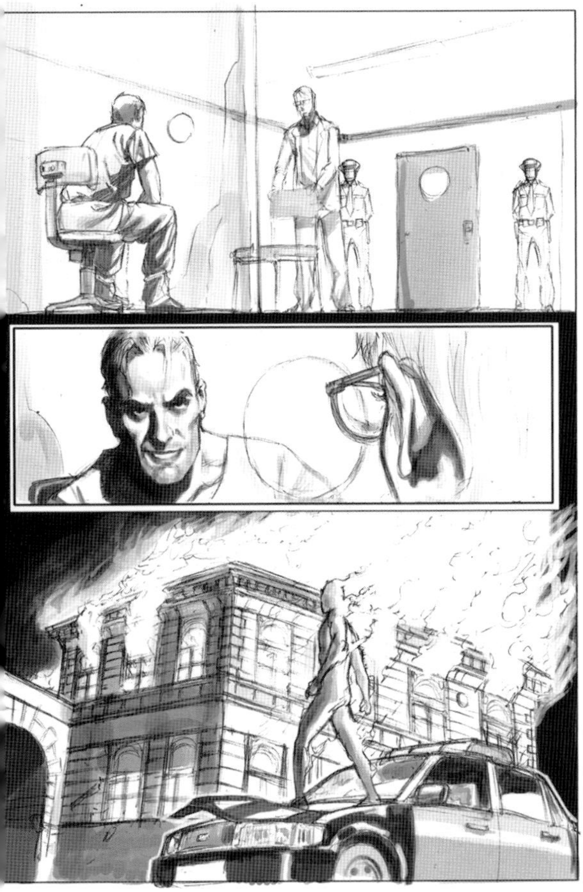

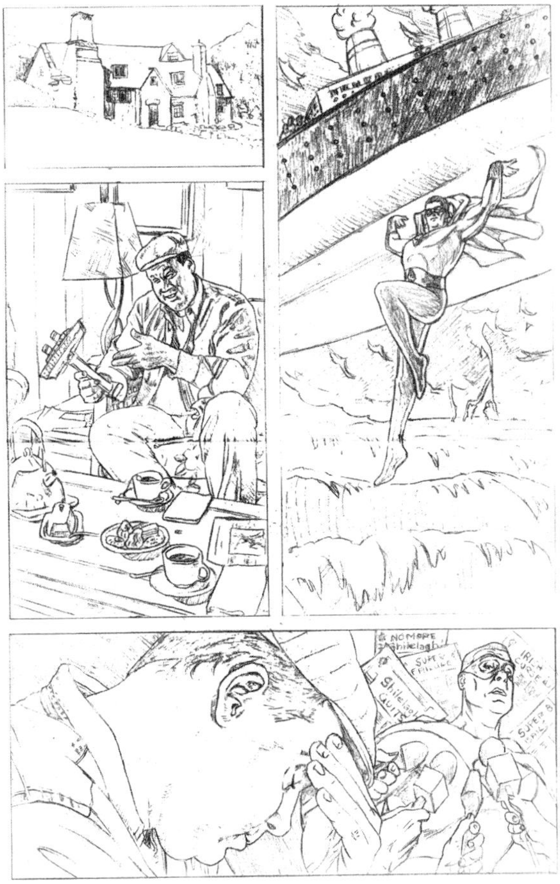

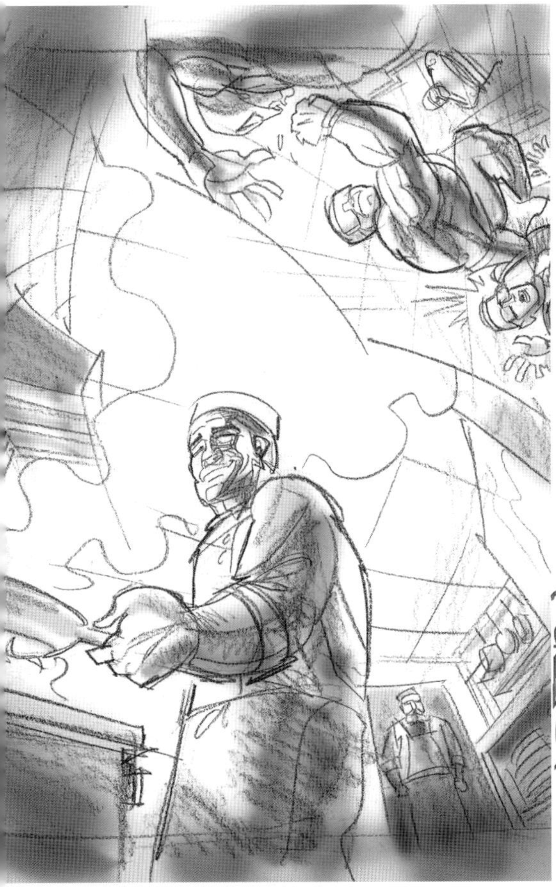

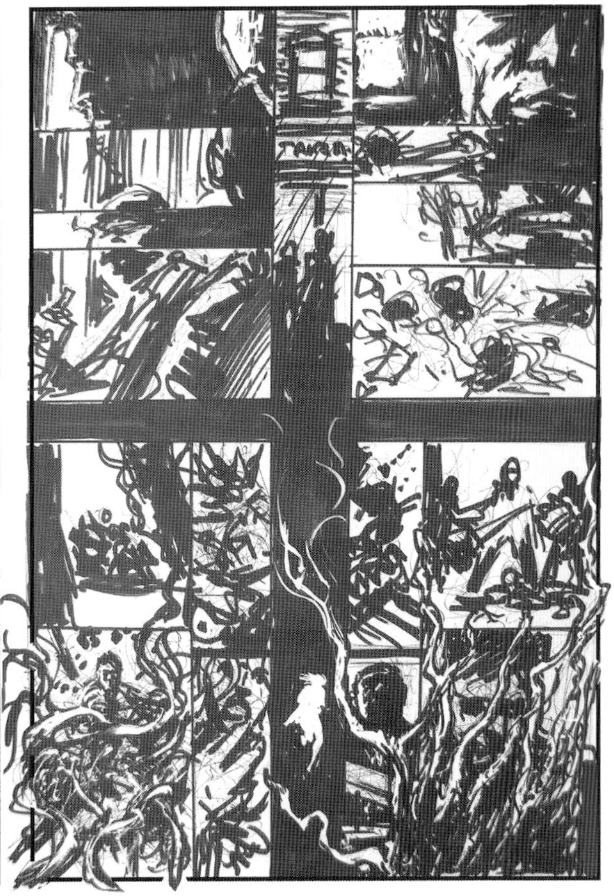

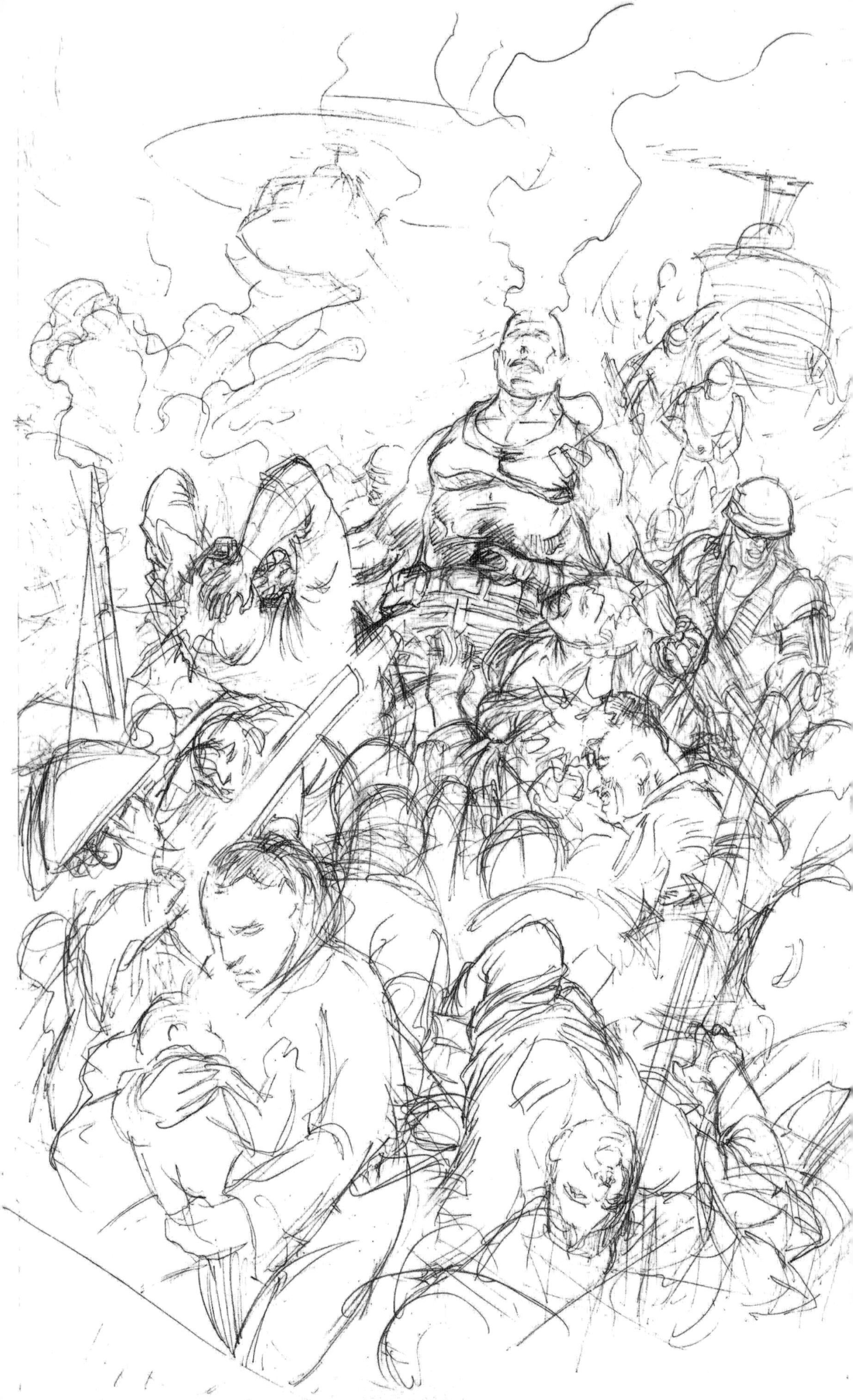

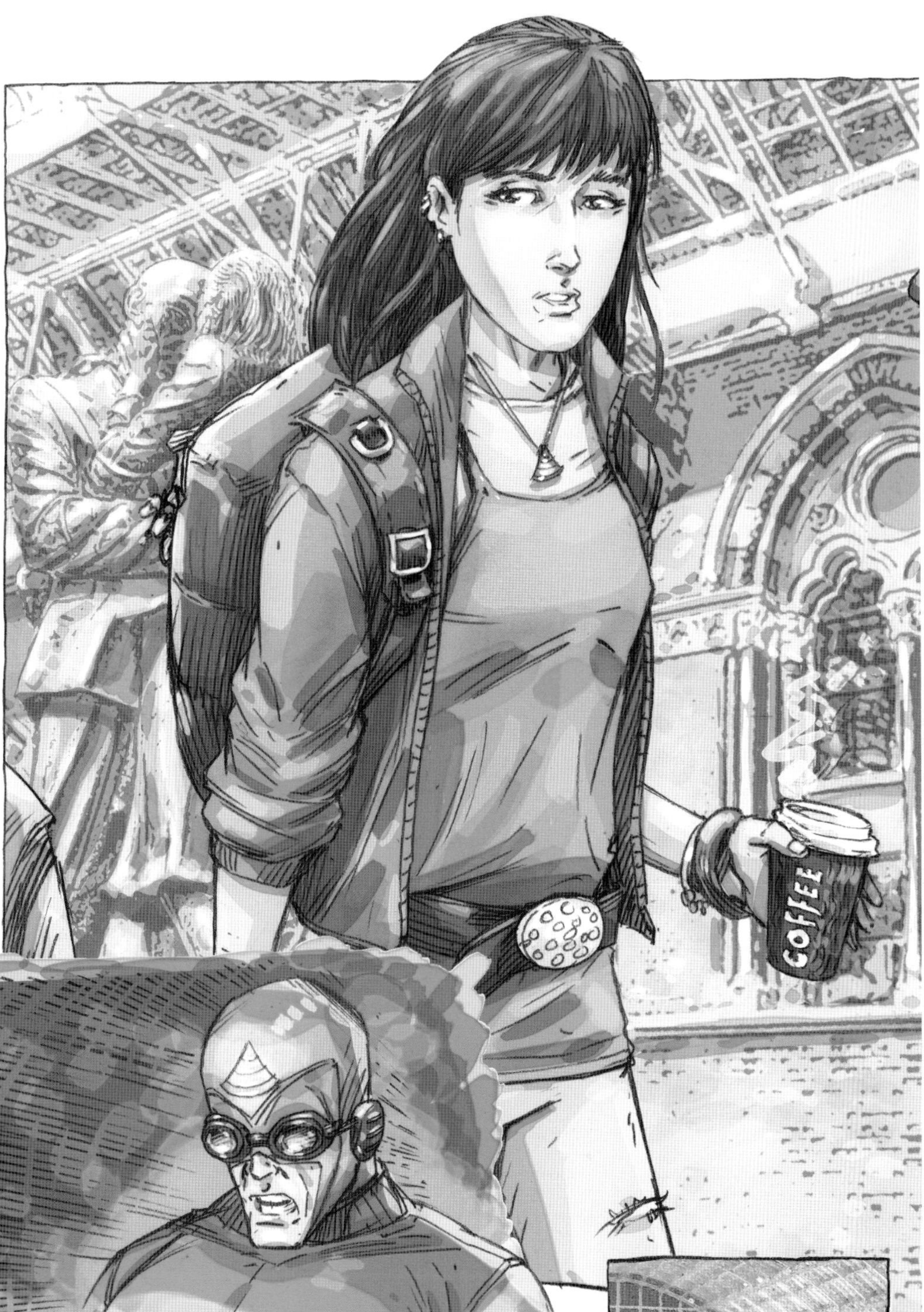
COFFEE

HANNAH HAWKINS CHARACTER CONCEPT
ARTWORK: ANDREW WILDMAN

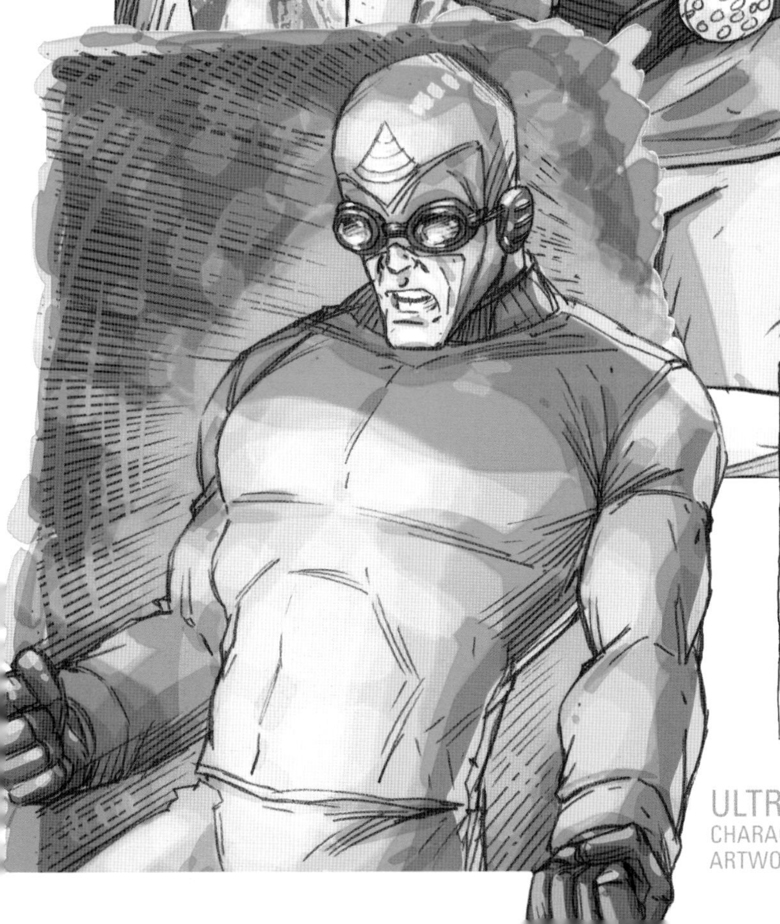

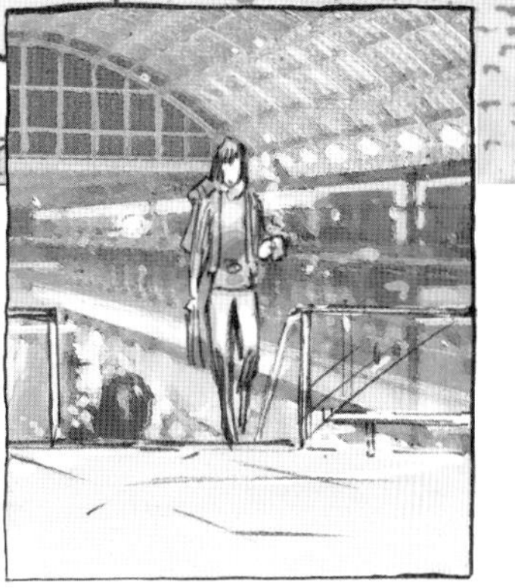

ULTRASONIC
CHARACTER CONCEPT
ARTWORK: ANDREW WILDMAN

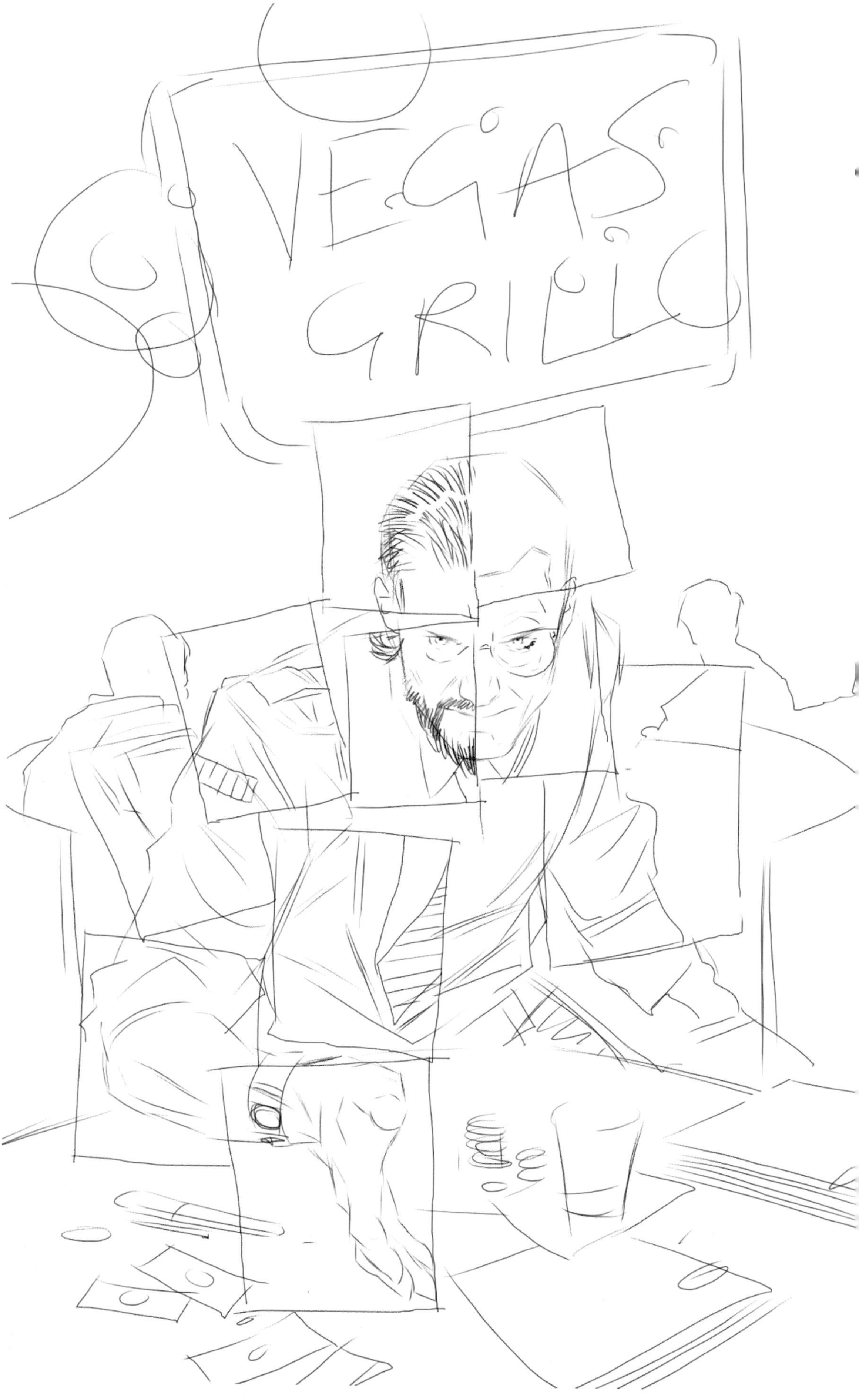
VEGAS
GRILL

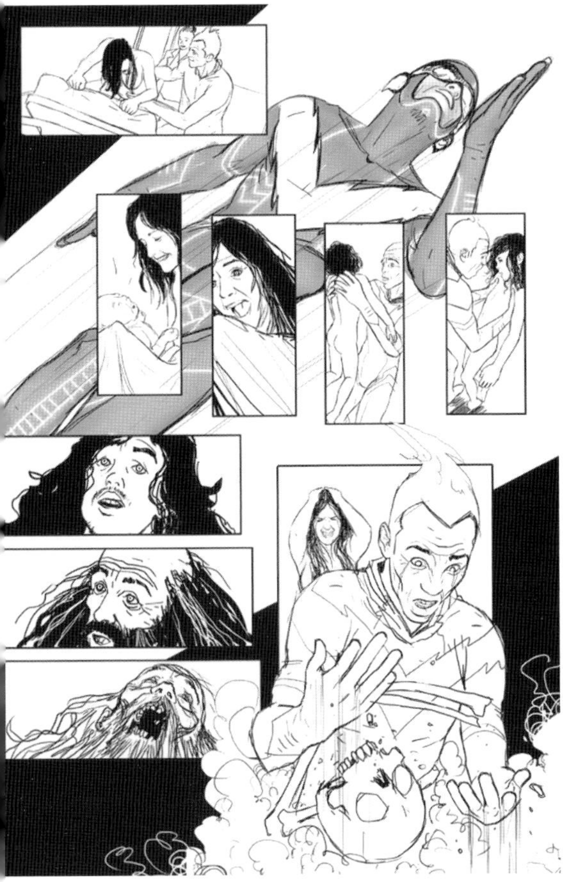

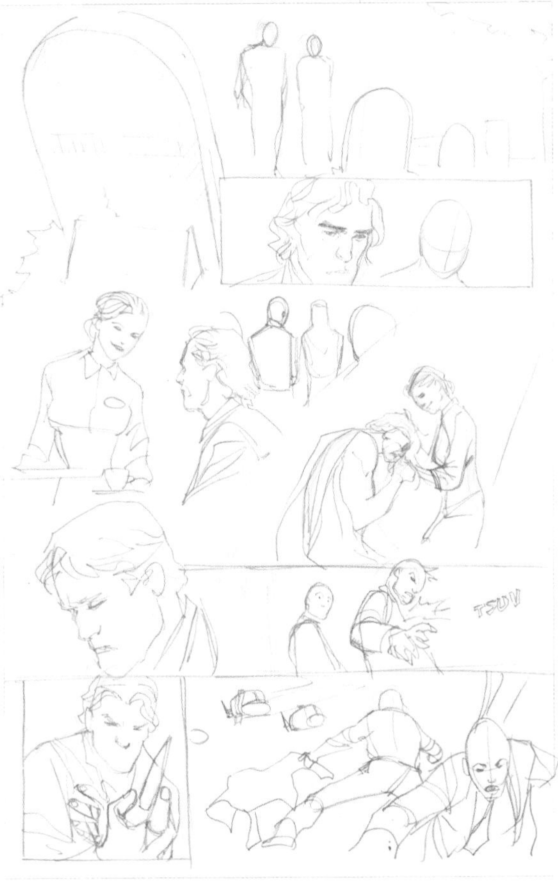
TSUV

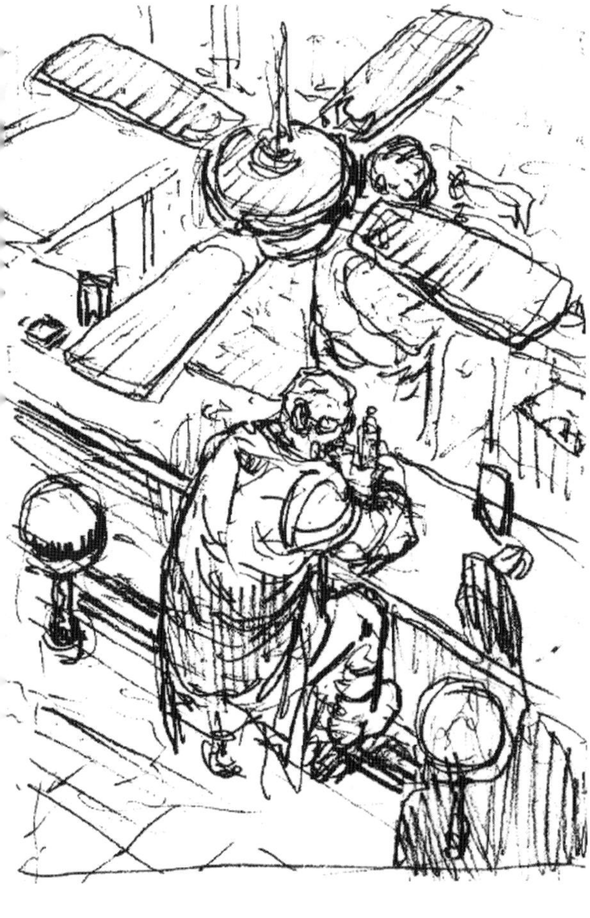

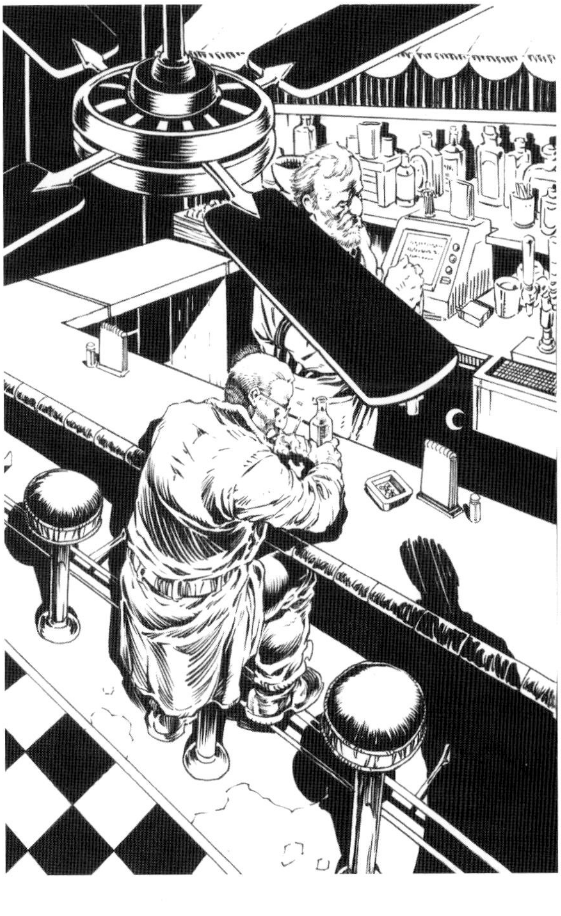

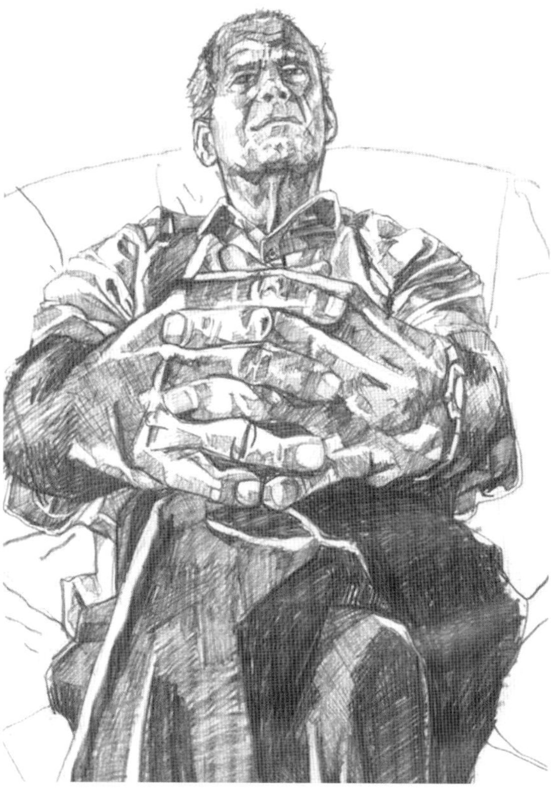

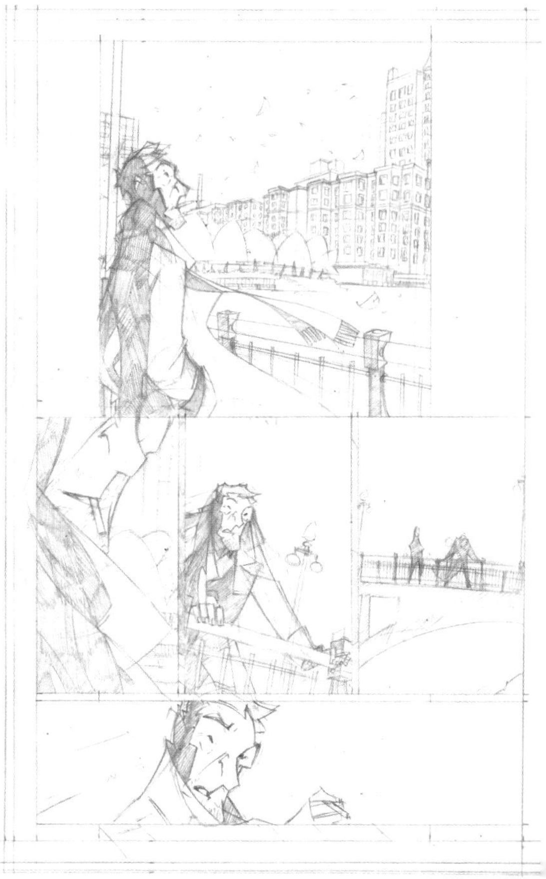

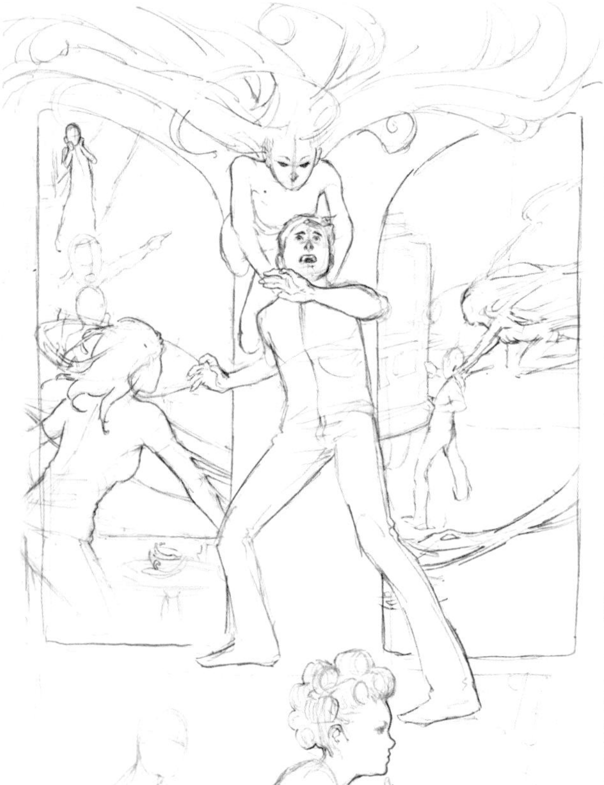

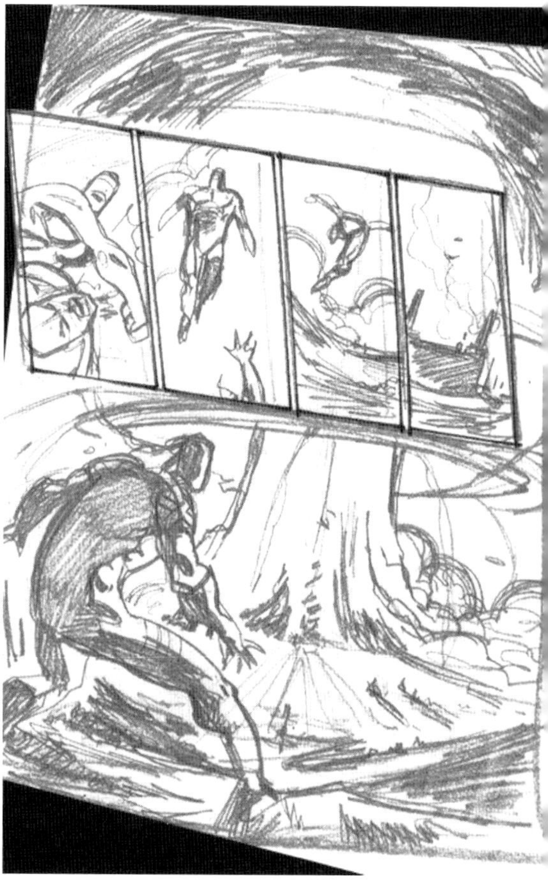

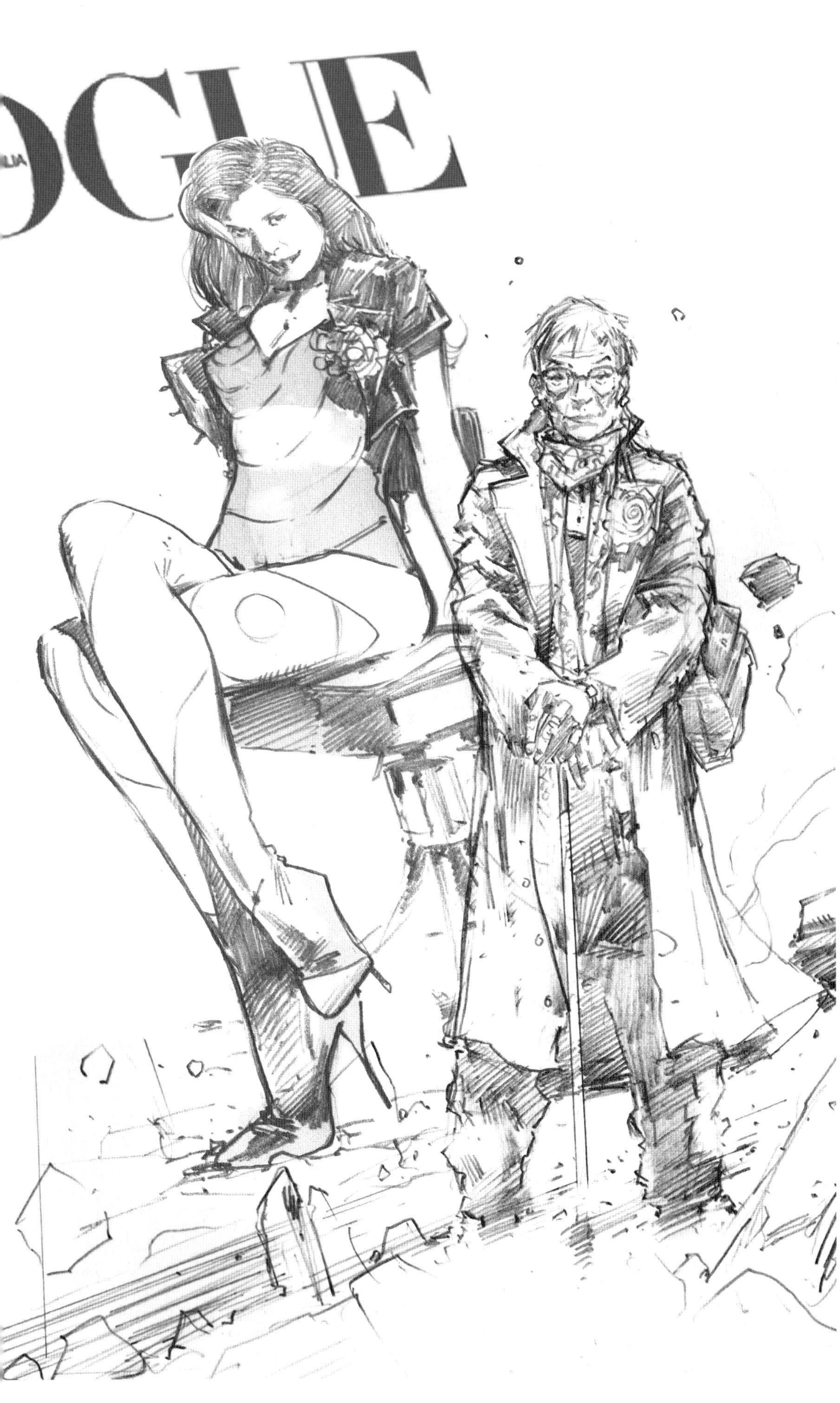
OGUE

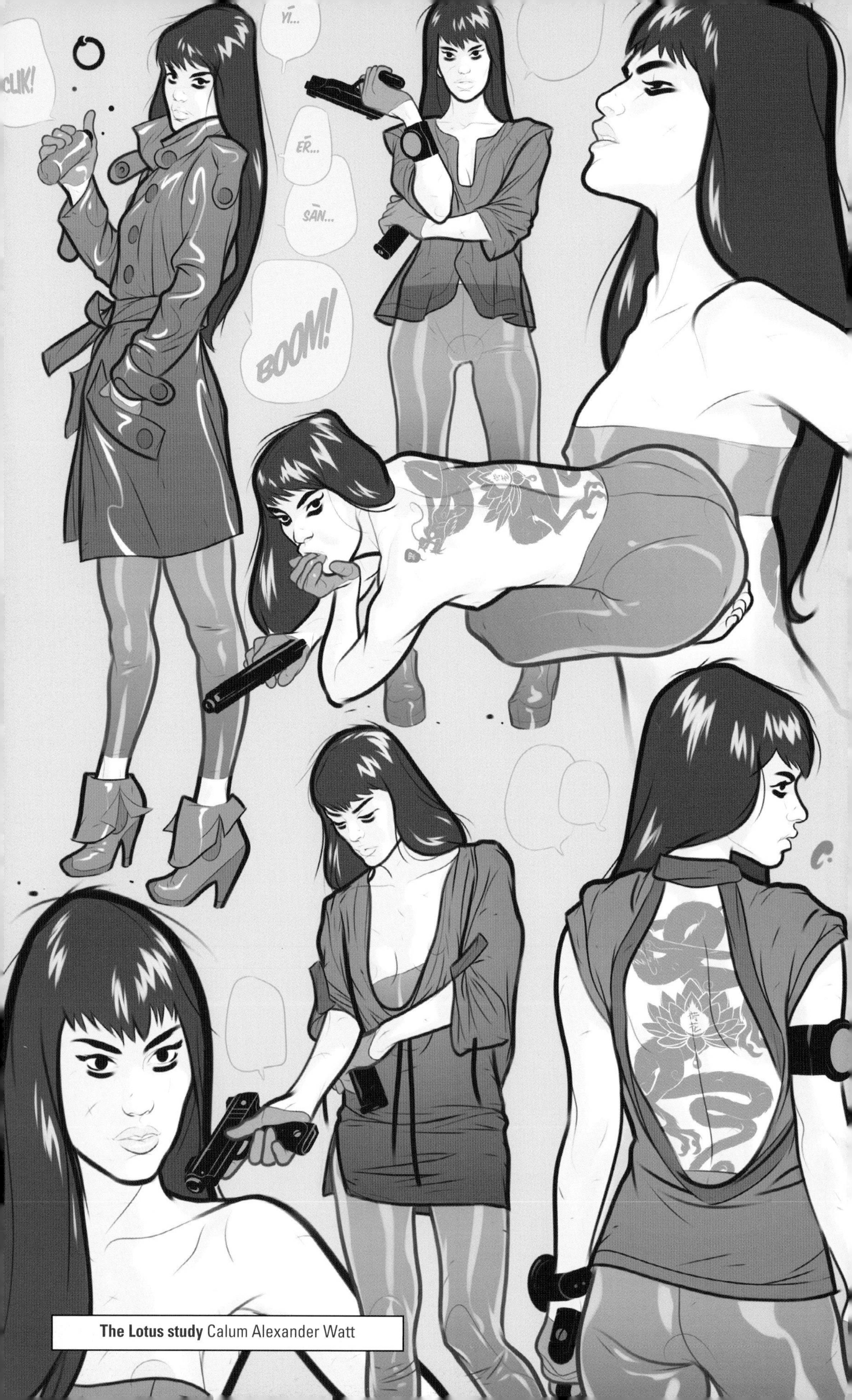
CLIK!
YĪ...
ÈR...
SĀN...
BOOM!

The Lotus study Calum Alexander Watt

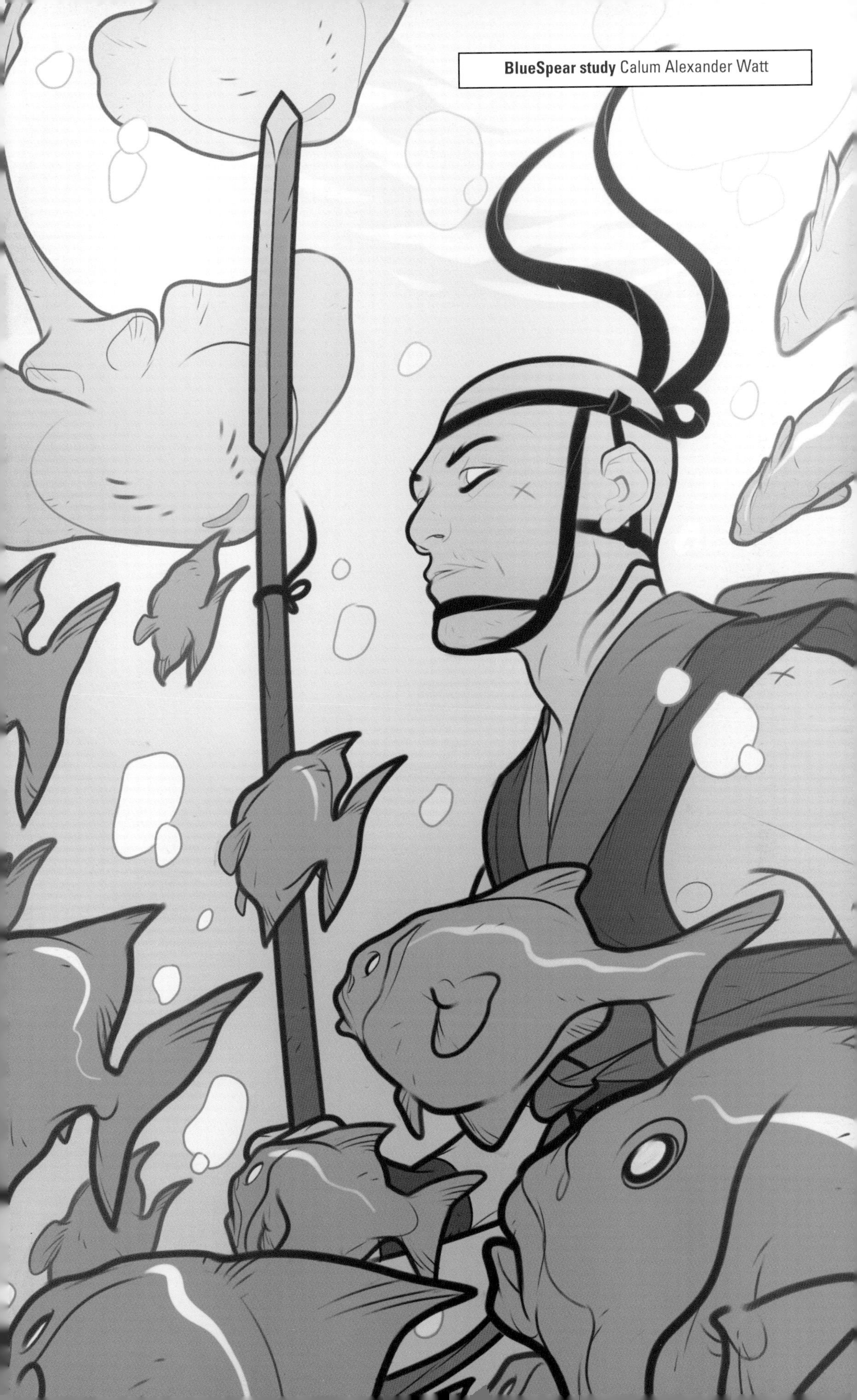

BlueSpear study Calum Alexander Watt

Biographies

Charlie Adlard is a "veteran" of the comics industry. In his 15 plus years of toil for comics, he's wound up on peaceful shores drawing zombies... many zombies. In between The Walking Dead – he's worked on many non-zombie projects including Le Souffle du Wendigo [Soleil], Rock Bottom [AiT/PlanetLar], Savage [2000AD] and, in the past, worked on most major characters for most major companies. In the future he plans to do more stuff for French comics – 'cos it's all sophisticated over there like – whilst carrying on drawing more zombies...

Jeff Anderson is from the North East of England. He has worked on Judge Dredd for Fleetway and Transformers for Marvel UK. A lot of the nineties were taken up working with scriptwriter Mike Maddox on the Graphic Bible, which was published in 1999 and they were fairly chuffed when it won an award at the Angouleme festival in 2000. He is now a vicar in Durham, slowly working on an adaptation of the Gospel of Luke.

Seb Antoniou is a freelance artist based in North London. He has worked as an animator, storyboard and background artist on projects ranging from Rupert the Bear to The Cramp Twins. He also paints portraits and landscapes which he exhibits at various galleries in London. 45 is his first published comic book work.

Robert Atkins has worked as a penciler, inker and colorist within the comic industry. His most recent work includes the penciling chores on IDW's relaunch of GI JOE! Recently Robert penciled stories for the Heroes online comic for NBC, as well as Ultimate Fantastic Four Requiem, coming out this summer 2009. He is also currently co-creating a series titled Elders of the RuneStone with writer Quinn Johnson (TMNT, Scrapyard Detectives) which is scheduled for release Jan 2010.

Dan Boultwood, Born on the stroke of midnight 1885, the irascible Dan Boultwood quickly decided a career in the ethereal was the only way forward, the only thing holding him back being the as un-yet discovered machinations of flight. On invention of the aeroplane and subsequent squiffy situation in Europe he had more than his fair share of brown trouser moments and was acquitted with accolades such as 'Moribund of the British Empire', 'the Victoria Secrets' and the 'Iron Cross', though this last one he claims is a clerical error. After failing yet again to land an SE5A intact he was unceremoniously ejected from the R.F.C and now sits in a shed and draws comics, some of which you have heard of and some of them you haven't but be assured he is there day in day out with no running water and a bucket.

Dan Brereton, a Native Californian, grew up afraid of the dark, was fascinated with catching snakes and ghosts, and constantly drawing monsters. Things haven't changed much since then, except he works at night so he can keep the lights on. Visit dan at *www.nocturnals.com*

Jason Cardy. A professional comicbook colourist, Jason has worked on a large range of British titles including Transformers UK, Spectacular Spiderman and graphic novels such as Frankenstein from Classical Comics. He has recently branched out into illustration and his art can currently be seen on the occasional cover of Titan's Transformers UK and Udon's Darkstalkers Tribute book. *jasoncardy.deviantart.com*

Lee Carter is a full time artist for leading video game developer Bizarre Creations whose credits included the "Project Gotham Racing" series and Segas "The Club". In his free time Lee has illustrated for 2000ad, Top Cow, Boom Studios, Gamesworkshop, imadginefx and Mam-tors award winning "event horizon" anthology.

Anthony Castrillo is currently working as a graphic designer. He has worked as a penciler for Marvel(X-Force), DC (IMPULSE, FLASH, HAWKMAN), VALIANT (TIMEWALKER, BLOODSHOT) and various other companies since he entered the industry in the early 90s. Anthony has contributed to DIGITAL WEBBING PRESENTS title Fist of Justice, designing the character and illustrating the initial 6 page introduction. He has also worked as cover and interior artist on the novel series THE ROOK. His illustration work can be found on various websites and print publications, working on the BIBLE HEROES strip for BOYS LIFE for the past 6 years. He has also contributed art and designs to several video game studios, the last being VICIOUS CYCLE. He lives in Brooklyn, N.Y. with his wife and daughter and 2 cats.

Tom Chu has over ten years of experience working with the two major companies in the business. While at Marvel Comics, he worked on series such as Deadpool, Avengers Forever, Iceman, and Weapon X, and at DC Comics, he was on the major weekly comic event Countdown to Final Crisis. He is now working on various projects for Marvel and DC. You can see more of his work at *colordojo.deviantart.com*

Simon Coleby's career began, in 1987, with work on Marvel UK titles such as Transformers, Thunder Cats and Action Force. Since then he has provided art for 2000AD, Marvel Comics, DC Comics and Games Workshop. His credits include Death's Head II, Punisher 2099, Inquisitor, Rogue Trooper, Judge Dredd and Low Life. Simon lives and works on the Suffolk coast, in England, and is currently drawing The Authority for Wildstorm Comics.

Boo Cook. Born in Welwyn Garden City, raised on Dartmoor, trained at Cambridge, and spray painted bum holes onto ceramic beagles in Edinburgh. Having sprayed his last bum hole in 2000, he started working for 2000AD where it's been an honour to draw such childhood heroes as; Judge Dredd, Judge Anderson Psi, ABC Warriors, plus Asylum and Harry Kipling. He's done a slew of Marvel covers, and is ecstatic to be working on covers and interiors for the mighty Elephantmen for Image. He one day hopes to return to bum holes.

Frank D'Armata aka FGD. Currently works for Marvel on Captain America, Invincible Ironman, and Ender's Game Battle School adaptation, has been in the industry for 15 years and has very little free time!!

Rufus Dayglo. Artist on the new Tank Girl books, spends his time sharpening pencils, priming grenades, looking for the Airfix kit instructions, and sipping lukewarm tea. *www.tank-girl.com*

Ross Dearsley. A leading freelance illustrator & concept artist, Ross designs for print, film, television and video games (most recently the Harry Potter series). Past clients include Marvel Comics, 2000AD, the BBC, Jim Henson's Creature Shop & Electronic Arts. Ross runs his own design studio in Berkshire, UK. *http://www.rossdearsley.com/*

Eddie Deighton. After retiring as stunt coordinator on One Tree Hill, Eddie has spent the last two years developing the velcro strap on the flight attendants' helmet for the maiden voyage of Virgin Galactic's spacecraft crew. In his spare time, he enjoys playing water polo with Kim Wilde and is a staunch advocate of 'Adopt-A-Granny' at Christmas. He prefers to use Primark socks over Andrews Quilted Velvet Toilet Tissue for personal sanitation. They are, in fact, cheaper.

Neil Edwards. Born in 1973 in Wrexham, North Wales. I always loved drawing and always wanted comics to be the career that I wanted to do. First professional piece was for Marvel UK on Generation X, which I did a poster for in 1995 and from there worked on various projects for Marvel UK, 2000AD, Striker 3D strip, MR T comic, Starship Troopers, Marvel Heroes, Boom Studios, Marvel and DC. Oh and 45 – can't forget that one!!!

Gary Erskine. Gary is a comic book artist currently living in Glasgow, Scotland. He has been illustrating for twenty years and contributed character designs and storyboards for television, commercials and games. He has collaborated on The Filth with Grant Morrison and Chris Weston and most recently re-envisioned Dan Dare with Garth Ennis.

Rodin Esquejo is a freelance artist based out of the Bay Area, California. Since receiving his B.A. in Graphic Design in 2003, he has been providing work for Hasbro, Avatar Press, Vineyard Press, as well as private collectors and colleagues.

Andi Ewington. Born in Rush Green, raised in Hornchurch and now living out the remainder of his days as far away from Essex as possible. Forty-Five is his debut publication, though he has plenty of other ideas that need sharing with the world, like Limpit Muskin & Company and Post Mort'em. World domination is always just one book away! *http://thefortyfivecomic.blogspot.com*

Dan Fraga started his career in comics at the early age of 16 by drawing a comic strip called "the Adventurer" for his local paper, The Martinez News Gazette. Six months out of high school, Dan was hired by Image Comics to start on their second wave of books. His first professional book was a title called Bloodstrike published in May of 1993. Since then, Dan has had the pleasure of working on many of comics top titles including Spider-man, Wolverine, Superman, Black Panther and The X-men franchise. In 2003 Dan left the comics business to pursue his interests in other storytelling media. His credits include working on movies like Transporter 2, Fantastic Four 2, One Missed Call and Dragonball. Dan currently spends the majority of his time working as a consultant and 2nd unit director for music videos and commercials. Most notably designing sets and drawing storyboards for artists such as Justin Timberlake, Beyonce, Usher, Gwen Stefani, Jamiroquai, and T.I., to name a few. Expect to see more comics work from Dan in 2010 with two new creator-owned titles from Image comics. Dan currently resides in the Los Angeles area.

Eduardo Francisco is a Brazilian illustrator and author of comic books, born in Sao Paulo, Brazil; he has worked professionally in this industry since he was 17 years old. He published his co-authored comic book series Victory, the first Brazilian copyrighted comic book totally produced in Brazil, with one of the largest publishers in the US. Equivalent to successful comics such as Promethea by Alan Moore, Hellblazer (Vertigo), Black Panther (Marvel) and Superman miniseries-Metropolis (DC comics). Since then he has collaborated and worked for several studios and publishers from around the world, all from his house in Sao Paulo.

Lee Garbett made his comics debut in 2006 with the indie comic Dark Mists and two assignments for the venerable UK anthology 2000AD. From there he went on to draw the critically acclaimed miniseries THE HIGHWAYMEN and the monthly series THE MIDNIGHTER for WildStorm before taking on the DC universe in the DC/WildStorm crossover DREAMWAR. Now exclusive to DC, Lee has pencilled BATMAN - LAST RITES with writer Grant Morrison, THE OUTSIDERS and is currently hard at work with the relaunch of BATGIRL.

Randy Green. Since getting a start at Dark Horse, DC and Image many years ago, Randy has worked as a freelance artist for comics and some advertising that's usually comic related. Otherwise, he spends time with his wife and two kids, drawing or working on creator-owned projects, and mashing buttons on Ninja Gaiden 2. Some past projects include Witchblade, Emma Frost and New X-Men, The Dollz and Teen Titans. He's also done artwork for many independents, as well as trading cards, video games, and CD covers. He enjoys hopping around and working on various projects, and feels fortunate for the opportunities he has been blessed with.

Trev Hairsine has worked all sorts of books from Judge Dredd to Spiderman over the last 17 years. Mostly, he's had a very, very nice time indeed.

John Higgins. Born in Liverpool. Has lived a long time. Moved around a lot. Drank gallons of Guinness. Drawn loads of comics. Enjoyed working on his page for 45. Wants to live a lot longer. Needs to draw loads more comics. And wants another pint of Guinness.

Sally Hurst paints under the pseudonym Bo:K (bouquet), where bold graphics depicting botantics and stars of screen and song are her main focus. Within Loco Motive Studios/TCS she is responsible for comic colouring, as well as image design and manipulation. She is working on Darren Dead (Megazine) and has worked on Razorjack, Jonah Hex, Greysuit (2000AD) and The Hills Have Eyes. *www.loco-motive.net www.bok.brighton-rock.net*

Frazer Irving has worked for every top dog publisher in the world, drawing super heroes and monsters and sexy women and lots of other stuff, ever since the turn of the millenium. What this means is that he is a child of Aquarius, a herald for a new dawn, a prophet of things to come. Hopefully those things won't be the same things he has been drawing for the past 9 years, cos if it is then we are all screwed. He is currently working on GUTSVILLE and a new Batman comic with Grant Morrison, as well as being worshipped by his minions who gather at the foot of Irving Towers.

Jock started working in comics drawing JUDGE DREDD for 2000AD before creating the Eisner Award nominated THE LOSERS for DC/Vertigo with his frequent collaborator, writer Andy Diggle. He's also illustrated covers for many DC Comics titles including BATMAN, NIGHTWING and CATWOMAN and interior art for SWAMP THING and HELLBLAZER, as well as contributing designs and concept art for such feature films as BATMAN BEGINS, CHILDREN OF MEN, HANCOCK and DUNE. He lives and works in Devon with his wife, Jo, and son, Aubrey.

Dennis Johnson. Full-time friend of the author's. In his spare time teaches Religious Education at an inner London Catholic school. Suffers from a variety of grammatical neuroses after being locked up in Andi's bedroom for 3 days to edit 45. Likes: the Blessed Virgin Mary. Dislikes: the Devil. Favourite colour: I don't have one.

Kevin Kobasic started his career as an Assistant Editor at Marvel in the early 90's, and went on to pencil for THE PUNISHER, DEATHLOK, RAI, and MAGNUS ROBOT FIGHTER. Since then he's done animation design for Cartoon Network and a ton of storyboards for Madison Avenue. Kevin recently launched a webcomic, BEANBOTS, on act-i-vate.com, with which he hopes to prove conclusively that kids really do say the darndest things. He lives in New York with his wife and two daughters.

Wayne Nichols is an Aussie comic book artist/commercial illustrator and part time dabbler in frenetic electronic music composition. He's best known for his work pencilling Star Wars: The Force Unleashed, The Federal Vampire and Zombie Agency for Radical Comics and Church of Hell written by legendary scribe Alan Grant.

Kat Nicholson is a freelance artist based in Wales. Kat is mostly known for her comic colouring but hopes one day for the opportunity to make good use of her drawing skills too. Titles worked on include Marvel Heroes, Transformers Animated, and Spectacular Spiderman. Non-comic interests include animation, computer games, environmentalism and Yoga. http://thedreamwolf.deviantart.com

Sean O'Connor. London based writer and artist, currently working on Julius Caesar for Classical Comics, due Aug/Sept 2010, and Redshift. www.classicalcomics.com/books/juliuscaesar.html

Alex Owens grew up in the American South, inspired by Michael Turner. He developed his own unique style drawing, inking and painting in both conventional and digital mediums, which has led to a fulfilling career as a freelance graphic illustrator. His greatest joy remains penciling sequential art in the comic book tradition.

Carlo Pagulayan. An industrial engineering graduate, got his first comics rejection letter during his 2nd year. 5 years later got his break drawing Elektra. And following that; Hulk, Emma Frost, and currently Agents of Atlas. He lives in the Southern Tagalog region of the Philippines and enjoying the clean air very much.

Bob Pedroza. Born in Chicago, IL. Attended Ray College of Design (now Art Institute of Illinois) for 2 years. Started digital coloring in 2004. Body of work includes: Marvel Masterworks (Marvel), Lions, Tigers and Bears, Gimoles, ShadowHawk, and The Intimidators (Image Comics). Currently coloring Runestone (Ape Entertainment) and the Phantom (Moonstone).

Sean Phillips has been drawing comics for almost thirty years. It's all been downhill since "Bunty"...

Jordan Raskin. Jordan Raskin has been the penciler for Dark Horse Comics "Predator: Race War" and Top Cow's "Ripclaw". In the mid 1990's, Jordan focused his career in advertising and animation, but in 2005 Jordan returned to comics with his creator owned title INDUSTRY OF WAR. For more, please visit jordanraskin.com

Dom Reardon is an illustrator from Devon, he works mostly for 2000AD.

Kenneth Rocafort has worked in various fields of the entertainment industry such as: theatre, video game box art (PS2), storyboard for advertisement, comics, magazine, card game, toy box art and more. In his free time he surfs to achieve his purpose of finding a beautiful and sexy mermaid.

Dave "RoadHog" Ryan. When not catering to a vice, Dave passes his unemployed time making cheese puppets. Turn-ons include: "giving up" and potential energy. Turn offs are shoelaces and sobriety. Daydreaming of a debilitating accident or disease are his only comfort while trying to finish War of the Independents.

Steve Sampson. Born London. Living in Brighton, UK. Education: Chelsea Art School. Work: Sheet metal worker, Comic book artist, Games Artist and illustrator. The future: It's full of stars! www.sampsonart.com

Benjamin Shahrabani. Since joining Com.x in 2003, Benjamin has been focused on building and diversifying the company's development. He has also been a part of, or produced several hours of, feature film and television, most recently JUNE CABIN released by Warner Brothers on DVD, and the TRANSWORLD SURF CALENDER 2008. Benjamin holds a BA From Brandeis University, and an MFA in Producing from UCLA.

Liam Sharp. Liam made his debut in the late 1980s drawing Judge Dredd for 2000ad. He later moved to Marvel UK, where he drew the best-selling Marvel UK title ever, Death's Head II. In 2004 Sharp set up his own publishing company,

MamTor™ Publishing, with wife Christina. Liam recently finished the controversial DC Vertigo title Testament with best-selling novelist and media commentator Douglas Rushkoff, and is currently drawing the comic adaptation of the seminal Xbox game Gears of War. Liam also worked on designs for the movies Lost in Space, Small Soldiers and the animated series Batman Beyond.

Tom Smith has been one of the top comic book color artists for the last 21 years and has colored some of comic's best-selling titles and has done work for all the top comic companies including Marvel, DC, Image, Top Cow, IDW, Chaos, First, Mailbu, Platinum, Gorilla, Topps, and many others. He owns and operates his own color and pre-press Studio "Scorpion Studios" in the great state of New Jersey in the US. http://www.comicartfans.com/GalleryDetail.asp?GCat=1645

Barry Spiers, Designer by day, illustrator by night. Born in South Wales, he now lives in London designing his way through various magazine titles at Titan Publishing (DreamWatch, Smallville, Star Wars Comic & Supernatural). He's eagerly turned his creative hand to illustrating the mighty Transformers Comic, Wallace & Gromit and Shaun the Sheep comics too. Barry now aims to open more comic book and graphic novel doors so he can illustrate to his hearts content.

Fiona Staples. Canadian Fiona Staples is the artist of WildStorm's SECRET HISTORY of the AUTHORITY: JACK HAWKSMOOR and the upcoming NORTH 40. She's also worked on Marvel's ASTONISHING TALES and contributed covers to VAMPIRELLA and SHEENA: QUEEN OF THE JUNGLE.

Stephen Thompson lives and works in Dublin, Ireland. Since first getting work with Dark Horse on Star Wars: Rebellion he's also drawn Buckaroo Banzai, Star Trek, John McCain: Presidential Material, Life Undead and Die Hard: Year One. In 2008 he was one of the winners of Marvel's Chesterquest talent search.

Matt Timson. Matt is currently drawing Impaler for Top Cow Comics and is the co-creator of Deadeye (with Moore and Reppion), which was included in Popgun – a Harvey Award-winning anthology from Image Comics. He lives in the UK with his wife, their two children and a cat called, 'The Cat'.

Andie Tong enjoys saving the world from evil aliens bent on conquering the world. When the aliens slumber though, he tends to draw lots and lots of Spider-man for the UK contingent. From time to time, Andie moonlights as a secret triple agent for DC Comics and HarperCollins. His former allies also included the likes of Dark Horse comics, Mirage Studios, Image comics, Markosia, MV Creations, Digital Webbing and CrossGen comics.

Gus Vazquez is an American artist and actor, originally from NYC, now living in Los Angeles. He has been drawing comic books for Marvel and DC for over 18 years now, and has also worked in toy design and animation, working on projects such as the Teenage Mutant Ninja Turtles and the Boondocks. Look for his latest work in the new Marvel handbooks. www.pbase.com/hellboy

Tim Vigil. Great American artist.

Kit Wallis. My first professional work was my creator-owned comic Monster Club (1991). Since then I've been drawing one-off issues for various publishers, including a 4 issue mini series for Markosia called Breathe. As well as comic books, I've been doing character design, web design and animation. At the moment I'm working on several comic book projects of my own.

Calum Alexander Watt. Also known as salaryman, Calum Alexander Watt is currently a concept artist working in the games industry. The occasional comic book project supplies that all important extra outlet for imagination and creativity. He lives with his wife and twin daughters by the sea somewhere on the south coast of the UK. He uses a computer, a lot. calumalexanderwatt.com

Bob Wiacek. After 3 years at the School of Visual Arts where in my 3rd year I was taught by Will Eisner and Harvey Kurtzman, I received the opportunity via Mike Kaluta to work at Continuity Associates with Neal Adams and Dick Giordano inking backgrounds with the Crusty Bunkers then moving on to doing backgrounds on my own with other artists. This landed me the chance to ink Mike Grell on the Legion of Super Heroes for DC and Al Milgrom on The Guardians of the Galaxy for Marvel. I have gone on to ink just about every major title from Batman, Green Lantern, Orion, Brave and Bold and JSA for DC. Then at Marvel on Spiderman, Captain America, Fantastic Four, Hulk, X-Men and Man-Thing, plus many more. I have inked Walter Simonson, Frank Miller, George Perez, Jerry Ordway, Steve Ditko, Ron Garney and Paul Smith, to name a few. Also have penciled, inked and co-plotted with Simonson on an Iron Man 2020 book and penciled 2 Silver Burper stories that Stan Lee wrote for What The..... Did some acting with Rap Artist 50Cent in a commercial and storyboards for some music video's.

Admira Wijaya. Another survivor from the advertising world, Admira combines his painting skills with his digital imaging skills to help make his illustrations realistic enough to eat. Now if only if he'll draw food. Admira Wijaya is an extremely talented line artist who is also apt at coloring, so much so that he is one of DC's favorite artists often working exclusively on many DC Licensing projects. He lives in Jakarta, cites Travis Charest and Adam Hughes as his inspirations and can often be found doing his pencil work on traditional pen and paper before continuing the magic on Photoshop.

Andrew Wildman has long been associated with Transformers but there is other stuff ya know. Spider-Man, X-Men and Venom amongst others. He's also designed characters for TV animation, storyboarded for movies and worked as a video game Concept Artist as well as create the charity project, Draw The World Together. www.drawtheworldtogether.com www.andrewwildman.net

Matthew Wilson has been trying to pay off his way-too-expensive art school education by coloring comics since 2003. Since then he's worked for Lee Loughridge's Zylonol Studios coloring the majority of Y the Last Man along with various other projects. In the last two years Matt has tried making a name for himself by working on titles that include Phonogram: Singles Club, The End League, Gigantic, Dead Run, and others.

The Birth of "Forty-Five"

Coffee. Can't stand the stuff. Even the smell makes me gag. Though it didn't stop me trying my luck with Revels* when I was a kid. I would happily, if not a little warily, gorge my way through an entire packet, stopping only to spit out the coffee ones. If you were foolhardy and had allergies, you could play Russian Roulette with the peanut ones. Anyhow, I digress. Back to my hatred of coffee. It's ironic that, during a 'coffee break', I was given the opportunity to create 'Forty-Five.' You see, I work with Eddie Deighton. Eddie runs Com.x, one of the most – if not *the* most – popular, independent UK comic publishers out there. To further confuse you, I don't technically work for Com.x; I work for Eddie's design company as his Creative Director, doing funky things like designing advertising and packaging for computer games. (See kids, it pays to waste your free time playing computer games. My father used to say that I'd never make anything of myself playing computer games – I beg to differ). Back to the story. Eddie likes coffee. Often, he'll venture out for a skinny medio cappuccino (don't ask me what that is, I have no idea), and to break up my day I usually tag along. During our walks we chat about many things, but nothing whets Ed's appetite more than talking comics. Ed loves his comics. Not only does he love his comics, but he *knows* his comics. I hadn't read them for years but still, I thought I knew comics. That's where I was wrong.

Before I could say "double espresso", I had been enlightened to the worlds of Alex Ross, Jack Kirby, Dave Gibbons, Kurt Busiek, and Jim Krueger, to name but a few. Suddenly, I felt like I had been plugged back into the comic mains; we talked stories, characters, super-powers and here I was, pumped about comics again. In hindsight, I think Ed knew what he was doing; he knew I had been writing for many years and had the desire to become a published author before I shuffled off this mortal coil. So I badgered him about writing a comic. And Ed responded in the normal Com.x fashion – by telling me to find a story that was original and unique and worthy of publishing through his company! So off I went a-hunting. They say write about what you know. Well, my wife was twelve-weeks pregnant at the time, so I was a walking Encyclopaedia on birth and impending fatherhood. Coincidentally, I had just finished reading the very excellent 'World War Z' by Max Brooks* and the equally impressive 'Marvels' by Alex Ross and Kurt Busiek and out of these three, unrelated experiences, the idea for 'Forty-Five' began to take shape. I couldn't wait to tell Ed.

Fast-forward twenty-four hours – we're walking our familiar coffee route and I'm pitching the idea of 'Forty-Five'; about a regular journalist who's about to become a father and embarks on a mission to interview a plethora of superheroes. The reason? To try and comprehend what it would be like if his child is born with super-powers. He really liked it and further discussions ensued, whereupon Ed suggested going one step further and commissioning a different artist for each interview. It certainly hadn't been done on such a scale before and sounded like a challenge, which I was up for. Thus, the concept was born (even if my child wasn't yet). I researched, I wrote, and Ed, along with his business partner, Benjamin Shahrabani, 'hooked me up' with a host of talented individuals. From there it simply snowballed. As a debut writer, I'm indebted to the artists that came onboard. I guess it's a testament to the concept that so many creatives wanted to be involved; it gave me faith that I was doing something right, that I'd created something special. When you read through the book, please take an extra moment to savour the artwork; all did their best, some generously gave their time for free, but every one has been a joy to work with. I finished the book four hours after my son was born. I like to think it was fated to be that way. So, sit back, enjoy and remember, the only thing that is going to make the experience that much better is a nice cup of tea.

Andi Ewington December 2009

*For those that don't hang in Revel circles, they are chocolate-coated sweets, randomly flavoured with orange, caramel, Malteser, chocolate, peanut and, the much-hated, coffee fillings.

**Max if you are reading this – I've you to thank for us naming our son 'Zack'.